The Age of the Economist

Ninth Edition

The Addison-Wesley Series in Economics

Abel/Bernanke
Macroeconomics

Bade/Parkin
Foundations of Economics

Bierman/Fernandez
Game Theory with Economic Applications

Binger/Hoffman
Microeconomics with Calculus

Boyer
Principles of Transportation Economics

Branson
Macroeconomic Theory and Policy

Bruce
Public Finance and the American Economy

Burgess
The Economics of Regulation and Antitrust

Byrns/Stone
Economics

Carlton/Perloff
Modern Industrial Organization

Caves/Frankel/Jones
World Trade and Payments: An Introduction

Chapman
Environmental Economics: Theory, Application, and Policy

Cooter/Ulen
Law and Economics

Eaton/Mishkin
Online Readings to Accompany The Economics of Money, Banking, and Financial Markets

Ehrenberg/Smith
Modern Labor Economics

Ekelund/Tollison
Economics: Private Markets and Public Choice

Fusfeld
The Age of the Economist

Gerber
International Economics

Ghiara
Learning Economics: A Practical Workbook

Gordon
Macroeconomics

Gregory
Essentials of Economics

Gregory/Stuart
Russian and Soviet Economic Performance and Structure

Hartwick/Olewiler
The Economics of Natural Resource Use

Hubbard
Money, the Financial System, and the Economy

Hughes/Cain
American Economic History

Husted/Melvin
International Economics

Jehle/Reny
Advanced Microeconomic Theory

Klein
Mathematical Methods for Economics

Krugman/Obstfeld
International Economics: Theory and Policy

Laidler
The Demand for Money: Theories, Evidence, and Problems

Leeds/von Allmen
The Economics of Sports

Lesser/Dodds/Zerbe
Environmental Economics and Policy

Lipsey/Courant/Ragan
Economics

McCarty
Dollars and Sense: An Introduction to Economics

Melvin
International Money and Finance

Miller
Economics Today

Miller/Benjamin/North
The Economics of Public Issues

Mills/Hamilton
Urban Economics

Mishkin
The Economics of Money, Banking, and Financial Markets

Parkin
Economics

Parkin/Bade
Economics in Action Software

Perloff
Microeconomics

Phelps
Health Economics

Riddell/Shackelford/Stamos/ Schneider
Economics: A Tool for Critically Understanding Society

Ritter/Silber/Udell
Principles of Money, Banking, and Financial Markets

Rohlf
Introduction to Economic Reasoning

Ruffin/Gregory
Principles of Economics

Sargent
Rational Expectations and Inflation

Scherer
Industry Structure, Strategy, and Public Policy

Schotter
Microeconomics: A Modern Approach

Sherman/Kolk
Business Cycles and Forecasting

Smith
Case Studies in Economic Development

Studenmund
Using Econometrics: A Practical Guide

Su
Economic Fluctuations and Forecasting

Tietenberg
Environmental and Natural Resource Economics

Tietenberg
Environmental Economics and Policy

Todaro
Economic Development

Waldman/Jensen
Industrial Organization: Theory and Practice

Williamson
Macroeconomics

The Age of the Economist

Ninth Edition

Daniel R. Fusfeld
The University of Michigan

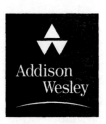

Boston San Francisco New York
London Toronto Sydney Tokyo Singapore Madrid
Mexico City Munich Paris Cape Town Hong Kong Montreal

Editor-in-Chief: Denise Clinton
Editorial Assistant: Jennifer Jefferson
Senior Production Supervisor: Juliet Silveri
Production Services: Kathy Smith
Marketing Manager: Adrienne D'Ambrosio
Cover Designer: Linda Wade
Composition: Gillian Hall, The Aardvark Group
Manufacturing Supervisor: Hugh Crawford

Photo credits for chapter-opening photos: Chapters 1, 3, 4, 5, 6, and 11: The
Granger Collection; Chapter 2: Historical Pictures Service; Chapter 7: Biblio-
thèque Cantonale et Universitaire, Lausanne; Chapter 8: The Bettmann
Archive; Chapter 9: North Wind Picture Archives; Chapters 10 and 14:
UPI/Bettmann; Chapters 12 and 15: Corbis–Bettman; Chapter 13: Stock
Boston.

Library of Congress Cataloging-in-Publication Data

Fusfeld, Daniel Roland, 1922–
    The age of the economist / Daniel R. Fusfeld.—9th ed.
        p.   cm.
    Includes bibliographical references and indexes.
    ISBN 0-321-08812-3 (pbk.)
        1. Economics—History. I. Title.
    HB75.F87   2002
    330'.09—dc21   2001026679

Preface

The Age of the Economist surveys the history of economics from the time of Adam Smith and some of his predecessors to today. This book is written for all those who wish to familiarize themselves with the background of modern economics but have no initial knowledge of the more complex aspects of the subject. It should prove as useful to the interested layperson as to the student of economics, history, or introductory social sciences.

By examining the historical development of economics, one can understand how the minds of the great economists worked—how the grand themes they dealt with were developed out of efforts to understand the problems and issues of their times, competing social philosophies, economic and social conflicts and a changing economic structure. The discipline that emerged gives us a fuller understanding of today's intricate and dynamic world. The ideas and events that influenced the great economists over the last 250 years are still at work. By examining the interplay between past and present events and ideas, we can begin to understand what today's economists are saying and why they are saying it. Inquiry into the past helps us understand the present.

The first edition of this book was published in 1966, at a time when the world economy was approaching the peak of the great economic-growth surge that followed World War II and just prior to the slowdown in economic growth and troubled times that began in the late 1960s. In the mid-1960s economic policies seemed to be working well, on the whole, and there was a broad consensus among economists about what was important and useful. When economic conditions turned sour from the late 1960s into the 1980s, however, the consensus dissolved. The accepted economic truths of the 1960s became the material for controversy. In the process, the view of the past as reflected in this small volume has changed.

Not much has been changed in the chapters that discuss the development of economics prior to the Second World War except for a section on Simone de Sismondi and Social Economics in the chapter on Classical Economics. The most important change was the addition of a chapter on the New Economy, which chronicles the development of economics in today's world of new technology, free trade, and globalization. The story, however, will not end there. The economics of the future will emerge out of the same hurly-burly events, policy issues, ideological debate, and scholarly inquiry that brought the discipline to its present state.

By the end of the book the reader will be drawn into some complex ideas. Economics has developed into what one philosopher called "one of the most elaborate constructions of sustained philosophical reasoning in existence." The important building blocks of the subject are introduced in the early chapters in relatively simple form, and complexities are gradually introduced, as they were in reality, by examining their evolution in historical context. One way to arrive at an understanding of intricate ideas is to study their chronological development from simple to complex. The careful reader should acquire a broad understanding of the more important ideas of modern economics by progressing through the book.

Throughout *The Age of the Economist* the emphasis is on the large conceptual framework of economic ideas, to show how economics is related to the great issues that have troubled people in every age—order versus freedom, riches and poverty, privilege and equality, power and its control, human welfare, and material and moral values, among others. It is easy to get so involved in the intricacies of economics that we lose sight of these large issues. Here they are pushed to stage front, for economics has always been an instrument through which we may better understand some of the great problems that have troubled humankind.

This book, then, chronicles the development of modern economics. In doing so, it presents the chief ideas and concepts of the discipline, those that would be explained in more rigorously analytic form in a typical introductory economics textbook. Most importantly, it shows the relevance of those ideas to the great debates about the world we live in—debates that continue to trouble thoughtful people everywhere.

Daniel R. Fusfeld

Contents

Introduction

Edmund Burke called the eighteenth century "the age of the economist," and the label is equally appropriate for our own time. The writings of economists have defined the major social philosophies of the past two hundred years. The chief ideological debates of the modern era involve the basic ideas of great economists like Adam Smith, Karl Marx, and John Maynard Keynes, who achieved their stature primarily because of the social philosophies involved in their economic theories rather than the scientific advances they made.

This fact was well understood by Keynes himself, who, doing battle with ideas he was convinced were wrong and pernicious, wrote:

> The ideas of economists and political philosophers, both when they are right and when they are wrong, are more powerful than is commonly understood. Indeed the world is ruled by little else. Practical men, who believe themselves to be quite exempt from any intellectual influences, are usually the slaves of some defunct economist. Madmen in authority, who hear voices in the air, are distilling their frenzy from some academic scribbler of a few years back.

Economists became the high priests of a world of money, wealth, and aspirations for material goods. Like the Schoolmen of the Middle Ages, they defined for a secular world the relationships between people, the individual and nature, and the individual and society. Their often esoteric and highly complex theories were translated into a folklore understood by millions and into policies adopted by nations. Although their base was usually in the relatively secluded atmosphere of the university, distinguished economists have served in recent years as prime ministers of England, France, Germany,

1

Italy, and Greece and as secretary general of the United Nations. It would be hard to name another discipline that has exerted as much influence on the modern world.

This was not always the case. Only two hundred and fifty years ago there were no economists known as such, and economic theory was a branch of moral philosophy. Economics as we know it today hardly existed, and what did exist was called "political economy," indicating that it was part of national policy more than anything else and that it dealt with such matters as taxes, public debts, and foreign trade.

Until very recently economics was the only social science with a generally accepted body of theory whose validity almost every practitioner accepted. Although economists sometimes joked about obtaining five different opinions on any topic from any four economists, or about the old professor who asked the same examination questions year after year but changed the answers, the disputes among economists were not about fundamental principles. The disagreements arose over applications, over the proper policies to be adopted in given circumstances, and over judgments about the importance of various factors in particular situations.

There was one major exception to this rule—the Marxists, who considered Western economics to be merely ideological justification of an exploitive system. They believed their own analysis of capitalism to be the correct one, laying bare the flaws that would lead ultimately to the downfall of the capitalist system. Their contempt for mainstream economics was reciprocated by the attitude toward Marxism of the orthodox economists, who considered that doctrine so wrong that most didn't even bother to read Marx.

Today, however, the accepted principles of orthodox economics are in trouble. The issues and problems for which economics provided answers— the way a market economy functions, how to maintain prosperity—have given way to new problems and issues for which answers are not readily available. Growth of big business, big government, and big unions brings economic power to the fore as a determinant of economic events. Economic growth and affluence bring problems of resources, pollution, and energy. An exploding world population seems to be a particularly intractable problem. Great disparities in income and wealth within nations and among nations create political and ideological conflicts over how economic benefits are distributed. Although the collapse of the Soviet economy leaves private-enterprise capitalism dominant in today's world, many issues remain unresolved about how these problems will be managed, what the proper mix of public and private control should be, and what our future will be like. The debates and policies that emerge will be shaped, in part, by the work of economists, and economics as a discipline will itself be forged in today's cauldron of events.

This process is not surprising, since economics is a social science. Both events and ideological debates have always been important to its development. This presents a great paradox: Some of the most important advances in economics have resulted from political debates over social policy. In this respect economics—like all other social sciences—differs radically from the physical and biological sciences, which grew step by step from facts and experimental evidence to theory, and from theory to further experiment and more general theories. Both the social and the physical sciences developed by means of grand integrating schemes, or *systems*, intended to explain large interrelated portions of a discipline. In the physical sciences, the grand designs emerged primarily out of an ordering of facts and evidence; in economics, that source of scientific theory was supplemented by great political and philosophical debates. Ideological systems, each with its supporting facts, assumptions, and body of theory, spawned much that is valuable in economics.

The ideas developed by Adam Smith in the eighteenth century comprised one of those systems, and the theory of markets developed by Smith and his followers represented the first great body of generally accepted principles in modern economics. Challenged by Marx and others in the mid-nineteenth century, this "classical" system and its laissez-faire ideology were remade in the last quarter of the century into a new orthodoxy that prevailed until the 1930s, when John Maynard Keynes almost single-handedly built the modern theory of national income and justified a policy of government intervention in economic affairs. Between these two developments, a variety of writers laid the foundations for today's welfare policies by criticizing the economic societies and theories of their time. Throughout these debates ideas emerged that were useful either in supporting or in attacking the existing order, its distribution of income and wealth, and its structure of power.

One of the great themes in the development of economics, then, is the interaction of ideology and theory. Without ideological conflict the discipline would not have evolved as it did. And because economics was forged in the fire of ideological debate, it will always arouse emotions, no matter how "pure" and "scientific" its representatives may try to keep it.

A second great theme is the relationship between economic theories and practical problems. People everywhere have sought prosperity and justice, freedom and order, individual betterment and the social good. The quest for these sometimes contradictory goals has always involved choices, and the theory of choice is a basic part of economic theory. One of the maxims of economics is that the greater the economic surplus, the more numerous are the alternative courses of action and the easier it is to achieve a multiplicity of goals. As society brought a recalcitrant nature more effectively under its control, ways and means of organizing and utilizing economic resources became more numerous, and public policy toward economic affairs became more important. With control comes choice, and choice begets policy. The need for policy decisions brought forth the economist—to analyze and advise and to develop a rational basis for choices.

For example, at the close of World War II the American people debated whether to institute an extensive program of loans to aid the reconstruction of Europe. The issue would have been strictly academic had not the United States produced a large surplus above its minimum needs that could be allocated to foreign aid. Since the surplus was available, however, economists were called in to advise how best to mobilize it (whether under public or private auspices), the form it should take (loans or grants, or both), and the uses to which it should be put (consumer goods or machinery, or both). Indeed, many economists look upon their discipline as the science of rational choice among alternatives, both by individuals and in public policy.

A third theme in the development of economics is its close relationship to the climate of opinion. A problem is never analyzed in a vacuum. One function of theory is to provide a context in which facts can be systematically organized. But solutions to problems must be practical and acceptable to the general public as well as to political leaders. If economics is to have any usefulness, the economic theory of an era must be consistent with the beliefs and concerns of the public, and it must provide beneficial results. In this sense, economics has always been political economy.

Scholars often overlook the importance of the climate of opinion. They seek the origins of ideas in the solid advances made by earlier scholars, tracing an intellectual genealogy from one generation of thinkers to another, finding the origins of modern ideas in the Old Testament, Aesop, and the Upanishads. In some respects this is a worthwhile task, for older generations were just as intelligent as we are; it is true, more often than not, that if an idea is good someone else thought of it first. Yet in the social sciences, at least, the more meaningful question is not "when did the idea first appear?" but "why is the idea important now?" The answer to this question involves the uses to which the idea can be put, the special interests of those who use it, and its consistency with other beliefs of the people affected by it. This climate of opinion is often more important than logical consistency for the development and survival of ideas—more important in the case of economic ideas, perhaps, than of those in any other social science, owing mainly to the close relationship between economics and public policy. Economists cannot escape the times in which they live—the times determine the very questions asked—and nearly every adult is, in some respect, an economist.

A fourth theme is the development of economics as a discipline. Over a period of 250 years—a quarter of a millennium—basic principles were developed concerning the ways in which markets function, the process of economic growth, and the determinants of the level of economic activity, among others. Like any discipline, a vocabulary of economic concepts has evolved that defines its subject matter, and methods by which hypotheses are tested, modified, and verified are adopted. Generations of theorists developed systematic analyses, demonstrable conclusions, and broad propositions.

There is a tendency to write the history of any discipline as if the entire past were prologue, leading inevitably to the discovery of the truths of the present, with the implication that the process will continue into the future as scholars move ever closer to a fuller understanding of the subject. To some extent that is true of economics—we know today far more about how a market-oriented economy functions than we did a hundred or two hundred years ago—but this view is an oversimplification. People in past eras were intelligent, too, and, although their technology was perhaps simpler, the problems they had to wrestle with were just as intricate as ours are today. Their world was different from ours, and their view of that world also differed. Inevitably, the social theories of the past were different from those of today. Whether our theories are "better" or more advanced is debatable.

For example, the "classical" economists of the early nineteenth century emphasized the economics of production and distribution in their analyses of the economy, and assumed that the level of economic activity was not a significant problem. That view is rejected today, as the emphasis is now on exchange rather than production and on how to maintain "full employment" levels of output. We might describe classical economics as if it were merely a prelude to today's truths, but that would be a distortion of both classical economics and the process by which we came to our present understanding of market economies. It would also distort our understanding of the path into the future, for if the past really is prologue we know that many of the truths of the present will become the falsehoods of the future.

Economics is an ever-changing discipline. Partly a product of the great ideological debates about the way human society ought to be organized, it also influences the outcome of those debates. Partly based on a theoretical search for abstract truths, it is also rooted in the realities of public policy and the climate of opinion. Partly an explanation of how and why an economic system functions, it is affected by the ways in which economic systems change. Economics is a complex amalgam of scientific theory, political ideology, public policy, and accepted truths.

Yet development of the discipline to its present position could not have taken place without the work of many ordinary and extraordinary individuals. The story of economics is also the story of a Scottish philosopher, a London stockbroker, an Episcopalian minister, a German philosopher and revolutionary, a Cambridge professor, a Norwegian-American skeptic, and a host of others. The story reflects their personalities and their convictions, their strengths and their weaknesses, their successes and their failures. *The Age of the Economist* is an account of their work and of the discipline they helped to build, of the interaction between facts, problems, policy, philosophy, and institutions in the building process, and of how we have come to think as we do about one of the most important aspects of our lives.

ONE

ECONOMICS AND THE MARKET ECONOMY

Thomas Aquinas (c. 1225–1274), a Catholic theologian, analyzed the ethical foundations of market exchange

The Rise of the Market Economy

The modern market economy is such an intimate part of our way of life that most of us do not realize that it is a relatively recent development. The organization of economic life around an interrelated system of markets—markets that adjust prices, output, and incomes in an impersonal system—did not emerge on a large scale until after the Middle Ages, that is, from the fifteenth century onward. Prior to that time most of Europe's population lived in an economy largely based on a social system of rights and obligations rather than on an acquisitive, profit-oriented economy of buying and selling.

The transformation of this society and its economy was observed by contemporaries. Thomas Becon, an English cleric of the mid-sixteenth century, for example, decried the growing materialism of his era and inveighed against "greedy gentlemen, which are sheepmongers and graziers" who "study for their own private commodity." Thomas Wilson, writing fifty years later, noted how even the aristocracy was affected by the change:

> The gentlemen, which were wont to addict themselves to warres, are now for the most part growen to become good husbands and know well how to improve their lands to the uttermost as the farmer or countryman, so that they take their farmes into their handes as the leases expire, and eyther till themselves or else lett them out to those who will give most.

Becon and Wilson observed what many others of the time could also see. The traditional pattern, in which each person was born to a definite place and fulfilled a definite function throughout life, was passing away. Peasants, long

7

accustomed to providing services and agricultural output for the lord of the manor, increasingly paid money rents and sold a portion of their product in order to get the money to do so. More than ever before, the lord used the rents to buy needed goods, and the more progressive landowners began to produce readily marketable products such as wool. Others gradually raised the rents charged their tenants, who were forced similarly to orient their crops toward marketable products. Middleman traders increased in number, wealth, and importance as a result of the growing market.

The Middle Ages—the era from the breakdown of the ancient Roman Empire to the mid-fifteenth century in Europe—were not without trade, commerce, and markets, but the trade was, in large part, a long-distance and interregional trade in luxury products consumed by the nobility and the wealthy. Peasant communities, rural and largely self-sufficient, produced a surplus paid to the lord in products, in labor, and sometimes in cash. This surplus was the basis for purchases of luxuries by the aristocracy—fine textiles, metal products, wine, and other items of the "good life." A dual economy grew up, comprising the peasant village on the one hand and the commercial town on the other. It was a regulated economy of organized groups, such as manor, town, and guild, rather than one that operated through free decisions freely negotiated. In its fundamental structure it was much like the economic system that prevailed throughout the Near and Middle East, Southeast Asia, and the Far East.

The great transformation of Europe to a market economy began in the fifteenth century. The geographical discoveries of the fifteenth and sixteenth centuries opened up tremendous opportunities for trade and commerce and set in motion a large flow of capital into Europe in the form of gold and silver treasures from both the New World and the East. The rise of national states largely destroyed the political power of two bulwarks of the old order, the nobility and the Church. New methods of warfare used by the emerging rulers, featuring paid armies and large navies, required money and administration: national tax systems emerged, and a flow of purchasing power from taxpayer through government and back to the public further stimulated the growth of markets. Cities like London and Amsterdam became centers of commerce; they looked overseas for profits and expansion, and they were supported by governments eager to increase the tax base by expanding the wealth of the nation.

The new economy generated new attitudes. Medieval people, accustomed to thinking and acting in traditional ways, gave way to market-oriented people who would sink or swim by virtue of their individual decisions. The successful ones were those who saved, who plowed profits back into the enterprise, who calculated prices and costs carefully, who took risks in order to make gains. In particular, there was little place for the attitudes of feudal warfare and jousting. The future lay with commercial profits and commercial wealth.

The new economy also generated the study of economics. The developing market orientation of production and distribution led to a new relationship between the individual and society, and between individuals, with all the ethical issues that those relationships imply. The morality of the new economic order had to be carefully analyzed and accepted rules for ethical behavior devised. Theologians became the first "economists."

Religion and Economic Life

The theologians were concerned with reconstructing the ethical basis of economic life. The older, medieval point of view had subordinated economic life to both individual salvation and the needs of society as a whole. Theologians had argued that earthly life was merely a prelude to eternity, and moral laws had to prevail in all aspects of human endeavor. This meant that in all human relationships, including the economic, the individual had to keep the law of God continually in mind. The Church knew that people must eat and clothe and house themselves, that the ordinary functions of production and distribution had to be carried on; but those functions had to be placed in proper perspective—salvation was the proper business of life, and one must never forget it. Seeking wealth for its own sake was sinful, since it took one's attention away from salvation and pursuit of the moral life.

Nevertheless, the growth of trade and commerce from the eleventh century onward forced theologians to come to terms with the growing market orientation of life. Relationships between people were increasingly being shaped by markets for goods, prices, and the ups and downs of business conditions, rather than by the moral principles taught by the Church, and the Church itself was becoming increasingly involved. The Catholic theologians saw clearly that market price, more than moral law, was becoming an important influence on human relationships. They began to search for the ethical foundations of market exchange—a just price.

By the thirteenth century three closely related ideas had been developed by the Schoolmen, the Catholic philosophers and professors. One idea, popular in central Europe, identified the just price as that which would provide for the continued reproduction of the social order. It would return to the producer just enough to provide for the necessaries of life and maintenance of the family, and to the merchant just enough profit to continue in trade. The buyer, meanwhile, would obtain needed goods without depriving the seller of the income necessary to continue in trade or production.

A more sophisticated analysis, but one consistent with the idea of reproduction of the social order, identified the just price as the price a modern economist would call the long-run price in a competitive market. With all forms of monopoly and market control eliminated, competition among sellers would hold the market price to a level that covered only the costs of production and a normal profit. Costs of production would be high enough to provide subsistence for the worker, including family maintenance, education, and acquisition of necessary skills. If less were paid to the worker, the working population would decline, supplies in the market would diminish, and prices would rise until the necessary work force was reproducing itself in the long run. A similar process would occur if profits were too low to enable traders to supply the amounts desired by buyers. On the other hand, if prices rose above the necessary production costs, supplies would increase and competition would drive prices down. In the long run, competitive markets would generate prices of goods just equal to the socially necessary costs of production. This argument, stated in different language, is found in that great treatise on theology, the *Summa Theologica* of Thomas Aquinas (about 1225–1274), an Italian theologian who taught at Cologne and Paris. The analysis of market price, a key element in modern economics, was begun by the Schoolmen.

The Schoolmen were also aware of the welfare aspects of market exchange. An English monk of the thirteenth century, Thomas Middleton, and a Scots theologian, Duns Scotus (about 1265–1308), who taught at Oxford as well as Cologne and Paris and was a strong critic of Aquinas on theological matters, developed the idea that both buyer and seller benefited from market exchange: if they didn't, they wouldn't trade. Buying, selling, and market exchange were seen as increasing individual welfare.

The economic attitudes embodied in the orthodox moral philosophy of the Middle Ages were summed up in a famous parable. A monk on a pilgrimage to Rome purchased a silver chalice for his cathedral. Traveling back to Germany with a band of merchants, he showed them the vessel and told what he had paid for it. The merchants congratulated him on his purchase, telling him that he had bought it for far less than its true value, and laughed that an unworldly monk could drive a better bargain than any of them. Horrified, the monk left immediately, made his way back to Rome, and paid the seller of the chalice enough to make up the fair price. It was the only moral thing to do.

Such attitudes may have been consistent with an economy of customary prices and accepted economic relationships, but they were out of tune with the success-oriented, profit-motivated behavior of the market economy. They may have been appropriate to people concerned with eternal salvation, but they did not suit people who sought material wealth and success. They may have worked in a society organized in stable groups, but they were incompatible with an individualistic social order and a desire to rise in wealth and status.

The rise of a market economy created a moral dilemma for the people of the early modern era. On the one hand, the ethical teachings of religion told them that each individual was morally responsible for others. These ideas were found in the Old Testament story of Cain and Abel and in the New Testament parable of the Good Samaritan, to cite only two widely known examples. On the other hand, survival and success in a market economy required that each person try to outreach, outsmart, and overcome others.

Rivalry, not brotherhood, was the necessary mode of behavior, and the principle of *caveat emptor*—"let the buyer beware"—prevailed. Market relationships were impersonal and transient compared with the permanent and face-to-face relationships of an unchanging rural village. People were judged more by their success in acquiring wealth than by the morality of their behavior.

This moral dilemma—the conflict between salvation and success—was an important factor in setting the stage for the Reformation. It was hard for an urban merchant to believe that the business way of life was less proper than any other. It was difficult to understand that the competition necessary for survival was antagonistic to the moral law, that the single-minded pursuit of profit that was fundamental to the very livelihood of business people was frowned upon by the divines. So doubts arose. Were the theologians right in their teachings about the modes of conduct required for salvation? After all, they were only human, like everyone else, and subject to human error. What did the Bible itself say about these matters? Such questions led to the Protestant heresy—doubt of the infallibility of the Church and a desire to go directly to the Bible as the repository of God's law, without the priest as intermediary.

The theological arguments of the Reformation are of little interest to us here, but out of them came a new economic ethic that gave the profit-motivated market economy its moral letters of credit. Underlying the new morality was the idea that God had intended a place on earth for each individual, through which the individual could work out his or her destiny. This place, or "calling," had to be sought and found by personal soul-searching, and once found, it had to be diligently pursued. Salvation was earned by hard work in one's calling, and any calling—even that of the merchant—was equal in merit to any other in the eyes of God. But how was one to identify one's calling? The theologians answered: partly through inner feeling and partly through success. Worldly success indicated that one had found the calling that God had approved. To achieve success, avoid idleness, temptation, and luxury: work hard and save. These were the prescriptions for ethical behavior hammered out during a half-century of religious controversy, sermonizing, and polemics. They fitted the needs of the growing urban middle class and promoted the hard work and capital accumulation that led to economic expansion.

By the eighteenth century the new economic ethic had lost much of its religious sanction and had become an almost universal way of life. That American sage, Benjamin Franklin, stated it in the form of aphorisms, which were repeated endlessly to generations of young people:

> Early to bed, early to rise, makes a man healthy, wealthy, and wise.

> The sound of your hammer at five in the morning, or at nine at night, heard by a creditor, makes him easy six months longer.

> What maintains one vice would bring up two children.

The new ethic was the basis of a secular and materialistic value system that has dominated the climate of opinion in western Europe and North America ever since.

But even though attitudes changed and the accepted goals of individual action became heavily materialistic, a moral problem remained. Was it true that economic failure meant unworthiness, that success and salvation were synonymous? Did not the individual have a responsibility to others that went beyond merely meeting one's contractual obligations in the market-place? Had the monk been correct in returning to Rome to pay the merchant more for the chalice than his bargain called for?

The problem arises because of the inherent conflict between an ethical principle—all humanity is one—and the competitive rivalry of the market economy expressed in the legal principle of *caveat emptor*. The ethical principle requires individuals to take responsibility for others, while the legal principle calls for individuals to look out only for themselves.

This moral dilemma has puzzled philosophers and ecclesiastics from the sixteenth century onward. Various solutions appeared in the religious controversies of the sixteenth century, in the eighteenth-century philosophy of *noblesse oblige*, in the writings of nineteenth-century socialists, and in the welfare legislation of the twentieth century. Present in all these approaches to the problem is a belief that the social system should not allow an individual to be crushed and destroyed by the operation of impersonal market forces. But the dilemma remains, and economists must be, in part, moral philosophers, while philosophers must also deal with economic issues.

TWO
THE EARLY
DAYS

*Jean-Baptiste Colbert (1619–1683)
was a French minister of finance
who established a program of
regulation of trade and commerce
in seventeenth-century France.*

Practical people often argue over the most esoteric of subjects, for policy decisions sometimes rest upon the most intricate of theories. One of these debates took place during the eighteenth century, and from it emerged the foundations of modern economics. The question at issue was the ultimate source of national wealth, which some saw in trade, others in agriculture and the natural forces of life, and still others in human labor. Although the issue may seem, at first glance, to be devoid of practical significance, the whole range of government economic policy depended on the outcome.

The Mercantilists

The mercantilists were the first to take the field. These writers were concerned with the national states that developed during the sixteenth and seventeenth centuries. They faced two different but related problems, one internal and one external.

The domestic problem was one of unity. National power had to be built from the localism of the Middle Ages. For the economy this meant a unified monetary system and coinage, a national system of weights and measures, elimination of internal tolls on roads and rivers, and a national system of taxes and tariffs. These institutions, which today we take for granted, were slowly forged by national rulers against the opposition of feudal lords, who tried to keep as much control as possible over the economy of their regions. The building of a national economy was predicated on the growing political power of the monarchs against the great nobles.

In this struggle the monarchs found natural allies in several places. First in importance were the rising commercial interests of towns and cities. Merchants benefited from the widened trade made possible by a unified economy in which local barriers to commerce were reduced. In turn, the merchants augmented the monarchs' power by helping finance the armies needed to subordinate the nobility. The interests of monarchs and merchants further coincided in that both benefited from expanded foreign trade. Merchants earned profits from trade with the newly opened lands in Asia and the New World. To the extent that the merchants of one country dominated trade with another area, profits would flow to the homeland and domestic manufacturers would be stimulated by the export market. The state gained from the tariff revenues derived from large trade, from the sale of trade monopolies, from the development of strategic military industries and personnel—shipbuilding and ship supplies, sailors and captains—and from the general economic growth that provided a firm base for national power. Two of the basic goals of national policy, therefore, were the development of commerce and its counterpart, the growth of power in international affairs.

A second group allied with the monarchs consisted of the smaller landowners, who looked to the state as a counterweight to the powers of the barons. This group was more interested in commercial agriculture than in warfare, jousting, and family power, and wanted the monarchs to maintain order and promote the growing markets from which they profited. They knew that as the power of the state increased vis-à-vis that of the great lords, their own wealth and power in local affairs would also increase.

Two other groups emerged from the rising market economy and national states. One was the legal profession, whose members were needed to interpret and define the vastly complicated economic relationships that developed out of free association and private contract in the market environment. Old and familiar legal relationships were being replaced by new ones, and lawyers were needed to systematize them. The second group comprised public administrators and the royal court. Although small in numbers, these two groups were of great strategic importance. A "white-collar" superstructure, allied with and dependent upon business and government, supported the policies designed to strengthen unity and national power.

Out of the political and economic alliances between crown, merchants, rural gentry, and professional people emerged economic policies designed to unify the nation under a single strong ruler, develop its military and naval strength, and increase its wealth through both domestic production and foreign trade. These policies and the theories underlying them have come to be called *mercantilism*, the first systematic body of modern economic thought.

One of the clearest statements of mercantilist policy was made by Phillip von Hornick (1638–1712), an Austrian civil servant writing for a backward country constantly threatened by the Turks. He wrote, in 1684, a widely read tract called *Austria over All, If She Only Will*, listing "nine principal rules of national economy":

To inspect the country's soil with the greatest care, and not to leave the agricultural possibilities of a single corner or clod of earth unconsidered . . . . All commodities found in a country, which cannot be used in their natural state, should be worked up within the country. . . . Attention should be given to the population, that it may be as large as the country can support . . . gold and silver once in the country are under no circumstances to be taken out for any purpose. . . . The inhabitants should make every effort to get along with their domestic products. . . . [Foreign commodities] should be obtained not for gold or silver, but in exchange for other domestic wares . . . and should be imported in unfinished form, and worked up within the country. . . . Opportunities should be sought night and day for selling the country's superfluous goods to these foreigners in manufactured form. . . . No importation should be allowed under any circumstances of which there is a sufficient supply of suitable quality at home.

These basic policies of nationalism, self-sufficiency, and national power were adopted in varying degrees by all the states of Europe. Manufacturing was encouraged by subsidies, special privileges, patents, and monopolies. Foreign trade was stimulated by acquisition of colonies and efforts to keep wages down, and it was regulated by tariffs, navigation laws, and trade restrictions. Agriculture was fostered by a variety of policies: in England imports of food were taxed in order to keep out foreign competition, while in France exports of agricultural products were taxed in order to keep domestic production at home. In particular, the munitions industries were promoted—guns, gunpowder, ships, and ship supplies.

In England, where trade quickly became the basis for increased wealth and national power, a great deal of emphasis was placed on expansion of the money supply as a stimulus to economic growth. In those days of limited markets and inadequate purchasing power, one of the barriers to economic growth was a lack of both hard cash in the hands of consumers and credit available for business. Rulers often needed to borrow, and they would similarly benefit from readily available cash and credit and from low interest rates. Modern banking was only in its infancy, and the availability of money and credit depended very heavily on the cash available—and that meant gold and silver coins. It was inevitable, then, that monetary policy was a major concern of the mercantilist economists. Basically, they favored what we would call an "easy money" policy—plenty of available cash to stimulate trade and keep interest rates down. On the other hand, they had to keep inflationary pressures in check, for two reasons: (1) rising prices created difficulties for the workers and the poor, because wage rates tended to lag behind price increases, and political unrest would therefore follow; and (2) rising prices would reduce foreign demand for domestic manufactures and ultimately result in worsened economic conditions at home.

Domestic and international economic policies, therefore, became closely intertwined, and the English mercantilists were quick to realize that the world economy was a web of interconnections. Hard experience as well as sharp analysis taught them that if the domestic money supply and purchasing power expanded more rapidly than the supply of goods available for sale, domestic prices would rise, imports would increase, and exports would fall. The fall in exports and rise in imports would then result in an export of gold and silver to make up for the "unfavorable" balance of trade. This in turn would reduce the money supply at home and cause the domestic economy to languish. These relationships were soon well understood, and a cardinal tenet of the mercantilists was encouragement of a "favorable" balance of trade. If exports exceeded imports, they argued, gold and silver would enter the country, money would be available, economic growth would be stimulated, and national wealth would grow.

The best statement of English mercantilism is found in a brief book by Thomas Mun (1571–1641), a businessman whose *England's Treasure by Forraign Trade* was not published until 1663, almost a quarter century after his death, although it circulated in manuscript long before then. Mun suggested a variety of ways by which the English government could stimulate trade, encourage exports, and promote a favorable balance of trade and imports of gold to increase the money supply. By modern standards the argument is crude, but the book remains a classic statement of the idea that the economy needs direction from a strong government if desired goals are to be achieved.

It should not be assumed that mercantilism was the same everywhere. There were great differences between countries. In France, for example, where luxury products such as silks and linens, tapestries, furniture, and wine were of major importance, close regulation of the quality of goods was emphasized. Under the leadership of Jean-Baptiste Colbert (1619–1683), minister of finance for more than twenty years during the reign of Louis XIV, national guilds were set up to regulate the major industries. Only craftsmen who were guild members could operate, and they were subject to the regulations of the national organization. The royal power, supported by steady revenues from the salt tax, was strong enough to enforce the regulations effectively, and the guilds remained powerful until the French Revolution at the end of the eighteenth century.

Unlike France, the efforts of her Iberian neighbors, Spain and Portugal, are a classic example of failure in applying the principles of mercantilism. So much liquid wealth came into these countries from their empire possessions that both nations felt little need in their complacency to turn to new domestic manufacture to balance their economies. In a different vein, Russia, the largest country in Europe, was backward agriculturally and would remain so until the dynamic rule of Peter the Great in the early eighteenth century.

In England, in contrast to France, regulation of domestic industry was not successful because the government, always short of money, was never strong enough to administer regulations effectively. English mercantilism was devoted primarily to expansion of trade and encouragement of manufactures. One result of this situation was that the medieval guilds disintegrated, especially when cloth production developed in rural areas, and industrial processes were far freer of restrictions than were those of France. When the Industrial Revolution began in the late eighteenth century, this absence of guilds and guild regulations gave English industry a long head start over France and the other continental countries that had copied the French example.

Nor was there always agreement on policies within nations. Popular revulsion in England against government grants of monopoly to individuals and companies was so great that in 1598 Queen Elizabeth I promised reforms and in 1601 proclaimed the end of many monopoly privileges. Two years later, in the famous "Case of Monopolies," the courts decided, in a path-breaking decision, that even monopoly grants by the Crown were subject to the common-law prohibitions on restraint of trade. Parliament finally prohibited government grants of monopoly in 1624, completing the legal foundations on which American antitrust laws are based.

The mercantilists recognized that wealth was produced by human effort, in general, but felt that it would not be realized unless trade and commerce were encouraged—unless exchange of goods enabled producers to make a profit. For this reason they emphasized the growth of trade and commerce as the key to increased national wealth, and expansion of the money supply as the key to increased trade. To the question, "What is the source of the wealth of nations?" the mercantilists gave the first answer, "Commerce."

In many respects they were right for their time. In the sixteenth and seventeenth centuries the most powerful nations of Europe were those that had developed their international and overseas trade to the greatest extent. Trade seemed to stimulate both manufacturing and agriculture and to bring prosperity, wealth, and power to the entire nation. Mercantilist doctrines had a commonsense validity derived from what people could see going on around them.

Opposition to Mercantilism

By the middle of the eighteenth century the mercantilists' preoccupation with trade and national power had begun to grate on some of the economic interests of the growing market economy. Mercantilist policies were fine for the great merchants and financiers who operated in the international economy; the basic goals of national power suited the rulers; and government administrators and courtiers were often able to benefit substantially, either directly or through bribes, from government grants of special economic privilege. But the economy became more varied as it grew, and both agricultural and industrial interests were increasingly coming to find that mercantilist policies were often not in their best interest. The policies were subjected to substantial criticism, and the theories on which they were based were questioned.

Small businesses, in particular, felt hemmed in by the monopolistic privileges granted to a few big financial and trading companies, and both they and the smaller farmers resented the taxes imposed to maintain a national power alien to their individual interests. A classic example is the issue of "taxation without representation" in Britain's American colonies. When the French and Indian Wars ended in 1763, the western frontiers of the colonies were relatively safe for colonization and development, and the colonists were well aware that much of their economic future lay in the West. The British government, however, long committed to development of the fur trade and favoring the interests of the Hudson's Bay Company,* had prohibited settlement beyond the Allegheny Mountains. Troops were stationed in the colonies to protect the frontier and enforce the prohibition, which protected the colonists from the Indians before 1763, but which restricted colonial economic growth after the frontier was pacified. To make matters worse, taxes on legal documents and tea were imposed in the colonies to pay for the troops, who were sometimes quartered in the homes of colonials. The colonists had to support the very troops who were protecting English business interests against their own! One wonders what attitude the colonists would have taken had the tax revenues been used to open the frontier rather than close it.

The case of the American colonies, where the issue became political and helped lead to the American Revolution, was a striking example of opposition to mercantilist policies. In Europe, however, a debate about purely economic issues arose. Was it true that economic expansion and growth were best achieved through regulation and direction? Would not better results be achieved in a free economy unhampered by the directing force of a mercantilist government? The debate over these questions was particularly strong in France and England.

In France, government regulation of production was so detailed that, for example, it specified the number of threads per inch in the manufacture of cloth. There was a multiplicity of taxes and tolls, and regulation of imports and exports was strict. Yet the nobility was exempt from taxation, while substantial taxes were levied on peasants and independent farmers. Moreover, the government was corrupt and inefficient—indeed, this probably made the system workable: the regulations and taxes could often be evaded by judicious bribes or clever evasions. The situation was so bad that one government inspector of trademarks, Vincent de Gournay (1712–1759), disenchanted with mercantilist regulation, is reputed to have originated the famous phrase *laissez faire, laissez passer,* or "free enterprise, free trade," in a free translation.

The Physiocrats

The most important French antimercantilists called themselves *Physiocrats.* Their leader was François Quesnay (1694–1774), court physician to Louis XV. Quesnay disagreed with the mercantilist assumption that wealth originated in industry and trade. He argued that only agriculture, by virtue of the life-giving aspects of nature, could produce a surplus over and above the

*The royal family and members of the nobility were major stockholders in the Hudson's Bay Company.

effort invested in production. Quesnay then went on in his famous *Economic Table* of 1758 to show how the surplus from agriculture flowed through the entire economy in the form of rent, wages, and purchases, supporting all the social classes as it went. Two policy conclusions stemmed from his analysis: (1) regulation of trade and industry impeded economic development by hindering the flow of income and commodities on which the economy depended; and (2) all taxes should be paid by landowners, as distinguished from farmers, partly because they were not productive and partly because their luxurious way of living distorted the flow of income.

Quesnay had been greatly impressed by the discovery of the circulation of blood in the human body and likened the circulation of money and products to that biological process. He believed profoundly that all wealth came ultimately from the life-giving process created by God. A strong believer in the supremacy of natural law, he felt that a regime of economic freedom not only was natural but also would be both beneficial and self-regulating.

Another Physiocrat, Jacques Turgot (1727–1781), rose to become minister of finance. In two short years he introduced a variety of antifeudal and antimercantilist reforms and was supported by the king, but opposition from the nobility forced him out of office. Even the "absolute" ruler of France was unable to push through reforms over the opposition of the nobility, and a few years later the old regime was swept away.*

All the Physiocrats agreed on one basic proposition, that wealth came ultimately from the land. Only land contained the life-giving forces of nature. Manufacturing could change only the form of wealth derived from nature, and commerce could change only its location and ownership. Land alone could produce a surplus. This was the second major theory of the source of wealth.

The Economic Liberals

The physiocratic interlude was short, although its influence was felt even in the United States, where a long line of statesmen from Thomas Jefferson to Abraham Lincoln were convinced that the nation's future depended on encouraging the small farmer. Far more important was the rise of *economic liberalism.* From small beginnings in the late seventeenth and early eighteenth centuries, it became the mainstream of economic thought in the nineteenth century and lives on today as the classic capitalist ideology.

The early economic liberals—those who advocated the doctrine before it was systematized by Adam Smith in the latter part of the eighteenth century—attacked restrictions on international trade and fought for an end to

---

*During the Revolution another prominent Physiocrat, Pierre du Pont de Nemours, emigrated to the United States, where he stayed for several years. In 1802 his son founded a small gunpowder factory near Wilmington, Delaware, the beginning of the great Du Pont chemical enterprise.

tariffs, monopolies, and regulations. They based their argument on the social theory that individual motives, however selfish they might be, resulted in benefits to society as a whole.

The first important economic liberal in England was Dudley North (1641–1691), whose *Discourses upon Trade* was published anonymously in the year of his death. Because North was a wealthy merchant and landowner who became a treasury official, it is understandable that he was cautious in publishing an attack on the nationalistic policies of mercantilism. His book made a strong case for free trade and attacked the mercantilist assumption that a favorable balance of trade was necessarily desirable. People trade, he argued, because it is advantageous to both parties, promoting specialization, division of labor, and the increase of wealth. Regulation interfered with these benefits by reducing and restricting trade and inevitably reducing real wealth.

North's argument was supported by the philosopher and historian David Hume (1711–1776), who pointed out that an automatic economic process would cause any favorable balance of trade to disappear: a surplus of exports would be paid for by imports of gold and silver, which would increase the money supply and cause prices to rise, which, in turn, would cause a decline in exports until exports and imports were in balance. It was, therefore, impossible for mercantilist policy to continuously maintain both a favorable balance of trade and imports of gold and silver.

The logic of North and Hume destroyed the mercantilist arguments for regulation of foreign trade. According to Hume, the policies would not work, and North showed that the results would be undesirable if they did work.

In the meantime, a fascinating, popular, and controversial book had appeared in 1704, a doggerel poem called *The Fable of the Bees*, written by Bernard de Mandeville (1670–1733), a Dutch doctor who had emigrated to England. The poem's basic argument was that advances in civilization were the result of vices, not virtues. Progress came from the selfish interests of the individual—desire for ease and comfort, luxury and pleasure—not from any natural propensity to work hard and save or from benevolent concern for others. Prosperity and economic growth would be increased by giving free play to the selfish motives of the individual, limited only by the maintenance of justice. The vice of selfishness would spur people to maximize their gains and thereby add to the wealth of the nation:

> *Thus Vice nurs'd Ingenuity,*
> *Which joined with Time and Industry,*
> *Had carry'd Life's Conveniencies,*
> *Its real Pleasures, Comforts, Ease,*
> *To such a Height, the very Poor*
> *Liv'd better than the Rich before,*
> *And nothing could be added more.*

The book was suppressed by an embarrassed government, with the full support of the guardians of morality. Yet, together with the theory of natural economic adjustments described by North and Hume, the selfish motives lauded by Mandeville became the basis of the next great economic theory— economic liberalism.

The idea that rational self-interest, together with competitive market forces, could lead to a regime of social order in a world of individual action was beginning to develop. In the 1720s, Richard Cantillon (died 1734), an Irishman who became a merchant in London and later a banker in Paris, wrote *An Essay on the Nature of Commerce in General*. It was published only in French in 1755; an English translation did not appear until 1931. It was not an influential book in its time, but it illustrates how some people in the early eighteenth century were thinking about the problem of economic order in an individualistic society.

Cantillon generalized the ideas about competitive markets developed by the Schoolmen of the thirteenth century into an early and crude version of what a modern economist would call *general equilibrium theory*. The underlying argument of his *Essay* was that rational self-interest on the part of traders, operating within a system of freely adjusting competitive markets, would lead to a network of mutually compatible prices and quantities traded. Order would prevail in the economy through the operation of human reason and rationality—an idea typical of the Enlightenment of the eighteenth century. Cantillon consciously imitated the recently discovered mechanics of Isaac Newton's physics, but with human reason and market competition replacing the physical forces of inertia and gravity in creating a natural equilibrium.

As to the source of wealth, the economic liberals of the eighteenth century found it in neither trade nor agriculture, but in human labor. It was through individual effort, they argued, that production takes place and the wherewithal to satisfy human needs is provided. Nature produces few materials that people can use in natural form: almost all natural products must be transformed by human effort before they can satisfy human wants. Without productive effort natural products are worthless.

This theory became known as the *labor theory of value*. It emphasized that the production of wealth had as its ultimate purpose the satisfaction of human wants. Wealth could not be considered an end in itself, nor was the aggrandizement of national power its proper end. Wealth *was* wealth because it bettered people's lives. The production of wealth, furthermore, depended not on the fertility of the soil or on favorable trade balances but on the individual incentives of ordinary people. The motive for work was the need to provide food, clothing, shelter, and comforts. The greater the incentive to work, the greater would be the production of wealth, and the faster would humanity move toward a more abundant society.

John Locke (1632–1704), the English philosopher, tied together these ideas about labor and production of wealth with private property, and in doing so made the institution of property one of the cornerstones of the liberal ideology. By adding labor to natural resources, people added part of themselves to the final product, making the product "theirs" to use or consume. Both wealth and private property were simultaneously produced by human labor. In Locke's words:

> God hath given the world to men in common. . . . Yet every man has a property in his own person. The labour of his body and the work of his hands we may say are properly his. Whatsoever, then, he removes out of the state that nature hath provided and left it in, he hath mixed his labour with, and joined to it something that is his own, and thereby makes it his property.

Later economic liberals made much of these connections between labor, wealth, and property. They argued that the first requisite for national economic growth was the protection of private property, for unless the right to property was sustained the incentive to work was reduced and the production of wealth would decrease.

A favorite illustration of this principle was a comparison of the wealth of the English and the poverty of the Turks. In ancient times, liberals pointed out, the domain of the Turk was the wealthiest in the world, with flourishing cities, prosperous agriculture, large exports, and world-famous manufactures. But a despotic and arbitrary government seized wealth without justification, imposed confiscatory taxes, and operated both justice and government through a system of bribery. These actions brought an end to prosperity. The Turk languished in poverty thereafter, unwilling to work, to produce, or to accumulate capital because it would be seized or destroyed by a corrupt government. Happy and prosperous England, on the other hand, was growing in wealth because individual initiative was protected by a rule of law that preserved for the individual the wealth he or she produced and saved. Justice was evenhanded, not arbitrary. The sanctity of private contracts was preserved, and no property could be taken for public use without just compensation. Whatever one earned could be used as the individual alone saw fit—within the limits of legality and decency. According to the economic liberal, the functions of government were few: protection of property, maintenance of justice, and national defense. The economy would operate within this framework without additional aid or regulation. Individual incentives would produce national wealth.

There were many variations on this theme. Some economic liberals would grant broader powers to the national government; others put more stress on the strength of individual incentives and competition, and still others on the operation of supply and demand in free markets. But all agreed on the need to free individual initiative from the limitations imposed by mercantilist restrictions, on the importance of work in producing wealth, and on the necessity of protecting and preserving property rights as the cornerstone of economic policy.

THREE
ADAM SMITH

Adam Smith (1723–1790) was the great Scottish expounder of economic liberalism and the policy of laissez-faire.

Adam Smith was the greatest of the economic liberals. A philosopher and college professor, he is considered today to be the founder of modern economics. Strangely, in his own lifetime he was known primarily for his writings in philosophy rather than economics and had little influence on public policy. He cultivated his academic garden, and his flowers did not bloom until later.

The Philosophical Life

Smith was born in Kirkcaldy, Scotland, in 1723, a few months after his father's death. His childhood was quiet and uneventful, and at age fourteen he entered the University of Glasgow. He did well enough to win a scholarship to Oxford, where he spent six years, dismayed by what he considered to be the low level of intellectual activity and the immorality of his fellow students. In 1751 he went to the University of Edinburgh to lecture, and the following year he became professor of logic at Glasgow when an opening suddenly appeared. Luck seemed to follow the young professor, for the next year the professorship of moral philosophy—Smith's favorite subject—became vacant and he was appointed to that post. He lectured on ethics, and his book *The Theory of Moral Sentiments* was published in 1759. To the modern reader it seems old-fashioned but interesting. Its basic idea is that ethical systems develop by a natural process out of individual personal relationships—a view that reflects the eighteenth-century interest in natural law. The individual decides that certain actions are proper or improper by observing the reactions of others to his or her behavior. A social consensus then develops, approving those patterns of behavior that benefit both society and the individual. The process amounts to an early "other-directed" theory of human action. The book was an immediate success and caught on well with the intelligentsia. Smith's reputation grew, and students even came from the Continent to study under him. He set to work writing a book on economics and began lecturing on "Police, Justice, Revenue, and Arms" at the university.

Then came his greatest stroke of luck, but one that he had thoroughly earned. Charles Townshend, the politician who later as chancellor of the exchequer was responsible for the tea tax and other taxes that helped bring on the American Revolution, married a wealthy widow and acquired a teenage stepson. An appropriate education for the young Duke of Buccleuch became important, and Townshend resolved to get the best. He had been very impressed by Adam Smith's book—and by the popular and critical esteem in which it was held—so he asked the forty-year-old philosopher to take a position as the young duke's tutor. To the surprise of his friends, including the philosopher David Hume, Smith accepted the post: it involved a three-year sojourn in France and a lifetime pension of three hundred pounds a year (about fifteen hundred dollars, a large sum in those days).

Much of the time in France was spent in Toulouse, where Smith, bored, began writing a book on economics. Later, in Paris, Smith met the leading physiocrats Quesnay and Turgot and discussed their doctrines.

Returning to Scotland, Smith lived on his pension and continued writing his book. His friends wondered when it would be finished, for he seemed to work on it interminably. Finally, in 1776, *An Inquiry into the Nature and Causes of the Wealth of Nations* was published.* The book was successful but not popular. Although it was read and appreciated by some, the general public ignored it. William Pitt seems to have based some of his tax proposals of the late 1780s on Smith's ideas, but it was not until twenty years after Smith's death that a new generation of writers, intent on building a new science of political economy, established Smith as the founder of their science and a major genius. In the meantime, the author in 1778 was appointed a commissioner of the customs, a post his father had held. His death in 1790 passed almost unnoticed by his contemporaries.

Adam Smith did not lead a spectacular life. As a child of three he was kidnapped by gypsies for a few hours, and, as a grown man, he was once confronted briefly by a robber, but otherwise he had few adventures. Typically, he was absentminded. Strolling in his garden at Kirkcaldy one Sunday morning, wearing a dressing gown and lost in concentration, he took a wrong turn down the turnpike and walked fifteen miles to Dunfermline be-

---

*Other important events occurred in 1776. Jeremy Bentham's *Fragment on Government* and Richard Price's *On Civil Liberty* were published, as was Edward Gibbon's *The History of the Decline and Fall of the Roman Empire*. Parliament rejected a bill that would have provided for universal male suffrage. Discontent continued in the American colonies. And the Boulton and Watt steam engine was applied to factory machinery for the first time.

fore his thoughts were interrupted by church bells. But, despite the colorless personality of its author, the *Wealth of Nations* is a great book because it resolved a key problem of social philosophy in its time.

The Problem in Social Philosophy: Order or Chaos in Society

The key problem of social philosophy in the eighteenth century was how social order emerges out of the potential chaos of an individualistic society. The problem arose because the spreading market economy, penetrating deeply into the daily lives of ordinary people, was gradually eliminating the medieval patterns of social status and defined obligations.

In medieval times each person had a place as part of one or more organized groups, each with its rights and duties. Lord and peasant, miller and priest, were each part of a village community that continued to function on the basis of traditional and often inherited obligations to others. Artisan and merchant were members of guilds and citizens of towns, and each had a place and function, at least in theory if not in practice, based on the charter of guild or town. Religious doctrine held that there was a universal natural order, ordained by God, that underlay both the order of nature and the order of society. If many people worked to support the few who governed and fought, while others prayed, it was because God had established a social order designed to carry out all of those needed tasks.

Yet the medieval social system was rapidly passing and by the mid-eighteenth century had largely disappeared in bustling cities such as London, which were largely oriented toward international trade, banking and finance, and the making of money. What was to take the place of a social system of organized groups and established rights and duties? Could society function at all when composed only of individual units—and selfish ones at that—following their own bents and trying to outreach one another? How could social harmony be achieved in this environment of individualistic chaos?

Individualism in English Life

England in the eighteenth century was an open society in almost every area of life outside of politics. Individual initiative and innovation were becoming mass phenomena. In the practical and fine arts, it was the golden age of English pottery and of the great furniture makers such as Chippendale and Sheraton. English painting reached its greatest heights with Gainsborough, Reynolds and Romney, and Handel composed his great oratorios. New forms of literature appeared: the novel (Defoe's *Robinson Crusoe*, Richardson's *Pamela*, and Fielding's *Tom Jones*), biography of a new type (Boswell's *Life of Samuel Johnson*), popular history (Hume's *History of England* and Gibbon's *The History of the Decline and Fall of the Roman Empire*), and the periodical essay (those of Addision and Steele in *The Tatler* and *The Spectator*). The first daily newspapers were established in London, and the first monthly magazine appeared.

The British Empire was extended by the acquisition of Canada, Gibraltar, Malta, and Ceylon. Robert Clive and Warren Hastings achieved supremacy in India for the British. Captain James Cook explored the Pacific from Australia and New Zealand to California and Hawaii for more than a decade. George Vancouver explored the northwest coast of America. James Bruce penetrated Africa in a daring expedition and found the source of the Blue Nile. Commercial and naval supremacy were won from the Dutch early in the century, and London replaced Amsterdam as the foremost center of shipping and finance in Europe.

Technological changes were building the foundations of industrialism. The cotton textile industry was transformed by a series of innovations that created the modern form of cloth manufacture, ushered in the Industrial Revolution, and made Lancashire and Liverpool great manufacturing and shipping centers. In 1738 John Kay invented a "flying shuttle" that greatly speeded up weaving and created a shortage of yarn. This led to the development of a spinning machine in the mid-1760s by James Hargreaves, an illiterate weaver and carpenter. An improved spinning machine developed by Richard Arkwright, a former barber, appeared a few years later. By 1770 Samuel Crompton, son of a farmer, had perfected a spinning "mule" that could produce the finest yarn in much larger quantities than was previously possible. Crompton's invention was stolen, and he died in poverty, but he gave the English cotton textile industry its greatest stimulus. The ability to produce yarn in larger amounts vastly increased the demand for cotton, and in America Eli Whitney developed the cotton gin, which mechanically cleaned the cotton boll. The growing of cotton throughout the world was greatly expanded, as was the plantation slavery system in America.

Industrial innovations had been preceded by the development of new machinery and methods in agriculture. Early in the eighteenth century Jethro Tull, a gentleman farmer, developed a drill for planting seeds and introduced the practice of planting in rows. Formerly, seed had to be scattered by hand across the field. Charles Townshend, grandfather of Adam Smith's benefactor and a prominent statesman, retired from political life in 1730 to devote his time to the development of new crops, especially fodder crops such as turnips and clover. This was an important breakthrough. Formerly land had to remain fallow to recoup its fertility, but now it could grow animal feed crops and still be "rested" for a year. Robert Bakewell, another successful farmer, developed techniques of stock breeding and introduced improved methods of livestock management. Arthur Young, a great writer on agriculture, spent most of his life publicizing the new methods and advocating enclosed fields as necessary to their adoption. The new agricultural techniques required larger farms, increased capital, and fenced-in fields, so from 1760 to 1830 the open lands of England were extensively fenced and hedged. Small farms and the village common lands disappeared in favor of larger acreage. Increased agricultural output and lower costs of production meant that greater numbers of the population could join the labor force in the growing industrial cities.

These are only a few of the leading events and major personalities associated with them. Thousands of other people in commerce and industry, agriculture, exploration and empire building, the arts, and other aspects of English life took advantage of opportunities with initiative and imagination. Many were of humble origin. Even in politics, the last stronghold of privilege, a few newcomers, like Edmund Burke, were able to work up to positions of prominence and power.

This was the practical, everyday side of the social process that philosophers like Smith tried to analyze. They could see all around them an economy in ferment, with change the order of the day. Progress was being made because of the individual efforts of thousands of people acting for themselves alone. There seemed to be no order or no reason behind the process, yet humanity was certainly moving onward—perhaps haltingly, but nevertheless onward—to what appeared to be a better world. In one respect there was a theoretical problem to solve—what were the principles that produced orderly social relationships in an individualistic, competitive, changing society? In another respect the problem was quite practical—would government regulation and control impede or advance the progress of such a society?

Natural Law in Science and Political Theory

A new view of the world was emerging in Adam Smith's time, and within its framework writers in the social sciences were beginning to construct new explanations of human and social relationships. The Renaissance (fifteenth and sixteenth centuries) introduced a rational, scientific point of view, and the Reformation (sixteenth century) greatly weakened religious explanations of natural and social phenomena. In the seventeenth and eighteenth centuries the development of science and mathematics greatly strengthened naturalistic rather than theological explanations and led to theories in which natural forces alone were sufficient to explain events.

The greatest advance in the natural sciences was made by the English physicist Isaac Newton (1642–1727). His *Mathematical Principles of Natural Philosophy* (1687) pictured a mechanical universe operating under the influence of basic natural laws of motion, gravitation, and conservation of energy to achieve a balance of forces, or equilibrium, in which all objects had their proper place. A great theory, it was proved to the public by the return of Halley's Comet in 1759, just as Edmund Halley had predicted after calculating its orbit in 1682.

Other sciences were similarly developed on the basis of natural laws. Robert Boyle discovered in 1660 that the volume of a gas varies inversely with its pressure. Antoine Lavoisier proved the law of conservation of matter through quantitative chemical analysis: matter changes its form but not its quantity. In biology, William Harvey discovered and demonstrated the circulation of blood; and the regularity of nature was emphasized when plant and animal forms were systematically classified in interrelated groups by botanists and zoologists of the time.

Political theory was the first area in the social sciences to develop an emphasis on natural law, regularity, and equilibrium. Hugo Grotius (1583–1645), the Dutch legal theorist and father of modern international law, stated the basic ideas. Grotius postulated that humans are inherently social beings and cannot survive without some form of social organization. Therefore, he argued, certain minimal conditions, or natural laws of society, must be realized if human society is to exist. Grotius listed the natural conditions of society as security of property, good faith and fair dealing, and correspondence between individual efforts and rewards.

It was in England, however, that natural-law theories of the state evolved most fully. The English were engaged, throughout the seventeenth and eighteenth centuries, in changing a monarchy that claimed absolute authority based on divine right to a constitutional government based on the consent of the governed. The classical theory of democracy emerged from these events and this debate.

People are inherently selfish, it was argued, and they institute governments in order to protect their natural rights as individuals—life, liberty, and ownership of property. A supporter of absolute monarchy, Thomas Hobbes (1588–1679) argued for absolutism on the ground that the stronger the power exercised by the sovereign, the more successful would be the social restraint on the selfish, combative element in human nature. In opposition to Hobbes, John Locke argued that order and freedom were compatible: people institute governments to avoid chaos and preserve their natural rights, but absolute power is granted to no one. The function of the state is to enforce the laws of nature and punish infractions, the laws of nature being superior even to acts of the state. Within this structure, Locke said, individual action could be given free play. To these foundations of democratic theory Locke and his followers added the theory of majority rule: the interests of everyone in preservation of order were essentially similar, and the best method of determining the common good was decision making by a majority. Only the individual could know what was in his or her best interest, and while a single person could be wrong in any one instance, it was highly unlikely that the consensus of a large group would be seriously in error. Finally, the Dutch philosopher Baruch Spinoza (1632–1677) added the last link to the liberal political philosophy: checks and balances within the government were necessary to temper power with justice. English political theorists quickly integrated that idea into democratic theory.

By the early years of the eighteenth century the political philosophers had developed a theory of liberal democracy based on natural-law precepts. An analysis of the economy in similar terms was next on the agenda. Toward the middle of the century there were several unsuccessful attempts by a variety of writers to produce systematic treatises on the natural laws of economic life and their relationship to individual freedom and government action. It was to this problem in social philosophy that Adam Smith directed his efforts. *An Inquiry into the Nature and Causes of the Wealth of Nations* was the result.

Smith's System of Natural Liberty

Adam Smith advocated a "system of natural liberty," in which everyone would be left free to pursue and advance their own interests. This system, he argued, would result in the greatest wealth for both the individual and society. Indeed, individual effort would bring maximum benefits for society as a whole and for other individuals. This was the simple principle that would enable social order to develop in an individualistic society.

The advocates of mercantilism and government regulation had assumed that the selfish desires of individuals would lead to less wealth for all unless human actions were regulated and controlled. More for me means less for you, was the assumption, unless efforts were directed toward more for all.

This argument was wrong, said Smith. If I want something from you, I must produce something you want and exchange it for what you have. Both of us benefit, because we both give up something that has less value to us than does the product we receive in exchange. The welfare of both is increased over what it would otherwise be. As Smith phrased it:

> It is not from the benevolence of the butcher, the brewer, or the baker, that we expect our dinner, but from their regard to their own interest. We address ourselves, not to their humanity but to their self-love, and never talk to them of our own necessities but of their advantages.

According to Smith, self-interest in a free society would lead to the most rapid progress and growth a nation was capable of achieving. People would save in order to improve their own positions and in so doing would add capital to the nation's resources. They would use that capital in the most profitable way to produce the things that others wanted most. Even where laws and regulations impeded freedom to invest, these motives would be so strong that they would still lead to growth and wealth:

> The uniform, constant, and uninterrupted effort of every man to better his condition, the principle from which public and national, as well as private opulence is originally derived, is frequently powerful enough to maintain the natural progress of things toward improvement, in spite both of the extravagance of government, and of the greatest errors of administration.

In Adam Smith's view, the greatest hindrance to economic progress was government. In the system of natural liberty there were only three legitimate functions of government: the establishment and maintenance of justice, national defense, and "erecting and maintaining certain public works and certain public institutions, which it can never be for the interest of any individual, or small number of individuals, to erect and maintain." Smith did not admit much into this last category, however. Roads and communications, yes—but their cost should be borne by the user through tolls rather than by the general taxpayer. Education and religious instruction, maybe—they were of general benefit, but could be provided by private enterprise or voluntary contributions as well as by government. Any other government undertaking would be more harmful than beneficial, even though the best of motives were behind it:

> Every system which endeavors . . . to draw towards a particular species of industry a greater share of the capital of the society than what would naturally go to it . . . retards, instead of accelerating, the progress of the society toward real wealth and greatness.

Although Smith definitely looked with disfavor upon government enterprise, it should not be supposed that he would give business a completely free hand. He was aware of the tendency of business people to conspire to their own advantage against the public:

> People of the same trade seldom meet together, even for merriment and diversion, but the conversation ends in a conspiracy against the public, or in some contrivance to raise prices.

Nevertheless, Smith was not afraid of private monopoly. He lived in a simpler age than ours, before the growth of great enterprises and giant industrial plants. The only example of industrial production in his book is a pin factory in which some two dozen handicraft workers were employed. In those days the capital required for entry into most trades was small, technology was simple and available to all, and monopoly existed only where special privileges were granted and protected by government. Smith was confident that no private monopoly unprotected by government could long endure: monopoly profits would immediately invite competition, which would destroy the monopoly.

The Self-Adjusting Market

If self-interest was the driving force of the economy, the mechanism through which it worked was a system of self-adjusting markets. Competition among sellers in an effort to make profits would naturally result in a pattern of production fitted to the needs and desires of consumers, while competition would hold profits to a minimum amount just large enough to motivate producers.

Every commodity, according to Smith, has a "natural" price. In primitive societies it is determined by the amount of labor needed for production. In more advanced societies, those in which private property has developed, the natural price depends on costs of production—the amount that must be paid for wages, rent, and profit. Whenever the market price of a commodity differs from its natural price, market forces are set in motion to move it back. As Smith explained it:

> When the price of any commodity is neither more nor less than what is sufficient to pay the rent of the land, the wages of the labour, and the profits of the stock [capital] employed in raising, preparing, and bringing it to market, according to their natural rates, the commodity is then sold for what may be called its natural price . . . precisely for what it is worth, or for what it really costs the person who brings it to market. . . .
>
> When the quantity of any commodity which is brought to market falls short of the effectual demand, all those who are willing to pay . . . cannot be supplied with the quantity which they want. . . . Some of them will be willing to give more. A competition will immediately begin among them, and the market price will rise. . . .
>
> When the quantity brought to market exceeds the effectual demand, it cannot be all sold to those who are willing to pay the whole value of the rent, wages and profit, which must be paid in order to bring it thither. . . . The market price will sink. . . .

These changes in price set in motion corresponding changes in the amount produced. When the market price of a commodity is greater than its natural price, more of that commodity will be produced and brought to market. On the other hand, production will fall when the market price is below the natural price and when, therefore, the resources used in production cannot be paid at their natural rates. Again, Smith describes how production responds to price relationships:

> The quantity of every commodity brought to market naturally suits itself to the effectual demand. . . . If at anytime it exceeds the effectual demand, some of the component parts of its price must be paid below their natural rate. If it is rent, the interest of the landlords will immediately prompt them to withdraw a part of their land; and if it is wages or profit, the interest of the labourers in the one case, and of their employers in the other, will prompt them to withdraw a part of their labour or stock from this employment. The quantity brought to market will soon be no more than sufficient to supply the effectual demand. All the different parts of its price will rise to their natural rate, and the whole price to its natural price.
>
> If on the contrary, the quantity brought to market should at any time fall short of the effectual demand, some of the component parts of its price must rise above their natural rate. If it is rent, the interest of all other landlords will naturally prompt them to prepare more land for the raising of this commodity; if it is wages or profit, the interest of all other labourers and dealers will soon prompt them to employ more labour and stock in preparing and bringing it to market. The quantity brought thither will soon be sufficient to supply the effectual demand. All the different parts of its price will soon sink to their natural rate, and its whole price to its natural price.

The natural price, therefore, is, as it were, the central price, to which the prices of all commodities are continually gravitating. Different accidents may sometimes keep them suspended a good deal above it, and sometimes force them down even somewhat below it. But whatever may be the obstacles which hinder them from settling in this center of repose and continuance, they are constantly tending towards it.

The whole quantity of industry annually employed in order to bring any commodity to market, naturally suits itself in this manner to the effectual demand. It naturally aims at bringing always the precise quantity thither which may be sufficient to supply, and no more than supply, that demand.

In the last two centuries little has been added to this description of market equilibrium. Contemporary economists use the term *normal* rather than *natural* price, and they are more careful to spell out the exact conditions under which it prevails. A much more complex analysis of production costs has been developed, and the process by which the level of output responds to price has been analyzed in greater detail. But the basic descriptions of how supply and demand determine an equilibrium price, of how competition pushes that price to a level that just covers production costs, and of how production responds to demand have remained fundamentally unchanged in the writings of successive generations of economists.

Smith's analysis of the self-adjusting market economy had tremendous significance. It showed that production will automatically adjust to the pattern of consumer demand, whatever that demand may be and however it may shift and change. It showed that competition among sellers will drive prices down to the lowest possible level consistent with continued production at levels satisfactory to consumers. It showed that resources will be used in the most efficient and economical manner—using as the criterion of efficiency and economy the satisfaction of consumer wants at the lowest possible prices consistent with continued production at the desired levels. And it showed that all this could be accomplished through the free operation of market forces, with no interference or direction from government or any other agency of economic management.

Smith emphasized, however, that these ideal results could be precluded by abridgments of full freedom in economic activity, such as "secrets in manufactures," "secrets in trade," "singularity of soil and situation," "monopoly," and "all those laws which restrain . . . competition." Smith was particularly opposed to monopoly in all of its forms, and some of his most pungent comments point to its evils:

> The monopolists, by keeping the market continually understocked, by never fully supplying the effectual demand, sell their commodities much above the natural price, and raise their emoluments, whether they consist in wages or profit, greatly above their natural rate.
>
> The price of monopoly . . . is upon every occasion the highest which can be squeezed out of the buyers. . . .

Whatever the source of the restrictions on economic freedom that led to monopoly—whether government, business, or labor—Adam Smith was opposed to it.

Two Qualifications

At this point it is important to note two limitations of Smith's analysis of the free market. These limitations were at the heart of criticisms developed by socialists of the nineteenth century, and theories of later economists have not satisfactorily overcome them.

The first limitation concerns the nature of "effectual demand" and its dependence on the pattern of income distribution. It is fine to argue that production will match the pattern of consumer demand, but if the distribution of income and wealth is highly unequal, that pattern will provide much to the rich and little to the poor. Unless the distribution of income is right and proper, it does little good to argue that production is efficient and economical. If the distribution of income is inequitable, the pattern of production will be inequitable as well, no matter how efficiently the free market works to match production with demand. This basic problem would soon be raised by the socialists spawned by the early Industrial Revolution, and it would shortly thereafter be expanded by Karl Marx into a theory of the breakdown of capitalism. Later generations of economists have attempted to provide answers to the problem—most successfully in the 1890–1910 period—with results that have not been fully satisfactory, as we shall presently see.

The second limitation, closely related to that of economic justice, concerns private property in land and capital. Adam Smith, as a good economic liberal, supported the institution of private property as both natural and necessary to the preservation of economic incentives. However, he granted its necessity only in advanced societies. In primitive society only labor needed a reward as a factor of production, and the cost of production consisted of wages alone. In advanced societies with private property, rent on land and profit on capital became part of the costs of production. In the case of rent and profit, the costs of production were clearly the products of *social organization,* not natural phenomena in the same sense as human labor and the motive of self-interest. This qualification spoiled Smith's grand scheme of an equilibrium of *natural* forces in the market.

Socialists were quick to seize upon these gaps in Smith's logic. Only a return to labor was natural, they argued, and only when the full value of output was gained by labor through social ownership of land and capital would the natural state of society be recaptured. Economic justice could then be achieved, since the entire product of society would go to those who worked, and the pattern of effectual demand would not be distorted by unearned income. In later chapters the dialogue on economic justice between the critics and the supporters of the existing order will be explored in greater detail.

Economic Growth

Adam Smith was not primarily concerned with these matters of justice in income distribution, and they did not become topics of major concern to economists until after the rise of socialism. Smith was far more concerned with economic growth and the advancement of society to higher levels, which he explained in terms of human motives inherent in the psychology of the individual and, hence, natural and inevitable in a free society.

The "progress of opulence," according to Smith, is the direct result of three factors: division of labor, widening markets, and accumulation of capital. As productivity rises because of these developments, "a general plenty diffuses itself through all the different ranks of the society."

Specialization in production and *division of labor* rest upon an inherent human "propensity to truck, barter and exchange one thing for another," according to Smith. Only humans show this propensity: "nobody ever saw a dog make a fair and deliberate exchange of one bone for another with another dog." Moreover the same psychological inclination that leads people to trade, and thus gives rise to specialization, also makes them dependent upon one another and thereby engenders the complex social fabric of the market economy. This is an old-fashioned view, however. The modern economist argues that people specialize in producing one thing rather than attempt to produce everything they need because their productivity and earnings are thereby increased.

Just as exchange gives rise to specialization and division of labor, Smith said, "The extent of this division must always be limited . . . by the extent of the market." When the market is small, no one can produce only one product. But when the market expands, producers can specialize and thereby gain the advantages of increased efficiency. Wider markets lead to greater specialization, higher productivity, and greater wealth, and to the use of money in an effort to overcome the difficulties of barter in a system of complex exchange relationships.

None of this economic growth can occur without large amounts of capital, gathered out of savings, and used to further increase productivity and promote still greater specialization and widening of markets. *Accumulation of capital* was seen as one key to economic expansion, but the whole process depended on security of property:

> In all countries where there is tolerable security, every man of common understanding will endeavor to employ whatever stock he can command, in procuring either present enjoyment or future profit. . . . A man must be perfectly crazy who, where there is tolerable security, does not employ all the stock which he commands, whether it be his own or borrowed of other people. . . .
>
> In those unfortunate countries, indeed, where men are continually afraid of the violence of their superiors, they frequently bury and conceal a great part of their stock . . . a common practice in Turkey, in Indostan, and I believe in most other governments of Asia.

Smith was well aware that economic growth brings change and diversity. As capital is accumulated, the natural progress of opulence proceeds from agriculture to manufacturing to commerce, and the affluent society exhibits prosperity in all three areas. A developing agriculture gives rise to the growth of towns, which in turn offer a larger market for agricultural products, and a developed urban and rural society offers widened opportunities for trade and shipping. Enlarged trade further stimulates manufacturing and specialized agricultural production for export. Population increases as productivity rises, facilitating still broader market expansion and stimulating still more specialization and capital accumulation.

By this process the economy moves forward to ever higher levels of development, raising the whole social order with it. It simultaneously maintains the orderly market equilibrium that continuously tends toward a pattern of production fitted to effectual demand. The system of natural liberty produces an equilibrium of forces moving always toward opulence.

Yet we should note an important aspect of Smith's ideas about economic growth that differs from some contemporary beliefs. Smith's vision was one of everyone working, saving, and specializing to increase his or her productivity and wealth—a mass movement of economic advancement. We do not find Smith arguing, as do some of today's apologists for great wealth, that economic progress is brought about by the innovative individual or the leaders of business and finance. Economic progress, according to Smith, stems from "the uniform, constant, and uninterrupted effort of every man to better his condition"—from a grass roots effort of the great mass of people—rather than from the actions of a few.

Although Smith strongly advocated a policy of laissez-faire and free trade without restrictions, his good Scottish common sense admitted some exceptions. Scotland had high tariffs and trade restrictions designed to limit the import of cheap English manufactures. These laws sought to protect the livelihood of Scottish handicraftsmen—hand weavers, for example—and the communities in which they lived. When Smith served as a commissioner of customs he supported vigorous enforcement of the Scottish tariffs and trade restrictions. He understood that economic development and technological change destroyed the old while creating the new. The effect of the agricultural revolution on village communities was widely known at the time: Oliver Goldsmith's narrative poem *The Deserted Village* had been published in 1770. Smith's theory glorified the progress generated by a growing and changing economy, but he recognized that in practice many could be seriously hurt as the new and better world developed. We shall meet this theme again.

Smith's Achievement

Adam Smith's analysis of the market economy emphasized that individualism resulted in order, not chaos. Even though each person competed with all others for wealth and profit, their very competition unleashed market forces that led to an orderly increase in the wealth of the nation. The desire for prosperity, coupled with a natural tendency to trade and exchange, led to specialization, investment of capital, and stable economic growth. The free economy served the individual, whose needs and desires were met by the natural tendency of producers to make and sell what consumers desired. The welfare of the community was thereby maximized.

The moral dilemma of earlier writers was resolved by Smith's analysis, in that there was no conflict between individual and social benefits. The whole structure rested on the free, competitive play of individual selfishness. The motives lauded by Mandeville a half-century earlier were shown by Smith to be the source of economic growth, social order, and general welfare. The path to brotherhood—at least in economic affairs—lay through competitive selfishness. Thus, Adam Smith provided social philosophers and moralists with answers to problems that had gone unresolved for a century.

In addition, Smith presented future economists with the analytical framework of the discipline of economics. His vision of a competitive market equilibrium following a path of growth to affluence and abundance defined the problems that economists have wrestled with ever since. His formulation of the solutions—the self-adjusting market and the process of capital accumulation—was the starting point for a complex theoretical system that later economists richly elaborated. Smith's purely scientific contribution has been vast, and in its basic structure his framework still remains the heart of modern economics.

It is easy to see why the *Wealth of Nations* is one of the great books of Western civilization. On one level, it is a polemic written for its own time and directed against the existing practices and policies of government. On another, it is a philosophical treatise that deals with fundamental problems of order and chaos in human society. Finally, it is a scholarly treatise that analyzes the principles on which the economic system functions. All three themes are so closely intertwined that no one aspect of the argument stands alone; rather, each supports the others. It is a fascinating amalgam of ideology, philosophy, and theoretic analysis.

FOUR

CLASSICAL

ECONOMICS

David Ricardo (1772–1823) was an English economist famous for his theories of economic development and international trade.

Adam Smith founded a "school" of economics. Particularly strong in England, Smith's followers dominated the field in both Europe and the United States for almost a century. They represented the orthodox approach to economic problems and policy until the last quarter of the nineteenth century and were united by their acceptance of Smith's liberalism and his system of natural liberty. Their analytical system was founded on Smith's equilibrium of supply and demand in competitive markets and on the labor theory of value. They generally favored freedom of action for business enterprise, strong limitations on government, free trade, and free movement of capital. *Classical economics* is the name usually given to this style of thinking.

Four other economists made major contributions to the classical system. They were Thomas R. Malthus, David Ricardo, Jeremy Bentham, and Jean-Baptiste Say. Working primarily in the turbulent first quarter of the nineteenth century, when the world economy was percolating with the changes wrought by war, revolution, economic change, population growth, new technologies, and political upheaval, they sought to analyze the economy in terms of a few basic underlying principles. In doing so, they turned economics into the first social "science."

England's Reaction to the French Revolution

Adam Smith's *Wealth of Nations* had just been published when an age of revolution began—the great political and social revolutions in the American colonies and later in France that wiped away the last vestige of European feudalism and the old aristocratic order. There was a good deal of sympathy in England for the American revolutionists, since many Englishmen felt that their own society retained unwanted remnants of the old order. One of the reasons for the success of the American Revolution was undoubtedly the opposition of English liberals to continuing the war. Political reform was a particularly strong issue in England, since many members of Parliament represented districts with very small populations, while some large cities, emerging as a result of economic change, had no representation at all.

Many Englishmen looked with favor upon the French Revolution, too. They thought it would bring democracy to France, develop a society similar to that of England, and establish peace between two nations that had been at war intermittently for more than a hundred years. Charles James Fox, leader of the liberal Whig party, praised the fall of the Bastille, calling it the "greatest event . . . that ever happened in the world." Even William Pitt, the Tory prime minister, felt that the Revolution would enable France to become more like England, and he forecast years of peace and tranquillity between the two nations.

There were, of course, conservatives who took a stand against the French Revolution from the very beginning. Edmund Burke, for example, in his *Reflections on the Revolution in France* (1790), opposed the treatment of the French king and aristocrats by the French mob and feared that freedom, justice, and order would be destroyed by the growing radicalism of the "swinish multitudes."[*] When the Reign of Terror began, British opinion shifted to support the conservative position. The intellectual leaders who favored the Revolution—such as Thomas Paine, who wrote *The Rights of Man* in 1790 as an answer to Burke—were discredited. Some changed their minds to support the conservative position. Prime Minister William Pitt had come into office on a platform of social and economic reform but turned to a policy of uncompromising conservatism. At one point he stated, "Seeing that where the greatest changes have taken place, the most dreadful consequences have ensued . . . and . . . seeing that in this general shock the constitution of Great Britain has remained pure and unchanged in its vital principles . . . I think it right to declare my most decided opinion, that . . . even the slightest change in such a constitution must be considered an evil." The policy of the British government became one of maintaining the status quo, resisting reform, and—worse—suppressing voices of dissent.

When the wars with France began, legal action was taken in England to "prevent disloyalty." In 1795 the Habeas Corpus Act was suspended for five years; all secret associations were banned; all lecture rooms where admission was charged were legally classified as brothels, in order to prevent meetings; any meeting attended by more than fifty persons had to be superintended by a magistrate; all printing presses had to be registered with the government; export of English newspapers was prohibited; the Correspond-

---

[*]The title of this book, *The Age of the Economist*, is taken from a passage in Burke's *Reflections:* "The age of chivalry is dead, that of sophisters, economists and calculators has succeeded, and the glory of Europe is extinguished forever." In those days the economist was considered to be a liberal reformer.

ing Society, a group of reformers who tried to spread news of their cause by writing letters, was suppressed in 1799. In that year and the next, the Anti-Combination Laws were passed, which prohibited any kind of combination of either workers or employers for the purpose of regulating conditions of employment. There is no record that the laws were enforced against employers, but workmen were prosecuted and nascent labor unions destroyed. An atmosphere of suppression prevailed.

Although reform was prevented, the march of events could not be halted. The war years of the late eighteenth and early nineteenth centuries were years of broad and rapid change. Industrialization was greatly stimulated by wartime demand. The agricultural revolution was speeded up by wartime increases in the price of food. Population was growing rapidly and shifting from rural to urban. As cities grew, slums, inadequate sewage and water systems, and other urban ills developed on a large scale. The multitude of economic and social problems generated by these vast changes went unsolved, while "the Establishment" concerned itself with holding the line and rooting out the "radicals."

Malthus and the Theory of Population

One of the most pressing problems that emerged during the years of the French wars concerned the poor. They had always been present in England, but in the former aristocratic, rural society, each parish had traditionally cared for its own. A tax on landowners was expected to provide relief funds for those who could not support themselves, while the parish was supposed to find work for the able-bodied poor. A philosophy of *noblesse oblige* prevailed.

This ancient system broke down, however. Wartime increases in food prices, the agricultural revolution and the enclosures of common land, which displaced many farmers from their small plots, the Industrial Revolution, and growing cities and population brought on serious poverty. Displaced farmers might have found work in handicraft manufacture of cloth, which had long been a rural occupation, but industrialization destroyed that opportunity; indeed, a whole generation of rural cottagers lost their livelihoods with the rise of textile mills in the growing cities. Growth of the armed forces offered a way out for some of the able-bodied young men, but it was not a general solution.

The conservative reaction engendered by the French Revolution meant that new measures to alleviate poverty were politically impossible. Anything smacking in the least degree of reform was anathema to English policymakers. Yet the great increase in the number of poor people put a tremendous financial burden on the wealthier landowners. Something had to give.

The solution was provided by an obscure young minister named Thomas Robert Malthus (1766–1834). Like all good conservatives in a time when serious problems abound, he found the cause of the crisis not in any recent developments or changes that might be amended by policy actions, but in large forces over which governments have little or no control. The problem of the poor was essentially moral, he argued, and had its origins in two fundamental propositions. First, "Food is necessary to the existence of man." Second, "The passion between the sexes is necessary and will remain nearly in its present state." These two facts led to the principle that "the power of population is infinitely greater than the power in the earth to produce subsistence for man." Any policies that attempted to alleviate poverty would be futile in the face of these natural laws.

In other words, population would tend to increase unless it was held in check by "misery and vice." If the supply of food were to increase, there would be a corresponding increase in population until the amount of food per person had fallen back to the subsistence level, at which point the increase in population would stop. Wages would always tend toward the subsistence level. Any increase in wages above that level would only cause the working population to grow and wages to fall back once more to subsistence. Conversely, if the price of food rose, wage rates would likewise be forced upward to maintain a subsistence level. One way or another, there was a natural rate of wages that always tended toward the level of subsistence.

Consider the implications of this doctrine. Paying relief would not solve the problem of poverty but would merely increase the income of the poor and enable them to raise more children. Poverty would continue because there would be no increase in food supplies for the larger population. It was not necessary, therefore, to look to economic or social causes to explain the problems of the poor. The old system of poor relief was itself responsible. The solution was obviously to eliminate the relief system.

Assistance to the poor worsened the situation in another way, according to Malthus. By increasing the numbers of the poor, the relief system shifted wealth from those who used it productively to an idle poverty-stricken population. Wealth that should have been invested to provide jobs was wasted on maintaining the poor in idleness, and the economic growth of the nation was slowed.

The Malthusian view had other important implications. The causes of poverty were not rooted in the structure of society, in the distribution of income, in inequalities in the ownership of wealth, or in any of the many institutions of society. Neither the wealthy nor society as a whole was at fault. The poor were responsible for their own fate. All they had to do to eliminate their poverty was to have fewer children.

Even the formation of labor unions was useless, according to Malthus. Higher wages would result only in a larger population and a rise in the cost of food as more people used the wage increases to bid up food prices. The end result would be a shift of wealth from businessmen through the hands of workers into the pockets of unproductive landowners. The amount of capital available for economic expansion would be reduced just as population increased, leaving the nation worse off in the long run. Furthermore, unions meant strikes, and strikes meant reduced output, lower profits, and less capital accumulation. No, labor unions were not a solution.

Malthus's principle of population was indeed a dismal theorem—for the poor. But it was a great doctrine for conservatives, because it gave them the best of reasons for doing nothing about a serious problem. Malthus himself, an educated, religious gentleman, felt compassion and pity for the poor. He expressed this many times, and there is no reason to doubt his sincerity. But his analysis told him that social action would hinder instead of help. The only permanent solution was moral reform of the individual that would hold sexual passions in check.

The Malthusian principle of population was to become one of the major building blocks of classical economics, and it remained the basis of wage theories for almost a century. Despite its essentially pessimistic point of view, however, it did provide one avenue of hope for economic growth. Economic expansion could provide increased food supplies that would then cause increases in the labor force necessary to achieve further economic growth. Malthus showed that the size of the labor force was not a barrier to economic expansion. Labor resources would increase as the economy grew. All that was needed was capital to get the process started.

Malthus also helped later economists clarify one of the key relationships necessary for betterment of the human condition. Production had to increase faster than population if there were to be any major improvement in living standards. Europe and North America, in the ensuing era of industrialization, succeeded in achieving that relationship and are vastly better off today than they were in Malthus's time. Many other countries, in which population growth exceeds expansion of production, have millions of people who are doomed to the "misery and vice" of the Malthusian analysis.

Ricardo and Economic Growth

David Ricardo (1772–1823) was the apostle of capital accumulation. In his view, the growth of capital was the great source of economic expansion, and all economic policy should be directed toward promoting it. To prove his point, he developed a theoretical model of the economy that dominated the thinking of economists for fifty years. He believed that economic freedom led to maximum profits, that profits were the source of investment capital, and that a competitive economy would lead to profit-maximizing investments. In Ricardo's view, policies that benefited business would lead to maximum economic growth.

Born in London of Jewish parents, Ricardo married a young Quaker woman when he reached the age of twenty-one, causing a break between himself and his stockbroker father. Financed by friends, he became a trader on the London Exchange. So adept was he at the intricate and risky business of speculation that by the age of twenty-six he had amassed a large fortune. He retired to a country estate in 1814, bought an Irish pocket-borough seat in Parliament in 1819, and devoted the remaining few years of his short life to public affairs and economics. A "millionaire radical," he advocated reforms in banking and currency, poor relief, and the tariff, and supported freedom of press and speech, as well as other reform causes. His only book on economics carries the formidable title *Principles of Political Economy and Taxation*. Its content is even more formidable, but it had tremendous influence in its day.

In the years around 1815, at the close of the Napoleonic wars, one of the great political and social issues in England was whether the nation should try to preserve its agriculturally based economy or become more heavily industrialized. Involved in the debate was the question of the place of the landed aristocracy in the English social and political system. The issue was fought out in Parliament over the Corn Laws, which dealt with the import of wheat into England. (The English call wheat and other grains "corn," and our corn is "Indian corn" or "maize.") English laws related to the import of wheat were intended to promote domestic agriculture without causing major increases in the price of food. When the price of wheat fell in England, tariffs were raised on imports of wheat in order to keep out the foreign grain that was depressing domestic prices and injuring the business of domestic farmers. When the price of wheat rose above a given level, import duties were reduced, thus encouraging more imports and keeping domestic prices from rising further. In short, the British government tried to keep grain prices between an upper and a lower limit by means of a sliding scale of tariffs.

Nevertheless, during the French wars the price of food rose substantially, and farmers were temporarily well off. Their production costs also rose and remained high when peace came, wartime demand slackened, and the price of food fell. Farmers began clamoring for higher duties on imported wheat, fearing that they faced ruin unless protected by enforcement of the Corn Laws. The landowner's point of view was reinforced by arguments that a sound agriculture was necessary for England's national defense and for the preservation of the old traditions and national vigor. There was a revival of the physiocratic doctrine that economic growth depended on the natural productivity of the soil. Pamphlets appeared, such as one entitled *England Independent of Commerce*, which argued for the protection and preservation of agricultural interests.

Business interests, on the other hand, opposed tariff increases, which, they declared, would raise food prices and force wages upward. The result would be reduced profits, decreased exports of manufactured products, and ruin for English industry. Business interests argued that England's future lay with industrial expansion, not with agriculture, and they demanded outright repeal of the Corn Laws.

This was the state of the issue when Ricardo and other economists entered the debate over Corn Law policy. Ricardo was on the business side of the argument. He believed that landowners, not farmers, would be the chief beneficiaries if the price of wheat in England was raised by a higher tariff. The high price of wheat would enable cultivation to be extended to areas that would otherwise be unprofitable. In older wheat-growing areas, rents would be raised to take advantage of the higher prices farmers were receiving. A larger proportion of the total national income would then flow into the hands of landowners, and this parasitic group would use its increased wealth for luxury expenditures such as servants and country houses, not for productive investment.

In addition, the enlarged cultivation of land would draw capital and labor away from industry and distort the whole production pattern of the country. Artificially high food prices would lead to a misallocation of productive resources into agriculture and out of manufacturing, thereby hindering the nation's natural development of industry.

Ricardo also pointed out that high prices for food would require high wage rates and high costs of production in manufacturing. Since England had to sell its manufactures throughout the world, competing with the products of other countries, higher costs in English industry would result in reduced business for English exports and a reduced level of output for English manufacturers. Profits would also be reduced, and there would be a slower pace of capital accumulation and economic expansion, due to the lack of both incentive and funds to invest.

This was Ricardo's indictment of the Corn Laws (although he did not advocate their complete repeal). It supported the business position on the issue with a theoretical model of the economy that gave substance and validity to his policy conclusions. Ricardo's theory was more than a treatment of a contemporary policy problem. If that were all it had been, it would have died as interest in the problem died. But Ricardo took it much further and generalized it into a comprehensive theory of economic growth.

In the early stages of a nation's growth, he argued, the population would be small and only a portion of the land would be cultivated. Under these conditions the rent paid to landowners would be a relatively small proportion, and profits a large proportion, of the total national income. The profits, plowed back into industrial development, would result in a greater demand for labor, which—following Malthus—would cause population to grow while wages remained at the subsistence level. The growth in population would require an extension of the cultivated area in order to provide larger amounts of food. This extension could be accomplished only by raising food prices to cover the higher costs of production incurred by bringing less fertile lands into cultivation. The higher price of food would enable landowners to raise the rents charged on the older cultivated lands, because the higher food prices charged could bear higher rents. At the same time, the higher cost of food would force employers to pay higher *money* wages in order to maintain wage rates at the subsistence level. This in turn would raise the cost of manufactured goods and thereby reduce the profits obtained by manufacturers. The reduced profits would then leave less wealth available for expansion and would also reduce incentives to invest. Ricardo envisaged that this process of economic growth would continue, with capital accumulation and growth gradually slowing down, until growth halted after many decades of expansion. At this stage of development the population would be large, cultivation extended, industry developed, production high—but savings and capital accumulation would be adequate only for replacement of capital, not for further expansion.

The picture Ricardo drew was one in which the economy, if left alone, would achieve the maximum growth possible. To that end, business would have to be freed of all restrictions that might reduce ability to maximize profits, so that the maximum amount of saving and capital accumulation could take place. Government intervention in the economy would lead to a lower rather than a higher level of economic activity. Right or wrong, the theory was on the side of the coming rulers of the social order—business interests—and this in itself ensured it long life.

The International Economy

One of the strengths of Ricardian economics was its applicability to the international economy. For the first time, an analysis of the domestic economy based on the fundamentals of land, labor, and capital could be applied rigorously to international economic relationships. This represented a major step forward in the development of economics as a social science. One of the goals of all scientific endeavor is the building of ever broader generalizations that encompass an ever widening body of phenomena. A discipline advances by stripping away details and constructing general laws, and Ricardian economics did this by reducing all economic phenomena to fundamental relationships between the factors of production.

The integration of the international economy into the Ricardian model was done in two ways. First, Ricardo showed that international specialization and division of labor was advantageous to all nations and that restrictive trade policies designed to protect domestic producers would injure the nation imposing them. Free trade was the road to economic well-being internationally as well as domestically. The argument for this position, embodied in the famous *law of comparative advantage,* is complex, but Ricardo was able to prove its validity. He showed, for example, that as long as it costs less to produce cloth in England than it does to produce wheat, *compared with costs in other countries*, it would pay the English to shift their resources to cloth manufactures, export cloth, and import wheat from other countries.

Suppose it takes an English worker one day's labor to produce a yard of cloth and two days' labor to grow a bushel of wheat; then a bushel of wheat would cost twice as much as a yard of cloth. Suppose also that it takes a French worker one day's labor to produce each product. In this case, England should produce cloth (one day's labor), export it to France, trade it one-for-one for wheat, and import the wheat back to England. In this way the English would get, for one day's labor, the wheat it would otherwise take them two days to produce. The French would also benefit. They could produce wheat, ship it to England, trade one bushel for *two* yards of cloth, and ship the cloth back to France. They would also receive products worth two days' effort for one day's actual work. Both sides would benefit from this specialization and free exchange.

But the process would not end there, as later economists showed. The export of English cloth to France would drive its selling price down in France, and increased domestic production would push costs of production up. The same would happen for French wheat in England. As these price changes took place, the growing import-export trade between the two countries would establish an equilibrium of prices and trade. England would produce and export much cloth, but its output of wheat would be small. Most of the wheat consumed in England would be imported. The opposite would be true of France. The two commodities would sell for equivalent prices in the two countries, for if they did not, further shifts in production, trade, prices, and costs would occur. In this way an international equilibrium would be established in which the world pattern of production would be optimized.

This analysis of international economic equilibrium was supplemented by a second approach, this time in the field of economic development. The preceding section of this chapter described the Ricardian theory of the fully developed stationary economy, in which the return to capital was so low that only replacement of worn-out capital equipment occurred. As the return to capital in one country fell, however, profit-maximizing investors would seek higher returns by investing in less well-developed countries abroad. Capital exports from the mature economies would flow quickly to the newly developing countries, and they in turn would be brought to higher levels of production and wealth. Of course, they would have to offer political stability and protection to private property, but aside from that qualification the classical economist could look forward to a whole world moving gradually toward opulence.

In this way economists applied Adam Smith's concepts of orderly growth and market equilibrium to the international economic system. Only national rivalry, with its tariffs, trade restrictions, and wars, could interfere with the development process. It is perhaps ironic that the part of his theory that Ricardo thought most important—the theory of economic growth—has been largely discarded by modern economists, although they retain his stress on capital accumulation. But the theory of international economic equilibrium, which was only a minor part of the original analysis, remains, almost in its original form, an integral part of modern economics.

Say's Law of Markets

Only one major element had to be added to classical economics to complete its systematic analysis of the economy: an examination of production and employment levels. It had been shown that a free market would allocate resources so that production would adjust to consumer needs and wants, that output would grow through savings and capital accumulation, that income would be distributed among social classes according to natural laws, and that the same principles applied to both domestic and international economic relationships. Still to be determined was whether a free market would also maintain full employment of workers and capital.

The issue was not merely academic. The Industrial Revolution had brought economic instability, aggravated in the early years of the nineteenth century by the on-again, off-again wars against Napoleon. When peace came in 1815 the economic stimulus of government spending was withdrawn from the economies of both England and the Continent. Demand for industrial products fell from its wartime levels, and England was faced with competition from the Continent for the worldwide markets it had kept largely to itself. Soldiers and sailors returning to the civilian economy and handicraft workers displaced by factory production increased the numbers of workers seeking employment. These problems were compounded in England by the fact that industrialization had proceeded furthest there.

England's economic situation was further aggravated by government monetary policies that resulted in "tight" money and a shortage of credit just when the economy needed a stimulus. During the war years prices had risen substantially, credit had been much expanded, and the Bank of England had stopped redeeming its paper currency in gold. Increases in the national debt had been one of the major causes of the credit expansion and the price increases. Economists, led by Ricardo, blamed the inflation on excessive issuance of paper money and when the war ended prescribed that the Bank of England again redeem paper currency in gold at the levels that had prevailed before the war, even though there was not enough gold to sustain the existing amounts of currency and credit then outstanding. This meant that the supply of money and credit would fall. The economy was to be given a dose of deflation.

This early application of principles of sound finance was based on an incorrect diagnosis of the economic illness, and the remedy turned out to be worse than the disease. Inflation had been largely due to expansion of total spending during the war years, promoted in part by increases in the money supply, at a time when output could be increased only slowly. Prices had to rise, and the amount of currency and credit reflected this expansion. By prescribing deflation as the cure for inflation, economists were able to bring prices down, but only at the expense of output and employment. Like any deflation after inflation, creditors and owners of financial assets benefited— to the detriment of unemployed workers and profitless businesses. The burden of England's economic difficulties was shifted from owners of monetary assets to producers.

Hardship was widespread, and business activity was in a generally depressed state for thirty years after 1815. The economy had its ups and downs during this period. Economic growth continued, but there was hardly a year in which England had full employment by modern standards. In some years, unemployment rose to 40 or 50 percent of the work force in the industrial cities of the midlands.

The instability of the economy had already aroused criticism of industrialism and the new economic order. Even before 1815 Jean Simonde de Sismondi (1773–1842), a Frenchman traveling in England, had seen the industrial depressions and predicted that capital investment would periodically force the capacity to produce to outrun the ability to consume. His argument was echoed by an English Physiocrat, William Spence (1783–1860), who pointed out in two pamphlets of 1807 and 1808 that capital investment in commerce and manufacturing created economic instability and insecurity, while the development of agriculture promoted economic stability and security. Spence called particular attention to the possibility that savings would reduce purchasing power and cause prosperity to disappear. Both Sismondi and Spence were disenchanted with industrialization, and each favored a different type of economic order—Spence the old aristocratic society and Sismondi a system that emphasized human and community values rather than individual gain. Their discussions of depressions were only part of more comprehensive attacks on the emerging business society.

Classical economists were quick to reply to these attacks. The basis of their rebuttal was a brief passage in a work by Jean-Baptiste Say (1767–1832), a French popularizer of Adam Smith's work, whose *A Treatise on Political Economy* had appeared in 1803. That work contained the first statement of the principle that came to be known as *Say's Law of Markets*, a concept that dominated the thinking of most economists about the level of economic activity until the Great Depression of the 1930s.

Say argued that there could never be a general deficiency of demand or a general glut of commodities throughout the whole economy. Certain industries or sectors of industry might be plagued by overproduction, because of miscalculation and excessive allocation of resources to those types of production, but elsewhere in the economy there would inevitably be shortages. The consequent fall of prices in one sector and their rise in others would induce business firms to shift production, and the imbalances would be quickly corrected.

People produce, he pointed out, not for the sake of producing, but to exchange their products for other goods they need and want. Since production *is* demand, it is impossible for production to outrun demand. "Production creates its own demand" became the answer of the classical economists to the problem of business depressions.

In England, Say's argument was put forth by James Mill (1773–1836), father of the renowned philosopher and economist John Stuart Mill, in an answer to Spence. The elder Mill wrote in 1807 that every increase in supply is an increase in demand—the more there is to sell, the more will be bought. The error in the theory of general glut, he maintained, is the confusion between a temporary dislocation in the process of exchange, which would be remedied by industry taking a new direction, and the impossibility of an excess of wealth in general.

One economist remained unconvinced: Thomas R. Malthus. In his *Principles of Political Economy* (1820) Malthus devoted a long last chapter to developing a theory of economic stagnation based on inadequate "effectual demand." His argument, in brief, was that wages, being less than the total costs of production, cannot purchase the total output of industry, and that this would cause prices to fall. The decline in prices reduces incentives to invest as well as profits that could be invested. The result is a general inadequacy of purchasing power that *could* continue indefinitely. A similar condition might result from excessive savings, which cause demand to fall, prices to decline, and stagnation to follow. The remedy, according to Malthus, was to reduce large incomes so that savings would not be excessive, to impose import tariffs and thereby promote a favorable balance of trade, and to spend for public works during bad times. A program of government intervention was needed because the free-market economy could not regularly provide for full employment.

Malthus's argument was not developed with clarity and preciseness—he was not a rigorous theoretician—and his good friend David Ricardo severely criticized his theory of general glut in letters written to Malthus, in "Notes on Malthus' Principles of Political Economy" circulated in manuscript among other economists, and in discussions at London's Political Economy Club. Since Ricardo's arguments *were* clear and precise, he carried the day.

Ricardo's answer to Malthus recapitulated Say's Law of Markets in slightly more elaborate form. Savings are made, not as an end in themselves, but in order to employ labor in production. Mistakes can lead to a glut of a single commodity, but demand for all other commodities is not thereby reduced. A reallocation of productive effort will occur. Furthermore, unemployment causes wages to fall, inducing business firms to hire the idle laborers with the capital created by savings. In this way, all capital is put back into use and all willing workers are once again employed. The basic cure, therefore, is not income redistribution and public works but lower wages and higher profits.

Ricardo's answer was supplemented by an extraordinarily perceptive volume originally published in 1802, Henry Thornton's *The Paper Credit of Great Britain*. This book had been written during the controversy over paper money, gold, and inflation, but its argument was adapted to Say's Law and the discussion of gluts. Thornton observed that if savings tended to become excessive, the supply of funds in the money market would rise relative to demand, and interest rates would fall. The lowered interest rates would both encourage investment and discourage savings, the process continuing until the two were equal. Any funds not used for consumption would, therefore, find their way into investment. Changes in the rate of interest would ensure that savings would be invested and the level of total spending maintained. There could be no surplus of savings and no general glut of commodities. Total spending on consumption and investment would then be adequate to purchase the total output of industry.

These complicated arguments were extraordinarily important. At the purely logical level they closed the theoretical system of classical economics by showing that a free-market economy would utilize all its resources. In terms of social philosophy or ideology they showed that unemployment and instability were not caused by a private-enterprise economy but were the result of noneconomic forces—psychological factors or other causes not associated with the institutional structure and natural processes of economic life. Finally, they prescribed a policy treatment for whatever depressions might occur: (1) strengthen the financial sector of the economy so that the processes determining saving and investment could work themselves out; and (2) endure the crisis until declining wages and prices ultimately encouraged enough investment to bring the economy back to normal. Such is the strength of a logical and precise theory that these policies prevailed for more than a century—at tremendous social cost, for the waiting period often brought waves of bankruptcy and long-continued unemployment—until the theory was finally demolished by a countertheory propounded during the Great Depression of the 1930s.

Bentham and Interventionist Liberalism

No discussion of classical economics is complete without an account of the ideas of Jeremy Bentham (1748–1832), a lifelong reformer and nonpracticing lawyer. His *Fragment on Government,* published anonymously in 1776 when he was twenty-eight, was a brilliant attack on the traditional legal interpretation of the English constitution as antithetical to progress. He sought to show how political reform toward greater democracy would promote "the greatest good for the greatest number." The book created a sensation, but when it was revealed that the author was only a young upstart and not one of the leading constitutional lawyers of the day, it was quickly dismissed. Disillusioned, Bentham began his great philosophical work, *An Introduction to the Principles of Morals and Legislation,* which was privately printed in 1780 but not published for the general public until 1789, after another of his books, *A Defense of Usury,* became a popular success.*

Principles of Morals and Legislation is the key work in utilitarian philosophy. In it Bentham argued that every act was morally valuable to the extent that it resulted in happiness. Both human actions and moral judgments were based on the poles of pleasure and pain:

> Nature had placed mankind under the governance of two sovereign masters, pain and pleasure. It is for them alone to point out what we ought to do, as well as to determine what we shall do. On the one hand the standard of right and wrong, on the other the chain of causes and effects are fastened to their throne.

*Bentham's major work had been completed before he reached his fortieth birthday, but he lived to be eighty-four and wielded great influence over a small band of devoted followers. He was never again to write an influential book but spent much of his later life devising complicated plans for prison reform, poor relief, education, and legislative reform. He founded the University of London with an endowment, and his will provided that his body be embalmed and once a year seated at the meeting of the university's trustees as a reminder of the principles on which the university was established. This grisly ritual continued to be performed until recently, using a wax head instead of the shrunken real one, which was kept in storage.

This simple principle was more complex than it appeared. Bentham meant that the social system should seek to maximize its total benefits and distribute them as widely as possible. A small increase in happiness for many was better than a large increase for a few. But, as critics were to point out, that conclusion is not self-evident.

An important problem raised by critics was that of measurement. Increasing human happiness involves choosing between alternatives. The cost of one course of action is the elimination of others; that is, we can't have everything. This means that comparisons of the magnitudes of benefits and costs must be made in order to determine the best, or optimal, solutions. As long as the discussion involved only total benefits, the problem was insoluble. Not until the economists of the last quarter of the nineteenth century began analyzing *increments* in benefits and costs—the famous marginal analysis—were even partial solutions found.

A related question was whether happiness, or utility, could be quantified. Bentham thought it could, at least in principle. Others argued that one could only make comparisons; for example, "I greatly prefer Mary to Jane, but my preference for chocolate over vanilla ice cream is not very strong." The absolute amounts of happiness derived from being with Mary or eating chocolate ice cream are, according to this view, impossible to measure and are, furthermore, irrelevant to the choices made.

These fine points were less important to Bentham than was his argument that people, *in fact*, made decisions on the basis of the amounts of utility derived from the alternative courses of action open to them. This "hedonistic calculus" was the principle underlying all human action, he declared, and the means by which the welfare of society was maximized. He believed that the selfishness of economic behavior was natural, rational, and desirable.

At this point in the argument, Bentham introduced morals and legislation. If people always act only for their own greatest pleasure when they *should* act for the greatest happiness of all, is not a contradiction involved? Bentham said there was not, because moral and legislative sanctions caused individual action to coincide with the public interest. The sanctions rewarded individual action that benefited all and punished action that diminished public welfare. Both morality and government action (if it was majority action) had a utilitarian foundation and rested on the principle of greatest happiness. Bentham, then, was not opposed to government action if it was based on democratic processes and did not reflect the narrow interests of special groups. At the same time, he wished to give free play to individual decision making within the framework of moral and legislative sanctions. His goal was to reconcile individualism and social action.

Bentham's significance goes far beyond his rather narrow and outdated view of human nature. In the first place, his ideas were important throughout the nineteenth century and profoundly affected later developments in economics. His view of humans as pleasure machines, continually calculating the advantages and disadvantages of alternative courses of action, became the accepted view, and rational economic behavior was defined in those terms. The assumption that individual decisions would lead to maximum public welfare was inherent, of course, in the work of Adam Smith and the other classical economists, but Bentham made it explicit. All the later conclusions of orthodox economics were solidly based on, or at least closely related to, this concept of human nature.

Even more important than his influence on economics was Bentham's impact on liberal social philosophy. He brought to it an interventionist emphasis quite at variance with the tradition of *laissez-faire*, creating a problem that even today remains unsolved.

The classical liberalism of the eighteenth century emphasized individual freedom as the ultimate goal of all policy. Reacting against political centralization and economic regulation, its advocates argued that any restriction on freedom hindered the achievement of maximum welfare. In the hands of Adam Smith, its greatest explicator, this philosophy advocated minimizing the role of government, strictly limiting it to such essentials as police, justice, and arms.

Bentham, however, saw that this philosophy was based on the assumption that only individual action could create welfare. His practical mind told him that the actions of one person in his or her own interest might reduce the welfare of another. His legal training and his study of constitutional law told him that the institutional arrangements within which people act could significantly determine the outcome of their actions. The very fact that human society was organized by institutional arrangements created by people—that a social system existed—meant that conscious action could create social forms that would enable people to live better lives. Benthamite utilitarianism was potentially an interventionist doctrine.

Bentham and his followers in England—they called themselves philosophical radicals—included the economists James Mill, David Ricardo, and, later, John Stuart Mill. Advocates of democratic government and majority rule, their major target for reform was the political system, which in their day excluded large numbers of people from the right to vote and did not provide fully for freedom of speech and the press. They believed that the social system could bring the greatest good to the greatest number only if it were fully democratic and subject to true majority rule. They were also classical economists and expounded the advantages of a freely competitive market system and laissez-faire policies. But their utilitarian political philosophy was to have the gravest consequences for their economic theories. Once political reform was achieved, the new power of the enfranchised voter was used as an instrument of economic reform, and the laissez-faire policy was discarded. The reforms were justified in terms of individual and social welfare, and the greatest-good argument was used again and again. The classical liberalism that had stressed individualism gave place to an interventionist liberalism that emphasized social welfare, and Bentham was its apostle.

In Bentham's time and later, there was a school of economists dedicated to preserving the distinction between economics as an objective science and the subjective judgments inherent in the law and government policy. These economists emphasized the natural-law aspects of individual freedom and rationality, along with the laissez-faire implications of that approach. For example, Nassau Senior (1790–1864), one of the later classical economists, argued that political economy should eliminate all value judgments and stick to the purely scientific analysis of how an economy works. The proper focus of economics should be "not happiness, but wealth." He strongly opposed the interventionist policies of Bentham and his followers.

Thus, the rise of Benthamite ideas gave rise to a division among economists that persists to this day. At one extreme is the thoroughgoing laissez-faire individualist. On the other is the dedicated social reformer. In between is a wide range of opinion that accommodates some portions of each view. Yet much the same theories, concepts, and methods of analysis are used. Differing conclusions, however, rest on varying preconceptions about the individual's place in the social order and the way in which economic outcomes are generated. Mainstream economics, both now and in its early days, could include a wide range of value judgments and policy positions.

Sismondi and Social Economics

Jean Charles Leonard Simonde de Sismondi (1773–1842), a Swiss native, lived during a period of revolutionary turmoil and armed conflict—the American and French Revolutions, the Napoleonic wars, and the events leading to the revolution of 1848. Apprenticed as a young man to a silk dealer in Lyons, he fled the French Revolution to a safe England, where he experienced the political and economic changes going on there. At the age of twenty-one he returned to Geneva, only to be jailed by the pro-French government and to have the family estate confiscated. Released from jail, he went to Italy, where he was jailed three more times by both sides in the political turmoil. Finally released, he discovered he was descended from a noble Italian family named Sismondi. He returned to Geneva in 1800 with a new surname, Simonde de Sismondi, and published a systematic exposition of Adam Smith's economics, *De la richesse commercial* (1803).

Sismondi modified Smith's economics by presenting a "absolutely new" way of looking at the level of economic activity. Output in a given year, he argued, was determined by investment in the previous year. This output, though, might not be large enough to employ all those who wanted to work. He illustrates this argument with arithmetic examples supported by algebraic formulas and footnotes. A modern economist, accustomed to the work of John Maynard Keynes a hundred years later, would be intrigued, but people in the early nineteenth century ignored the book. Jean Baptiste Say's *Traite d'economie politique*, in contrast, which presented Say's Law of Markets, was published in the same year and went through five editions in the next quarter century. Disappointed when his book did not sell, Sismondi spent the next decade writing an eight-volume history of Italy.

Sismondi returned to economics in 1814 with a long article on "Political Economy" for the *Edinburgh Encyclopedia*, in which he developed an analysis of what would be called "macroeconomics" today. This approach was greatly elaborated in Sismondi's next works, *Nouveaux principes d' economie politique* (1823), which appeared in the midst of the post-war depression and a growing controversy over Say's Law of Markets.

During the Napoleonic wars, when government spending was high and hundreds of thousands of young men were drawn into armies and navies, the economies of the contesting powers seemed to achieve the goals of full employment and an expanding economy. Private investment was correspondingly high in those early days of the Industrial Revolution. But when the Napoleonic wars ended in 1815, armies and navies were greatly reduced, government spending and private investment fell, unemployment rose and wages fell. The period from 1815 to about 1850 featured high unemployment and low wages while the economy fluctuated at less than full employment levels, culminating in the decade that would be called the "hungry forties."

Sismondi elaborated his theory of equilibrium income to fit these postwar problems. He argued that during a period of good times producers would invest to produce more, while consumers would buy only what they had bought in the previous period. Goods could not be sold at profitable prices and output and employment would fall. In essence, Sismondi was arguing that investment was volatile while consumption was relatively stable, leading to recurring periods of overproduction and underproduction.

The tendency toward the uneven fluctuations typical of business cycles was exacerbated by two other factors: underconsumption caused by the growing wealth of the business classes, and the substitution of machinery for labor. Low wages and technological change would keep consumption from growing as fast as needed. Sismondi agreed with the advocates of Say's Law of Markets that a satisfactory level of economic activity would be achieved in the long run, but the adjustment would take a long time, with "long and cruel sufferings." Both capital and labor adjust slowly to changes in demand, he argued, not quickly as Ricardo, Say, and others were saying. The process of market adjustment was imperfect and costly.

Sismondi's approach to economics differed from that of the English economists who were concerned about the growth of wealth. He stressed the enjoyment of wealth and its diffusion among the people at large. Government, he felt, had a positive role: limitations on child labor, regulations of hours of labor, public works to employ the unemployed, a minimum wage, worker co-ownership of business enterprise, and unemployment insurance paid for by the employer. These and other government actions were discussed in the final two chapters of Sismondi's *Nouveau principes*.

Largely ignored in his lifetime, Sismondi is now recognized as an important economist of his time. He was one of the first to show the limitations of *laissez-faire* and individual self-interest, to emphasize the need to have an economy sensitive to the needs of working people, and to demonstrate the need for government to take a positive role in economic affairs. He was the forerunner of a group of dissidents who advocated a positive role for government.

John Stuart Mill

No account of classical economics would be complete without discussion of John Stuart Mill (1806–1873). The eldest son of James Mill, whom we met earlier in explaining Say's Law of Markets, John Stuart received an extraordinary education at the hands of his father. He was started on Greek at age three and Latin at eight. By the age of fourteen he had read most of the Greek and Latin classics in the original languages and had read widely in history, logic, mathematics, and science. His father started him on economics at thirteen, with emphasis on Ricardo, Malthus, and Bentham. After a session on economics taught by his father, the young scholar was required to write a careful summary of the day's work. His father used these papers as the basis for his own textbook, *Elements of Political Economy* (1821), without mentioning that it was based on papers written by his son. The son was so convinced of the correctness of Malthusian population theory that at age seventeen he was arrested for publicly distributing pamphlets advocating birth control and contraception as means of improving the condition of the working class.

At sixteen John Stuart Mill went to work at the East India Company, where his father was employed. He rose to an important managerial position by the time the company was taken over by the British government in 1858. Two events early in those years had a profound influence on his life. At age twenty he passed through two years of what then was called a "mental crisis," but that now would be described as severe depression. He emerged with a mission in life, devoting himself to advocating political and economic reform. There followed a series of writings that made him the best known and most widely read nineteenth-century English philosopher. *A System of Logic* (2 volumes, 1843) made the case for empirical science as the source of knowledge, supplemented by logical deduction to arrive at general propositions, not the other way around. *On Liberty* (1859) made the case for the full freedom of each individual to develop his or her abilities without hindrance from others or from social or economic constraints. The only limitation was not to hurt others or limit their freedoms. *Considerations on Representative Government* (1861) made the case for democracy and majority rule but with the qualification that minorities must be protected from majority authoritarianism. *Utilitarianism* (1862) argued for a modified Benthamite society structured in ways that enabled everyone, including working people, to obtain the good things in life. *The Subjection of Women* (1869) advocated reforms that would end the laws and social customs that made women second-class citizens subject to rule by men. As a philosopher, John Stuart Mill focused on the great issues of his time, not on metaphysical theorizing.

The second great defining event in Mill's life came shortly after his bout of depression. He met Harriet Taylor (1808–1858). When the two first met, Mill was twenty-five and Harriet was twenty-three. She was married, with two children and a dull, unappreciative husband. The young man and woman immediately became close friends. The husband agreed not to interfere in the relationship so long as it remained platonic. The young people agreed, but the relationship was a scandal: the two lived and traveled together, ignoring gossipy tongues. When the husband died in 1851, John Stuart and Harriet waited an appropriate two years and then married.

John Stuart Mill always acknowledged Harriet Taylor's influence on his thinking. In his *Autobiography* (1873) Mill wrote that she was "the inspirer, and in part, the author, of all that is best in my writings." Her influence seems to have been particularly strong on his writings in economics, to which we now turn.

John Stuart Mill's *Principles of Political Economy* (2 volumes, 1848) was the most important economics textbook for over a quarter of a century. It was based on the Ricardian version of classical economics and on Malthusian population theory but with some important modifications and extensions. Where Ricardo had shown that international free trade provided gains to each country, Mill determined how the gains would be divided. Mill also showed that the market adjustment process involved changes in income as well as changes in prices, an idea that had much in common with the Keynesian economics of the 1930s and after. Mill also modified Say's Law of Markets by arguing that a general oversupply of goods could develop; but he also argued that such a condition would be a temporary one, thereby denying the possibility of Malthus's chronic stagnation.

However, the most important innovation in Mill's *Principles* was the distinction he drew between production and distribution. Following Ricardo, Mill agreed that the principles regulating the production of wealth are grounded in laws of nature and are therefore beyond human control. But breaking with Ricardo and Malthus, Mill argued that, unlike the laws of production, those of distribution are partly of human construction and are subject to change. This distinction, which may have been influenced by Harriet Taylor, is emphasized in the very first chapter and is followed later in the book by an analysis of the land tenure and property rights that influence the distribution of income and wealth. The poverty of Irish farmers, for example, is clearly shown to result from the way land is distributed—not a law of nature.

Mill argued that patterns of distribution of income and wealth were characteristic of a particular type of society and were not necessarily morally or ethically just. In an article on the revolution of 1848 in France, he wrote that "no rational person will maintain it to be abstractly just, that a small minority of mankind should be born to the enjoyment of all the external advantages which life can give . . . while the immense majority are condemned from their birth to a life of never-ending, never intermitting toil, requitted by a bare, and in general a precarious, subsistence."

Although Mill agreed that an economic system based on private property would continue to exist into the foreseeable future, he felt that it would eventually be superseded by "a system of cooperative production"—socialism! He welcomed an economy of worker cooperatives and worker-owned enterprises as the ultimate resolution of the social ills bred by a society composed of a class of employers and a class of laborers. Mill did not believe in revolution, however. He felt that enlightened action by free people would bring experiments with voluntary associations, such as worker's cooperatives and schemes for profit sharing, which would lead to a better social order. John Stuart Mill did not believe that an economy organized around individual enterprise, private property, freedom of contract, and a minimum of government action—however productive it might be—was the final consummation of economic progress.

Classical Economics Today

The great themes of classical economics are as important today as they were in Ricardo's time. The economy has changed, of course, from industrial revolution to mature industrial capitalism, but the interrelationships of resources, people, and capital remain central to problems of human welfare. As world population gallops strongly onward and upward, the Malthusian population trap takes on crucial importance. The advanced industrial nations were able to break the connecting link between production and population—rising output does not trigger the population growth that prevents income per person from rising. But many less-developed countries find that growing populations literally eat up the gains from economic expansion and billions of people remain embedded in poverty. As this twenty-first century begins, however, the birth rate for underdeveloped nations has fallen dramatically. Whether this continues or not remains to be seen.

Meanwhile, in the advanced countries the processes of capital accumulation and technological change continue to produce greater wealth and rising standards of living: the twenty-five years after World War II showed the largest and most sustained increases in material well-being in the history of Western civilization. But this growth was followed by twenty years of slowed growth and relative economic stagnation. Even in the United States economic growth after the late 1960s was only half as fast as in the preceding twenty years. At the same time, rapid technological change puts increased pressure on the natural environment through both pollution and increased use of exhaustible resources. A changing world economy brings greater instability to the production sector of the economy, affecting both workers and business firms. Through it all, trends toward big business and financial speculation seem to accelerate.

These developments in the world economy have brought back into prominence the fundamental relationships between population, accumulation of capital, technology, and economic growth that were the central concern of classical economics. Economic policy today is increasingly concerned with those relationships, and economists are returning both to them and to a renewed interest in the problems dealt with by the classical economists.

FIVE

SOCIALISM
AND
KARL MARX

Karl Marx (1818–1883) provided a revolutionary critique of capitalism and a theoretic foundation for socialism.

Modern socialism emerged as a response to the industrial era just as classical economics had, and just as the classical economists developed an ideology for the new order, the socialists developed a critique of it.

Some socialists were impractical, idealistic dreamers, some were hard-headed critics of the existing society, and others were revolutionists, but all were united by their criticisms of the new industrial society and by their belief in common rather than private ownership of the means of production. Socialists had a different view of the nature of society than did the classical economists, arguing that the social fabric was essentially an organic whole composed of classes, rather than a collection of independent individuals. They stressed the cooperative element in human nature, rather than the individualistic profit motive of private capitalism, and they advocated egalitarianism in place of the unequal distribution of income that prevailed. The socialists could often point to actual economic conditions—real defects in industrial capitalism—to support their arguments.

Socialism and the Climate of Opinion

The economic and political events of the half-century from 1775 to 1825 provide a background for understanding the rise of modern socialism. Of primary importance was the Industrial Revolution. It provided substantial increases in living standards and opportunities for acquisition of great wealth for the new middle class. It was clear that the reasons for economic growth were industrialization, capital investment, and higher productivity, and that every widening of market opportunities made still further advances possible.

To the socialist, however, industrialism had a different face. Workers in the new factories were paid low wages. Although factory pay was high enough to draw labor from the countryside, unemployment in rural areas meant that workers were willing to accept very low wages. Hours of work were long, women and children were employed in substantial numbers in difficult and dangerous jobs, factory discipline was often harsh and rigorous, and in some areas company-owned stores profited from exclusive selling rights among employees. Particularly in the textile and coal industries, competition kept selling prices low, and firms competed with each other by squeezing labor costs whenever possible. These shortcomings were particularly evident in the first half of the nineteenth century in England, where the Industrial Revolution began.

The realities of industrial life created sharp contrasts between the growing wealth of the new industrialists and bankers and the poverty of those without property who formed the work force in the factories of the slum-ridden cities. During the "hungry forties" in England Benjamin Disraeli wrote of "the two nations"—the rich and the poor—while Charles Dickens examined the business ethic in *Hard Times*. The public read Thomas Hood's pathetic poem of the sewing woman, *Song of the Shirt*.

Poverty there had always been, and rich and poor had lived side by side for ages. Many people always had to wrest a meager living from a stingy natural environment. But industrialization promised abundance. For the first time it seemed as though the economy might be able to produce everything people could want, and that the great struggle for existence could be resolved. Yet the gray slums of Manchester and the black country of the coal mines told a different story. The promise and the reality were vastly different.

A similar difference between ideals and reality prevailed in politics. The French revolutionists of 1789 had proclaimed "Liberty, Equality, Fraternity," and with that slogan the French had overthrown the privileges of the old order and marched through Europe to sweep away the last remnants of feudalism and aristocracy. New beliefs in freedom and equality seemed to be creating a political order of full democracy, just as the Industrial Revolution seemed to portend an end to poverty.

But the defeat of Napoleon brought reaction and repression—and reestablishment of the old system of place and privilege. Even where parliamentary government existed, as in England and France, participation was limited to persons with property, and working people were excluded from the vote. Democracy, apparently, was fine for the middle class but dangerous if extended to the worker.

The Industrial Revolution and the French Revolution appeared to many as means of realizing some of the ageless and ancient ideals of Western civilization—abundance, an end to excessive toil, and the triumph of brotherhood and equality. Yet in the darkness of the post-Napoleonic reaction all this was betrayed, and postwar depressions seemed to produce even greater poverty and want than before, since the unemployed worker did not have even a small plot of land on which to grow food. To the early socialists it was self-evident that private ownership of the means of production was the source of society's ills. Ownership of machines, factories, and other capital enabled the owner to reap rich rewards, to sit back and rake in profits while others worked. At the same time, economic position brought political power. In the eyes of the socialist, fifty years of social revolution had given wealth and power to a few owners of capital rather than to the great numbers of common people. Society as a whole had been betrayed for the benefit of a few.

Robert Owen, Utopian

The humanitarian and idealistic roots of early socialism are typified by the work and writings of the Englishman Robert Owen (1771–1858). Apprenticed to a linen-draper at ten years of age, he worked at various establishments in the textile industry throughout his youth, including one shop that "often worked their employees from 8 A.M. to 2 A.M." After failing in business for himself, he became manager of a textile mill when only nineteen years old. Seven years later he was able to buy control of textile mills at New Lanark, in Scotland, and in 1800 he took over their active management. The former management had used children from orphanages as part of its labor supply, along with adults, many of whom were "thieves, drunkards, and criminals of every sort." The workday ran from 6 A.M. to 7 P.M. for children as well as adults, and the company town was composed of wooden one-room houses. These working and living conditions were not considered bad for the time.

Owen was a religious man who believed that the workers of New Lanark were evil because of their surroundings, so he decided to turn New Lanark into a model community. He took no more children from workhouses or orphanages and allowed no child under ten to work. The workday was set at ten and one-half hours for both children and adults. He provided schools in the evening for the working children (imagine a child of ten going to school after working ten and one-half hours!) and set up nursery schools for younger ones. For his adult workers he established a "register of character," which recorded drunkenness and other delinquencies, such as illicit sexual behavior, so effectively that pubs quickly disappeared from the town, and there were only twenty-eight illegitimate births in nine years. An elected committee, called "bug hunters" by the women, inspected for domestic cleanliness once each week. A support fund for the injured, sick, and aged was established, into which workers were required to pay one-sixtieth of their wages. Thrift was encouraged by establishment of a savings bank and by provision of better houses for those who used the bank. Finally, Owen established a store that sold food and other products to workers, charging considerably lower prices and providing goods of higher quality than did private shopkeepers.

How could Owen do all this and still make money in the highly competitive textile industry? Apparently there were two reasons. First, his plants were located in an area of labor surplus and his wages were low: An investigating committee in 1819 reported that he paid 9 shillings, 11 pence—about $2.40—per week to men, and 6 shillings—about $1.50—per week to women, figures that were below average for the time. Second, even though his methods were paternalistic, the attention he paid to workers seems to have brought relatively high labor productivity. In 1819 profits were 12.5 percent of the invested capital.

Owen recognized that the reforms at New Lanark had come from the patron rather than from the workers themselves and that some form of industrial self-government would have to follow. He published his views in 1816 in one of the landmark books of the socialist movement, *The New View of Society*, at a time when England was debating the first factory act, designed to limit the hours of work and establish a minimum age for child labor. Owen lobbied hard for the act, but failure of the bill adequately to cover child labor disappointed him, and the unwillingness of other employers to imitate the example of New Lanark drove him to more radical schemes.

He tried to establish cooperative communities, in which land was owned in common, and in 1824 went to the United States to open one at New Harmony, Indiana. But the community in America, and others in England, failed, with substantial financial loss to Owen. More successful were the cooperative retail stores established under Owen's leadership in England, beginning the far-flung consumers' cooperative movement that has been highly successful in England and Scandinavia and has developed to some extent in the United States. Owen also tried to set up producers' cooperatives—groups of workers who owned the factory in which they worked—but these projects did not succeed.

Owen was a visionary who sought to reform society through worker-owned communities and enterprises in which profits were not permitted. He expected that in such communities the life of the individual would achieve a larger meaning through full integration into the cooperative life of the group. In an individualistic era, his efforts were doomed to fail. Perhaps he was right when he wrote to a business partner, "All the world is queer save thee and me, and methinks at times that thou art a little touched."

Karl Marx, Revolutionary

In sharp contrast to the idealistic and impractical Owen was the intense German, Karl Marx (1818–1883). Born and raised in the most economically advanced part of Germany, the Rhineland, and son of a petty legal official of the government, Marx displayed great intellectual ability at an early age. Sent to the universities at Bonn and Berlin, he first studied law with a view toward a governmental career, but his opposition to the autocratic governments in Germany precluded that. The young Marx then turned to philosophy, with the goal of a professorship, but his studies of philosophy and religion at Berlin—his doctoral dissertation was on the Stoic and Epicurean roots of Christian doctrine—led him to atheism, and this barred him from a university career. So Marx went into journalism and became editor of a liberal Cologne newspaper in 1842. It was there, while writing on economic problems, that he became convinced of the economic basis of politics—that underlying political theories and political power lay the economic interests of various groups in society. His newspaper was suppressed by the government for its liberal views, however, and Marx went to Paris where he married his childhood sweetheart, the daughter of a German baron,* and became acquainted with a number of socialists.

One of them was Pierre Joseph Proudhon (1809–1865), a socialist leader who influenced him very strongly. Proudhon's chief work was a book called *What Is Property?* ("Property is theft," he answered to his own question), a forceful statement that the whole product of industry should go to the worker, and that private property in the means of production enabled the capitalist to appropriate wealth that rightfully belonged to the worker. This concept—not original with Proudhon—was a basic tenet of nineteenth-century socialism and fundamental to Marx's own view of capitalism. Another of Proudhon's books, subtitled *The Philosophy of Poverty*, attacked the orthodox economics of his time and especially the "iron law of wages"—the Malthusian argument that wage rates tended toward the subsistence level because of population growth. Convinced that Proudhon's arguments were specious, Marx attacked his friend in a book sarcastically titled *The Poverty of Philosophy*, and legend has it that Proudhon never spoke to Marx again.

Another socialist whom Marx met in Paris was Friedrich Engels (1820–1895), son of a wealthy German textile manufacturer who owned mills in England and Germany. Marx and Engels formed a friendship that lasted until Marx's death, and the two men collaborated in developing the ideas that Marx was later to publish. Engels supported Marx and his family for most of the next thirty-five years.

While in Paris Marx continued his journalistic career, writing articles especially critical of Prussia, and he was soon expelled from France at the request of the Prussian government. Moving to Brussels in 1848, just before the outbreak of the revolutions of that year, Marx and Engels wrote *The Communist Manifesto:* "A spectre is haunting Europe . . . Workingmen of the world unite, you have nothing to lose but your chains!" Marx had entered on his career as active revolutionary.

When the revolution broke out, Marx returned to Cologne, began editing his newspaper again, and publicized the revolution sweeping Europe. But the revolt was suppressed and Marx, expelled from Germany and

---

*Jenny Marx was herself a fiery radical. After the family settled in London in 1849, a series of strongly stated revolutionary articles appeared in several leftist English papers, under male pseudonyms, which recent scholarship suggests were written by Jenny Marx. She also is reputed to have translated *The Communist Manifesto* into English. The couple's family life was marred when, in 1851, while Jenny was pregnant with their fifth child, Marx fathered a child by a household servant. The child was adopted by another family, with financial assistance from Marx's friend, Friedrich Engels, who announced that the child was his in order to shield Marx when rumors about the true parentage began to circulate. After that the pseudonymous radical articles stopped.

unwelcome in France, went to England, where he spent the rest of his life. He continued working in journalism from time to time. For a while he was English correspondent for the *New York Tribune,* and he wrote about the French Commune of 1871 for the *London Times.* But most of his time was spent in scholarship, doing research on economics in the library of the British Museum and writing his great work, *Capital.* This book was both a denunciation of capitalism—Marx invented the word—and an explanation of why it must fail. The first volume appeared in 1867 and was the only part completed by Marx himself. The second volume, edited by Engels, appeared in 1885, two years after Marx's death, while the third volume, edited by Karl Kautsky, was not issued until 1894.

Scholarship did not completely replace revolutionary agitation, however, for when the International—an international alliance of socialist parties—was formed in 1864, Marx took a leading part. It was not enough to be a theorist, he felt, for there had to be a revolutionary party to take control when capitalism collapsed. He wrote extensively in support of the proletarian revolutionary movement and in opposition to socialists whose views differed from his own. Marx set a precedent in the use of vitriolic denunciation that has continued to plague left-wing radicalism to the present day.

Marx died in 1883 after having given to revolutionary socialism its theoretical foundations. One wonders how different the world might be today had not the rigid authoritarianism of post-Napoleonic Prussia barred Marx from a career in government or university.

Marx's View of Capitalism

It is difficult to condense the grand scheme of Marx's thought without doing injustice to the power and consistency of his reasoning. The very fact that Marx's argument is long and intricate, with all parts of it logically connected and integrated, makes almost any short summary a falsification. Nevertheless, it is important that it be understood, if only because it is the basis of one of the most powerful ideologies in the modern world.

Marx begins with the idea that economic relationships are the fundamental driving force in any society. Particularly under capitalism, however, people are motivated primarily by their own economic interests—but let him say it in his own words, from the Preface to *A Contribution to the Critique of Political Economy* (1859):

> In the social production which men carry on they enter into definite relations that are indispensable and independent of their will; these relations of production correspond to a definite stage of development of their material powers of production. The sum total of these relations of production constitutes the economic structure of society—the real foundation, on which rise legal and political superstructures and to which correspond definite forms of social consciousness. The mode of production in material life determines the general character of the social, political and spiritual process of life.

In a capitalist society, according to Marx, the two great economic interests are those of capitalist and worker. These two classes stand in opposition to each other, since the capitalist can prosper only if the worker is exploited. In this respect capitalism is only the latest in a series of social organizations in which one class exists at the expense of another. *The Communist Manifesto* (1848) puts it bluntly:

> The history of all hitherto existing society is the history of class struggles. Freeman and slave, patrician and plebeian, lord and serf, guildmaster and journeyman, in a word, oppressor and oppressed, stood in constant opposition to one another. . . . The modern bourgeois society that has sprouted from the ruins of feudal society has not done away with class antagonisms. It has but established new classes, new conditions of oppression, new forms of struggle in place of the old ones.

Marx started his attack on capitalism with the *labor theory of value*. Recall that this theory, which was developed by the economic liberals and the classical economists, stated that the true value of any product or service was simply the amount of labor used in its production. A table that takes ten hours of labor to make is worth twice as much as a chair that requires five hours of labor, assuming labor of equal quality.

In Marx's view, labor under capitalism is exploited because it is not paid the full value of the products and services it produces. The capitalist employs workers at the current wage rate and works them for as many hours each day as possible, making sure that the value of the workers' output is greater than the wages paid. This difference between the wage and the value added by the worker, which Marx called "surplus value," becomes the capitalist's profit. Exploitation of the worker can be intensified, and the surplus value appropriated by the capitalist can be increased, by an employer's efforts to achieve lower wages, longer hours, and employment of a greater number of women and children. Thus Marx explained some of the more widely prevalent characteristics of the industrial economy of his time.

Exploitation exists in another sense as well. Marx saw capitalism as a gigantic mechanism through which the labor time of the worker is transformed first into profits and from profits into capital. Whereas labor time is owned by the worker, capital is the property of the capitalist. In this fashion the capitalist class grows increasingly wealthy out of the labor of the working class: "They coin our very life blood into gold," to quote a radical song from pre–World War I America.

This exploitation of workers is only the direct economic effect of capitalism on the working class. It has psychological effects as well. Marx viewed work as a continuing interaction between people, nature, and the product of labor. Work was an essential element in the development of the human personality, so a full realization of the self required a full and rich development of the individual's relationship with the means of production and the product. Yet under capitalism the worker is separated from both the fruits of labor and the tools of production, which are the property of the employer.

Full development of the self and the personality is prevented. The result is a pervasive *alienation* that dehumanizes all personal and social relationships. Market exchange and money payments take the place of human feelings and human relationships, and life becomes dehumanized and pointless. The result is a range of social and psychological pathology that pervades all capitalist society and is inherent in its basic economic relationships.*

Exploitation and alienation are one side of capitalism. The other is accumulation of capital and growth of wealth. This side of the economic process also develops out of the relationships between capital and labor. However much the employer tries to squeeze his labor, the labor market itself will determine the level of wage rates, while hours of work are limited by human endurance, and employment of women and children is affected by a combination of technological factors and labor-market conditions. The individual employer has relatively little flexibility in these matters and cannot readily gain a competitive advantage over other capitalists except by reinvesting profits (surplus value) in new machinery and equipment, which raises productivity of labor and increases profits still further. Indeed, the employer is compelled to do so to survive, because competitors will do the same. The result is a continuing drive to expand investment. In this way Marx explained the process of capital accumulation and the growing productivity and increased output it generates.

Capitalism, then, presents two faces: capital accumulation and growth on the one hand, exploitation and alienation on the other.

The Breakdown of Capitalism

Marx believed that capitalism was doomed, and he developed an intricate analysis of the "laws of motion" of capitalist society to prove it. At one level the argument has a moral basis: the inherent injustices of capitalism lead ultimately to economic and social conditions that cannot be maintained. At another level the argument is sociological: class conflict—between a decreasing number of increasingly wealthy capitalists and a growing and increasingly miserable working class—will lead ultimately to social revolution. And, finally, the argument is economic: the accumulation of capital in private hands makes possible economic abundance; yet accumulation also leads to depressions, chronic unemployment, and the economic breakdown of capitalism. At each level the idea of conflict is emphasized: conflict between ideal and reality, between capital and labor, and between growth and stagnation. Out of conflict comes change, and for this basic reason, accord-

---

*Marx did not give great emphasis to these extraordinary insights into modern society. He developed them in early essays that were not published until after World War II and in two chapters of *Capital* that deal with them in partial fashion. But even that was enough to profoundly influence many modern psychologists and give us the concept of alienation as a source of psychological disorders.

ing to Marx, capitalism must give way to another form of society in which conflict is replaced by ethical, social, and economic harmony. Change through conflict is the "dialectical process" by which socialism was ultimately to replace capitalism. Marx felt that the process had an economic basis in the division of society into workers and capitalists. Their relationship was exploitive, with the owners of the means of production having the upper hand. Conflict was inherent in this situation, he argued, and it would build up until the whole fabric of society was torn apart.

Exploitation of labor is the starting point. It leads to inadequate purchasing power and, through surplus value and capitalist competition, to accumulation of capital. There is an inconsistency here, however. When the economy is prosperous, business firms earn surplus value for their owners, who reinvest it for expanded output. But purchasing power eventually lags, partly because workers are not paid the full value of their labor and partly because capital investment pushes output capacity upward. Sooner or later a glut of unsold commodities appears on the market. Production is then cut back and prices fall: unemployment increases, profit declines and then disappears, and capital accumulation is halted. The capitalist "crisis" continues until the glut of commodities has been disposed of: prices recover, profits increase, and capital accumulation resumes once more, continuing until the next glut appears. This process, argued Marx, creates the recurring cycles of prosperity and depression that are an inherent failing of capitalism.

Marx also argued that the crises would become more severe—longer and deeper—as capitalism developed. The total capital and productive capacity of the economy increase from crisis to crisis, and the ratio of capital to labor rises. These changes cause the gluts to become larger and larger, to take longer and longer to be disposed of, and necessitate greater and greater cutbacks in production.

But why, one may ask, would the glut appear in the first place? Will not rising prosperity cause increases in employment, wage rates, and purchasing power? Marx answered that even during prosperity the "reserve army" of the unemployed receives recruits—workers whose jobs are taken over by machines. Capital investment leads to substitution of capital for labor. Indeed, this is the only way in which capitalists can increase the rate at which they accumulate surplus value. During prosperity, therefore, capital accumulation creates technological unemployment and pushes wages and purchasing power down, just as commodity gluts do during periods of depression. In either case, the result is the immiseration of the working class.

This is only half the picture, however. Changes also take place within the capitalist class. First, the rate of profit declines as investment in machinery and equipment gradually becomes an increasing proportion of total investment. (Marx was thoroughly convinced of this when he wrote the first volume of *Capital*, but the notes he left for Volume Three show that he was not quite so sure that profit rates must necessarily decline as capital accumulation proceeds.) Second, the business cycles engendered by capitalism enable the big capitalists to gobble up the little ones. The firms with the largest financial resources survive, and over the years the ownership of industry gradually becomes centralized in fewer and fewer hands until a few great financiers control all. This remaining capitalist class becomes increasingly wealthy, in contrast to the growing misery of the proletariat, which expands as small businesses fail and the owners join the ranks of the working class. The working class also becomes increasingly degraded as technological change breaks down complex jobs into simple ones, skilled jobs become semiskilled, and semiskilled become unskilled. Ultimately a revolution occurs, a popular uprising of the vast majority against the wealthy few. Led by communists, the working class seizes power and proceeds to build the new society.

Marx was quite aware of the possibility that these economic trends could be modified by political and social changes. Labor unions, originating in the conflict between capital and labor, could reduce exploitation of labor, but Marx feared that opportunistic union leaders might retreat from class conflict in favor of class accommodation. Governments, although dominated by capitalist political interests, could introduce social welfare legislation to strengthen the economic system as a whole. And parliamentary democracy could provide the appearance of popular participation even while the economic basis of political power was becoming more concentrated. Marx, however, was confident that the underlying economic trends and conflicts would predominate and ultimately create a revolutionary situation in which capitalism would be more or less rapidly transformed into socialism.

The Marxist Vision

Marx's analysis of capitalist development was based on the assumption that two great forces are continually at work in the development of human society. One is the struggle of people against nature to obtain subsistence and ease. The development of technology and improvements in methods of production are one result of that struggle, and in its early stages capitalism represented a major step toward abundance. Factory production and machine technology greatly increased human command over nature, and competitive capitalism forced business firms to reinvest their profits in new and better methods of production. Capitalism's failure lay in its inability to continue this process and in the periodic breakdowns, or crises, that occurred.

In Marx's view, the struggle for existence led to the second great force that causes economic and social change: the struggle of people against people. Human beings are one type of productive resource, and control over them is one way in which a few can increase their wealth and welfare. Therefore, argued Marx, the struggle for existence inevitably leads to exploitation of some by others. Early manifestations of this principle were the patriarchal family, the slave-based economy of ancient times, and feudalism. The last, in turn, developed into the wage system of capitalism. Each of

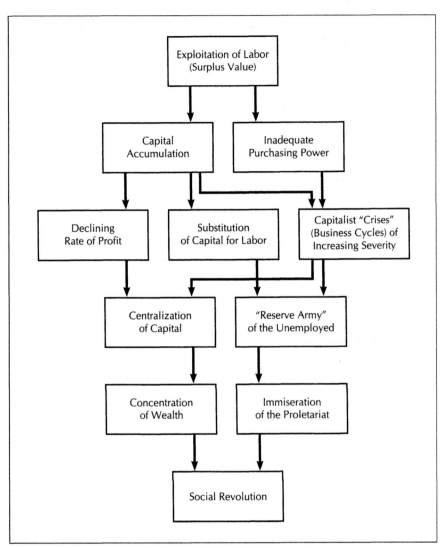

1-1. Schematic Diagram of Marx's Theory of Capitalist Development

THE PROCESS OF CAPITALIST DEVELOPMENT

Exploitation of labor is the source of capital accumulation by capitalist enterprises, which seek to increase surplus value by substituting capital for labor. Loss of jobs, overproduction, and inadequate purchasing power bring on business cycles, which tend to become increasingly severe as the economy matures. The long-run trends (capital accumulation, substitution of capital for labor, declining profit rates), together with worsening economic crises, lead to (1) an increasingly wealthy capitalist class among whom ownership of wealth tends to become more highly concentrated, and (2) an increasingly immiserated working class that gradually becomes conscious of its own class interests and its systematic exploitation under a capitalist system.

these social developments represented a victory in the battle against nature and marked an increase in human freedom—for some, if not all—and each was made possible by advances in technology and the social organization of production.

Ultimately, he argued, the economy could achieve widespread abundance and produce enough for all, and at that point in human history all people could be completely free, both politically and economically. Capitalism could not achieve this goal, because it prevented the full development of modern technology, resulted in the periodic stoppage of capital accumulation, and created the conditions of social revolution. But socialism could achieve the goal, because it eliminated exploitation and class distinctions and because it removed the roadblocks hindering the advance of production.

Marx concluded that an economy of abundance was possible only in a classless society. When the abundant economy arrived, there would no longer be any need for social or economic differences, and exploitation would long before have ended. Distribution of income would be based on the maxim "from each according to his abilities, to each according to his needs." At this point the two great struggles of humanity—people against nature and people against one another—would end. This was the positive side of Marxism—its vision of a great world of abundance, equality, and freedom.

Was Marx Right?

One of the least useful economic debates of the twentieth century has been over the correctness of Marx's analysis of capitalism. As proof of Marx's errors, his detractors point to the rising living standards of modern nations. The working class has not been subjected to growing misery, and labor unions have gained economic and political power in all the major industrialized countries. Moreover, the working class has shared the increased wealth, income, and economic benefits that have been spread widely throughout all social classes.

Marxists answer that the extremes of exploitation have been shifted from the domestic working class to that of colonial and less-developed nations. Peoples dominated politically or economically by great capitalist nations now bear the greatest burden of exploitation, enabling capitalists to ease their treatment of the working class at home and allow its living standards to rise. They also point to the continuing extremes of poverty and wealth within nations, to the rise of big business and the prevalence of monopoly, to the dominant influence wielded in politics by business interests, and to the failure of capitalist nations to find a cure for depressions and unemployment, as indications that the Marxist analysis was essentially correct. In spite of all the "concessions" that have been made to the working class— social welfare legislation, union organization, higher living standards— Marxists contend that the basic defects of capitalism remain, holding back

economic growth and postponing indefinitely the emergence of the abundant society.

Yet even if the Marxist predictions of increased misery and a polarized
society were wrong, Marx's arguments must give us pause. No society can
long endure that excludes a substantial group of its citizens from enjoying
its benefits, as was the case for many workers and their families in Marx's
day and during the nineteenth-century decades of discontent and potential
upheaval in Europe. In many respects Marx's analysis was a theoretical interpretation of actual conditions.

In the years after 1870, however, many important changes took place on
the European scene. The right to vote—political democracy—was gradually
extended to working people. National systems of welfare legislation provided protection against the worst effects of the industrial system. The
growth of labor unions and the appearance of political parties representing
the interests of labor gave a new dignity to the worker and signified the
place industrial labor was making for itself. The "safety valve" of emigra-
tion to North and South America and Australia enabled many dissatisfied
Europeans to start a new life in freer societies. And imperialism offered significant economic opportunities, whatever else might be said against it.

Social tensions would not have been sufficiently eased, however, in spite
of these developments, without growth in the European economy. Industrialism opened many doors to the intelligent and the ambitious—Robert
Owen is only one example. Although it has always been true that one gets
ahead more easily if one begins near the top, it is also true that a growing
and changing economy offers more opportunity than a stagnant one. Continued economic growth, both external and internal, gave Europe time to
adapt to the stresses of industrialization by instituting reforms that gave political rights to workers and protected them from some of the harshest effects
of the market economy. One moral to be derived from Marxism is that an
economy must provide dignity and broad opportunities for all if society is
to remain healthy.

The Marxist prediction of the triumph of socialism and the creation of a
democratic, egalitarian, and nonexploitive society has not proved accurate.
The prediction of increased concentration of economic power in the capitalist world has been borne out by events, although many economists would
argue that the reasons for that trend differ from those advanced by Marx.
And capitalism was placed on the defensive by the rise of communist
regimes in Russia and China, and by the spread of socialism through many
of the less-developed countries. But in most instances, these noncapitalist
economies developed authoritarian political regimes, new forms of economic and social inequality, and new aspects of exploitation. The humane
goals that underlay Marx's rage at capitalism seemed no closer to achievement in the noncapitalist regimes of the late twentieth century than in the
capitalist. This situation created something of a crisis among leftists in
the advanced capitalist countries, as they reevaluated Marxist theory in a
twentieth-century context.

We should also note that Marx had little to say about what specific forms socialism might take after the revolution. We should not attribute either the authoritarian command economy of the former Soviet Union or the democratic evolutionary socialism of Western Europe to Marx, although both claim him as godfather.

Marxism After Marx

Marx's critique of capitalism included a forecast of the inevitable breakdown of capitalism, leading to a period of social revolution out of which a classless, egalitarian, and communal society could emerge. Engels was later to call the process "historical materialism." The idea was that in the early days of capitalism the new "social relations" of capitalist and worker had freed the "forces of production" from the fetters of feudalism, leading to an era of growing abundance and freedom. But the contradictions and conflicts within capitalism—exploitation of workers, elimination of small enterprise, growth of big business, growing concentration of wealth in fewer and fewer hands, and financial crises of increasing severity—would lead to both an end to economic growth and authoritarian suppression of dissent. The social relations of late capitalism once again would hinder further development of the forces of production. Conflict, crisis, and economic upheaval would follow. The working class could take command and build a communal, egalitarian society in which conflict would be eliminated and the forces of production would be free once more to usher in a new era of abundance and freedom for all.

Marx's great vision was not to be. Marx had urged his followers not merely to interpret the world, but to change it. Take action! As mass political parties emerged on the left in the late nineteenth and twentieth centuries, particularly after the Russian revolution of 1917, historical materialism became not a theory of historical change but a rationale for revolutionary seizure of power. By the 1930s it had evolved into an apologetic for Stalinist authoritarianism in the Soviet Union.

Yet at the same time Marxist "revisionism" generated an entirely different strategy among more moderate socialists. The revisionists rejected Marx's theory of capitalist breakdown leading to a final crisis. Gradual reform and democratic elections rather than revolution and seizure of power characterized this outcome of the debates over Marxism after Marx.

The transformation of what came to be called "orthodox" Marxism started shortly after Marx's death in 1883. The German Social Democratic Party (SPD) was the largest socialist party in Europe in the late nineteenth and early twentieth centuries. It organized a meeting of all socialist groups in Paris in 1889, and another at Erfurt, Germany, in 1891, to produce a socialist manifesto. The Erfurt Programme, as it was called, had two parts. The first part was theoretical, written by Karl Kautsky (1854–1938), whom we met earlier as the editor of the third volume of *Capital*. The second part discussed policy, written by Eduard Bernstein (1850–1932), a journalist who became the chief spokesman for Marxist revisionism.

Kautsky's part of the Erfurt Programme was a simplified version of Marx's theory of capitalist breakdown. He wrote that society is breaking into two hostile groups: an ever-expanding working class and an ever-shrinking capitalist elite. The condition of the working class constantly deteriorates while the elite grow wealthier. Economic crises become increasingly severe. The goal of socialism moves closer as the final crisis of capitalism approaches.

Bernstein's statement of immediate objectives, however, said almost nothing about socialism or social ownership of the means of production. It was a list of political goals: extension to everyone—including women—of the right to vote; proportional representation in the legislature, referendums for direct votes by the public; popular election of judges; separation of church and state, particularly in education; control of foreign policy by the legislature; a bill of individual rights; freedom of association and press; and equal rights for men and women. There isn't much that is revolutionary here, at least to us more than a hundred years later. These political goals were supplemented by such measures as free medical care; legal aid programs; free burial; free education at all levels, including higher education; old age pensions; and full employment. Costs would be paid out of progressive income taxes, property taxes, and death duties. Indirect taxes, such as sales taxes, would be prohibited. There's not much here that's radical. All of Bernstein's practical program could be accomplished in a private-enterprise capitalist system—or by a communist party after a revolutionary seizure of power.

Orthodox Marxism took the latter path, despite the fact that both Marx and Engels recognized that England and the United States, for example, might avoid a revolutionary confrontation between capital and labor because of their democratic political institutions. Engels's later writings, however, emphasized Marx's theory of the breakdown of capitalism in an era of social revolution, leaving out, as Marx did not, the possibility of developments that might modify the trend toward breakdown, such as labor unions, welfare legislation, and parliamentary democracy.

Orthodox Marxists debated several strategies for seizing power in the name of the working class. Rosa Luxemburg (1870–1919) advocated mass action by the working class, using the general strike of all workers at a time of crisis to bring monopoly capitalism to its knees. In *Social Reform or Revolution?* (1900) she advocated revolution. In *The General Strike* (1907) she laid down her revolutionary strategy. In *Accumulation of Capital* (1913) she argued that the collapse of the capitalist system was imminent, carrying Kautsky's rigid version of Marx's historical materialsm to its logical conclusion. She was murdered by the military during the Spartacist revolt in Berlin in 1919, a failed effort to stimulate a general strike and seize power.

Although Marx had argued that the working class would develop a revolutionary consciousness, a program, and a strategy out of its experience in a capitalist society, the Russian, V. I. Lenin (Vladimir Ilyich Mlyanov, 1870–1924) doubted that would happen. In a 1902 pamphlet, *What Is To Be Done?—Burning*

Questions of Our Movement, he called for the formation of a party of dedicated revolutionaries who could lead the masses during a time of crisis, seize power, and proceed to build the new society. Members of the party would work full time for the party and would be thoroughly trained in revolutionary strategy and tactics—professional revolutionaries. The party would maintain contact with other groups and organizations among the working class and other exploited groups, but its members would remain an elite and secret leadership.

Meanwhile, an important modification of the theory of the breakdown of capitalism, by Rudolph Hilferding (1877–1941) in *Finance Capital* (1910), gave added impetus to those Marxists arguing for revolutionary seizure of power. While Marx had analyzed the development of competitive capitalism, Hilferding argued that capitalism had evolved into monopoly capitalism dominated by a few great financial institutions. This was the final stage, and the social revolution was imminent, he argued. Orthodox Marxists, including Lenin, immediately seized upon Hilferding's analysis as further justification for a revolutionary seizure of power. Lenin, in particular, used Hilferding's argument in his theory of revolution and political action.

Lenin's revolutionary strategy developed during the tumult of events of the World War (there was only one at the time). In *Imperialism, The Highest Stage of Capitalism* (1916) he characterized the war as essentially an imperialist war for control of investment opportunities in underdeveloped parts of the world. He argued that as investment opportunities and rates of profit declined in the advanced capitalist nations, and concessions were made to the working class to avoid strife, colonies became essential as outlets for surplus goods and surplus capital. Furthermore, exploitation of labor in the colonies was intensified as unions grew at home and exploitation of labor was relaxed. This analysis helped answer those critics of Marxism who argued that, contrary to Marx and orthodox Marxism, exploitation of labor was not increasing and the working class was not being immiserated. It also served another purpose within Russia, where Lenin could argue that Russian workers, in an underdeveloped country, were subject to more intensive exploitation than workers in more advanced western European countries and would therefore be more ripe for revolt. Marxist theory was placed in the service of a political program.

The State and Revolution (1917) was even more important in the formation of Lenin's political strategy. The revolution against capitalism would lead to a "dictatorship of the proletariat." This phrase had been used by Marx, but its meaning was not clear. Did it mean simply a government dominated by workers, analogous to bourgeois dominance of the state under capitalism, or did it mean an authoritarian government headed by a small revolutionary political party? Marx himself was not clear on this point, sometimes using the term in one context and sometimes in the other, and Engels had once written that the United States might move to a dictatorship of the proletariat by democratic elections, whatever that might mean. Nor was Lenin clear on exactly what he meant (he used exactly one page to discuss the issue). In practice, however, after the Bolshevik seizure of power in Russia in 1917, dictatorship of the proletariat meant authoritarian rule by a small group of revolutionaries acting in the name of the working class as a whole.[*]

The State and Revolution also made a distinction between the lower stage of communism and a higher stage.[**] Lenin argued that after the revolution, during which the communist party comes to control the state, the powers of government would be used to move toward socialism. But only after the socialist system increased production to achieve abundance would it be possible, in the higher stage, for the state to wither away and the principle of "from each according to his work, to each according to his need" to be applied. In the first stage—socialism—incomes would not be equal, and the dictatorship of the proletariat would prevail.

With Lenin, orthodox Marxism developed into an economic and political ideology that served the needs of Soviet authoritarianism. Engels's and Kautsky's emphasis on the inevitable breakdown of capitalism, plus Lenin's strategy of a revolutionary party and dictatorship of the proletariat, combined with the concept of socialism as a lower stage of communism, produced a bastard Marxism perfectly suited to Stalin and the authoritarian Soviet regime.

While this development of orthodox Marxism was going on, an entirely different path was pioneered by the revisionists. After the death of Engels in 1895, Karl Kautsky and Eduard Bernstein, the two authors of the Erfurt Programme of 1891, were widely considered to be the foremost Marxist theorists in Germany, where the Marxist tradition was strongest. Bernstein had been editor of one of the important socialist newspapers from 1881 to 1890, published first in Zurich and then in London because of Germany's laws banning socialism and socialist publications. While in London he became friendly with Engels and met some of the English socialist leaders. He served as co-executor of Engels's estate in 1895 and 1896. But Bernstein had already begun to question the theory of capitalist breakdown stated so forcefully by Engels. He returned to Germany when the antisocialism laws were repealed, and between 1896 and 1898 he published a series of articles on "Problems of Socialism" in the leading socialist newspaper *Die Neue Zeit.* They were later expanded into a book with the cumbersome title of *The Presuppositions of Socialism and the Tasks of Social Democracy* (1899). An abridged English version, *Evolutionary Socialism: A Criticism and Affirmation,* was published in 1931, at a time when the Great Depression and the rise of fascism revived interest in socialist alternatives.

---

[*]One of the early slogans of the Russian revolution of 1917 was "All power to the Soviets," which were local and factory governing bodies elected by workers. I once asked an economist from the Soviet Central Planning Commission, shortly after the death of Stalin, "What do you suppose the world would be like today if Lenin had placed power in the hands of the Soviets instead of in the Party?" I should have known better. His answer: "It was an historical necessity"—Marxist historical materialism as political ideology.

[**]Marx had made a similar distinction in an 1878 pamphlet, *The Critique of the Gotha Programme,* in which he pointed out that there would have to be an intermediate stage between capitalism and full communism. But he did not specify what that stage would be like, leaving that to be decided by those living and working at the time.

In his 1899 book Bernstein denied that he was rejecting the essential core of Marxism, while he sought to revise what he considered to be outdated, dogmatic, or ambiguous. In particular, he rejected the idea of an imminent collapse of capitalism. He disputed the Marxist predictions of increasing industrial concentration, the destruction of small business, and more acute economic crises (Germany had recovered quickly from the depression of the 1890s), as well as the theory of working-class immiseration. Instead, he argued that the working class was steadily advancing both economically and politically and a social reaction against capitalist exploitation was reforming economic life. There would be no catastrophic crash.

Bernstein called for the Social Democratic Party (SPD) to forego ideas of forcible revolution and the dictatorship of the proletariat and become a party of reform. It should emphasize transforming the state "in the direction of democracy" through extension of political and economic rights. Ultimately, when the SPD gained power through a democratic election, it could move toward socialist reform. Bernstein rejected both revolutionary seizure of power and dictatorship of the proletariat.

Successive party congresses rejected Bernstein's views, although in practice it adopted them. Bernstein was elected to the Reichstag and served as a socialist delegate from 1902 to 1906, 1912 to 1918, and 1920 to 1928. During World War I he called for a peace settlement and in 1915 voted against funds for the war effort. After the war he argued the case for democratic socialism on moral and ethical grounds.

Bernstein's evolutionary socialism of reform from within rather than revolution, of extending the scope of parliamentary democracy, of introducing the socialist program step by step thorough majority vote, was to become the program of socialist political parties in all of western Europe and North America in the twentieth century. After the Second World War socialist parties came to power everywhere in western Europe, usually in coalitions with other liberal groups, and were able to legislate a variety of socialist programs and economic reforms. Marxism after Marx took two paths. One led from Engels through Lenin to the ideology of the Soviet Union. The second, by way of Bernstein, evolved into the strategy of democratic socialism.

Marxism, as an idea, has been an important force in the modern world. It expresses a moral outrage at the condition of humanity. It holds up a grand vision of what the condition might be. It viewed modern capitalism as a dynamic system in which the very process of growth leads ultimately to a crisis in which the system as a whole could no longer sustain itself. Its class-oriented view of the social order provided a framework within which much of what happens in the modern world can be analyzed. It provided a basis for political action and an ideology around which dissent could rally. These aspects of Marxism are far more important than whether its analysis of individual issues is right or wrong. Wherever people feel oppressed, Marxism can express their outrage and hope and offer a path to something better. It is this characteristic of Marxism that made it a force to be reckoned with in the modern world.

SIX

THE
PHILOSOPHY
OF
INDIVIDUALISM

Herbert Spencer (1820–1903) was the leading philosopher of laissez-faire individualism.

The rise of socialism and its demands for social justice forced the supporters of the existing order to raise their defenses. A theoretical refutation was also needed, because Marx's critique of capitalism was based on the assumptions of classical economics itself—on the labor theory of value and the theory of capital accumulation. He used the weapons of the dominant ideology to attack the very system those weapons defended.

One answer to Marx and socialism was the nineteenth-century philosophy of individualism, which developed as the ideology of a business civilization in the years between 1850 and World War I. Just as Marxism had carried the disenchantment of the dispossessed and the alienated to a high level of theoretical analysis, so a revived and reinforced theory of laissez-faire expressed the interests of the successful. Few of the protagonists of the new individualism could be called economists in the strict sense of the word—the most important were philosophers, jurists, and business leaders—but their economic thought left a far greater impact on their world than did the work of hundreds of academicians.

A second reaction to Marx was a reconstruction of economics itself, accomplished by stripping away its weak elements, strengthening its theoretic rigor, generalizing its basic concepts, and adapting it to the contemporary world. Economics as a discipline was greatly strengthened by the impact of socialist theory and criticism. But the tenor of the times and the climate of opinion within which the reconstructed economics emerged were set by other, more practical men of affairs.

The Philosophy

An English philosopher, Herbert Spencer (1820–1903), and an American sociologist, William Graham Sumner (1840–1910), led the further development of the philosophy of individualism. These men worked out the ideology on which half a century of legislation, law, and folklore was based.

Spencer was an evolutionist before Darwin. As early as 1850, in his *Social Statics*, he maintained that all social systems develop and change by a natural process that results in a maximization of individual welfare. This process of natural development stems from competition between individuals, he argued, and any interference on the part of the government prevents full achievement of the ideal goal. Spencer's early statement was followed by essays and a ten-volume *Synthetic Philosophy*, which sought to show that evolutionary progress occurred in all phenomena—in the biological world, in the human mind, in society, and in ethics. Where Darwin explained evolution in terms of "natural selection," Spencer invented the phrase "survival of the fittest" as the source of progress:

> Any organism, including the social, changes through adaptation to outside influences, carried out in such a way as to benefit the organism involved. Those organisms which are best fitted to their environment, or which change to fit themselves to their environment, will survive. The least fit will die out, leaving the strongest and "best."

Progress is made in this way. The weakest individuals and the least useful social institutions gradually are eliminated. Since the individual member of society is the decision maker, the social organization that emerges from the process of change is more closely adapted to meeting the needs of the individual. Progress means that the welfare of the individual must be improved.

These ideas led to a description of the ideal society, conceived as a static equilibrium between people and their surroundings brought about by full exercise of individual natural rights. Government, a necessary evil, was severely limited to protection of people and property and enforcement of private contracts—nothing else. As society moved from a primitive state of violence and military control to higher levels of industrialization and peace, even the protective role of government could be reduced and would ultimately wither away in the final utopia of philosophical anarchism. In the transition, however, there should be no government regulation of industry, no state church, no organized colonization, no relief for the poor, no social legislation, no public mint, no government-owned postal system, and no public education. Unfettered individual action should be permitted, and nothing should be allowed to interfere with natural selection of the fittest—not even such measures as public sanitation, which protected and thereby perpetuated weaker types.

Spencer's philosophy had a greater impact in the United States than in his own country. His foremost American follower was William Graham Sumner, an Episcopal minister and Yale University economist who became one of the foremost sociologists of his time. His major work is a sociological classic, *Folkways* (1907), which argued that social institutions and conventions develop and continually change by a process of adaptation to individual and social needs. If such institutions do not contribute to individual welfare and survival, they are gradually replaced by more effective methods, and the social system evolves into a higher and better form. Social institutions that proved their usefulness in the past are given up only with reluctance, however, and only after new methods have been proven better. In Sumner's view, therefore, the social system is at one and the same time conservative and progressive, resistant to change and changing.

Within the social system, individuals are also rising and falling, according to Sumner. The person with ability, intelligence, and drive will rise to prominence by successfully competing with all others. The lazy, ignorant, and weak will fall out of sight. The emergence of leading individuals brings progress, because they are the ones who innovate, who think, and who develop new ideas. Competition between them results in both a more vigorous population and a better social structure.

In a long series of essays with such titles as "What Social Classes Owe to One Another," "The Forgotten Man," and "The Concentration of Wealth: Its Economic Justification," Sumner applied his theory of society to questions of contemporary policy. "The forgotten man" was the one who worked hard, produced, paid his taxes, saved, and invested, and thereby brought to society all the benefits of hard work and enterprise, in spite of bearing the burden of protective tariffs, government social services, and the high costs imposed by labor unions.* Concentrated wealth was justified because it was used to produce for others. Wealth that was squandered or allowed to lie idle never led to such concentration. The economic elite rose to the top only because, in competition with others, they expanded economic activity and produced the goods and services that society wanted and needed. Social classes owed nothing to one another; they had only to look out for themselves, and benefits to others would automatically follow.

This, then, was evolutionary philosophy applied to the social system. It justified unlimited individualism on the ground that only social good could come from competition. It justified great wealth on the ground that wealth existed only because it served others. It justified lack of responsibility for others on the ground that anyone destroyed by competition could be considered "unfit," not capable of making a large enough contribution to the social order to survive. It was a rigorous philosophy that associated success

---

*Ironically, Sumner's phrase "the forgotten man" was reversed by Franklin D. Roosevelt and used to describe the poor and downtrodden who would benefit by the welfare measures of the New Deal, an interventionist program that Sumner would have abhorred.

with right and failure with wrong, wealth with public service and poverty with uselessness.

Individualism and the Law

The philosophy of individualism was applied to economic affairs most fully in the United States. The Civil War (1861–1865) brought political dominance to the industrial interests of the northeast, and, during the conflict, several laws were passed that prepared the way for what one critic was to call "the great barbecue." The Morrill Tariff (1861) raised duties on imports and set the stage for high-tariff legislation after the war ended. The Homestead Act (1862) finally opened the West to large-scale settlement. The Pacific Railway Acts (1862 and 1864) provided federal subsidies for transcontinental railways. In 1864 contract labor was authorized to promote immigration by allowing employers to pay for the passage of immigrants in exchange for a work contract. The National Bank Act (1863) remade the monetary system to provide a limited and "sound" money supply. Finally, the ending of slavery created, once and for all, a free labor market for the entire country. The stage was set for the dominance of private enterprise in a business-oriented civilization, once the landed interests of the South went down to defeat in the war.

The philosophy of unrestricted individualism came to be embodied in the nation's fundamental constitutional law. The person most responsible for this development was a now almost forgotten justice of the United States Supreme Court, Stephen J. Field (1816–1899). Field was the son of a prominent Congregational clergyman and the brother of two equally eminent men, Cyrus Field, the businessman who laid the first trans-Atlantic telegraph cable in 1866, and David Dudley Field, a prominent New York lawyer who led the movement for reform of legal codes in the 1860s and who later became the leader of an international movement to substitute arbitration for war, a forerunner of the League of Nations and the United Nations.

In his early thirties Stephen Field joined the gold rush in California. He was elected to a judgeship and in 1850 to the state legislature. By 1857 he was on the state supreme court and became its chief justice in 1859. Field was a product of the developing West and its individualistic, open social structure in which a person could rise through his own efforts.

Abraham Lincoln appointed him to the United States Supreme Court in 1863, a position he held for thirty-four years, becoming one of the country's greatest authorities on constitutional law. In 1876 he was a member of the famous Electoral Commission that decided the presidency in favor of the Republican Rutherford B. Hayes against the Democrat Samuel J. Tilden, who had a larger total vote. During his career on the Supreme Court, Field's most important opinions related to protection of property and freedom of business enterprise, by application to corporations of the freedoms guaranteed to individuals by the Fourteenth Amendment to the Constitution. At first in the minority, Field soon became the most important majority spokesman for the view that the Constitution guarantees individual and business enterprise against government intervention.

The famous Slaughterhouse Cases of 1873 enabled Field to state his position in unequivocal terms. Louisiana had passed laws intending to protect public health in New Orleans by limiting the operation of slaughterhouses and giving a monopoly of the business to a single company. The act was opposed by butchers and cattle dealers, who asked for an injunction against enforcement on the ground that the act was unconstitutional. They argued, among other things, that the monopoly deprived them of the right to follow their usual employment and, contrary to the Fourteenth Amendment, deprived them of property without due process of law and denied them equal protection under the law. Supporters of the legislation argued that it represented a valid expression of the police power of the state government. The case was ultimately appealed to the Supreme Court, where the majority held that the state was legitimately using its police powers and that no civil rights had been violated. Field, however, wrote a vigorous dissent. He felt that the right to operate a slaughterhouse or any other legitimate business enterprise was a right that could not be removed by government. "I cannot believe that what is termed in the Declaration of Independence a God-given and inalienable right can thus be ruthlessly taken from citizens, or that there can be any abridgement of that right except by regulations alike affecting all persons of the same age, sex and condition."

The argument for property as a natural right that no government can appropriate without due process of law was tested further in the ensuing years. Field dissented vigorously on several occasions when the majority of the Supreme Court supported state intervention in economic affairs. But opinion changed, and by 1886 the whole Court had come to accept Field's position. In a case concerning the validity of special taxes imposed on the Southern Pacific Railway by a California county, Field could say, "The Court does not want to hear the argument on the question whether the provision of the 14th amendment applies to these corporations. We are all of the opinion that it does." The constitutional amendment that originally had been intended to protect freed slaves was then applied to corporations and to business enterprise, and in this case the local taxes were declared invalid.

Once Field's position became part of the constitutional law of the United States, much state legislation was struck down, including regulation of hours of work, child labor, factory conditions, and other aspects of economic life. At a time when industrial growth was creating many new problems, the philosophy of unrestricted laissez-faire was the law of the land, and little interference with private enterprise and freedom of contract was permitted. In vain did Justice Oliver Wendell Holmes complain in one famous dissenting opinion that "the fourteenth amendment does not enact Mr. Herbert Spencer's *Social Statics*."

The Folklore of Individualism

The philosophy of individualism was translated into folklore as well as legal principles. The lore told of the poor immigrant boy who started his career at the bottom of the business ladder, worked hard, saved his money, made shrewd investments, and ultimately rose to a position of business leadership. He married well, raised a happy family, and gained the respect of his fellows. Wise in his old age, he was an elder statesman consulted by presidents and loved by his grandchildren.

Although relatively few business leaders followed this path to the top—most were sons of business or professional men, had more than an average education, and did not start at the bottom—a growing economy in which individual enterprise was unhindered and that had no income taxes did offer a fertile field to those bent on obtaining riches. A few actually were living examples of the folklore, although they did not rise within existing enterprises but built their own businesses with shrewdness, ability, and luck.

Andrew Carnegie, for example, was born in Scotland, the son of a weaver who brought his family to America when power looms forced him out of business. The thirteen-year-old Andrew went to work in a textile plant near Pittsburgh as a bobbin boy at twenty cents a day. His hard work earned him a promotion to the engine room, and his knowledge of arithmetic and his penmanship earned him another promotion to the clerical staff. Seeking newer fields with greater opportunity, Andrew became a telegraph messenger boy, learned telegraphy, became an operator, and in his spare time earned extra money as a newspaper telegraph reporter. Moving again to greener fields, he became a telegraph train dispatcher for the Pennsylvania Railroad and then secretary to the general superintendent. When his boss became president of the company, Andrew, then all of twenty-five years old, was appointed superintendent of the railroad's western division. Saving his money, he invested in a sleeping-car company and in oil lands, two new and dynamic industries at the time. During the Civil War Carnegie was in charge of all the eastern military railroads and telegraphs, and he ran them with the efficiency he had applied to all of his work.

Forecasting the superiority of iron and steel bridges over those made of wood, he organized the Keystone Bridge Works in 1862. Shortly after the Civil War ended, he built his own steel plant to supply raw material to his company and in 1868 introduced the Bessemer steel process into the United States. Building and expanding further, he acquired more plants, iron and coal mines, railroads, and all the other elements of the first fully integrated steel company in the country. Rather than run it himself, he took care to hire the best managerial talent available and gave his managers incentives to work with initiative and progressiveness. In 1901 he sold his company to the newly formed United States Steel Corporation for almost half a billion dollars. Carnegie himself received over $300 million, a huge fortune in those days.

Carnegie believed and lived the philosophy that wealth is held by the individual only as a stewardship and that it is to be used ultimately for the benefit of society as a whole. After selling his company, he devoted the remainder of his life to supporting education and research. He established and financed the Carnegie Institute of Technology in Pittsburgh, the Carnegie Institution of Washington for purposes of scientific research, the Carnegie Corporation of New York as a trust fund for support of education and research, the Carnegie Foundation for the Advancement of Teaching, the Carnegie Endowment for International Peace, and the Carnegie Hero Fund to provide rewards for heroic deeds, in addition to endowing libraries in hundreds of cities across the country. In all these gifts he insisted on the principle of self-help: the recipient usually had to provide some money as well.

Carnegie wrote three popular books expressing his philosophy of individualism and stewardship of wealth: *Triumphant Democracy* (1886), *The Gospel of Wealth* (1900), and *The Empire of Business* (1902). All of these works extolled the business system, individualism, private enterprise, and the idea that wealth was not to be used solely for individual benefit but devoted to community betterment. Typical of his opinions were those expressed in his article "Wealth," published in the *North American Review* in 1889:

> The price which society pays for the law of competition . . . is also great; but the advantages of this law are also greater still, for it is to this law that we owe our wonderful material development, which brings improved conditions in its train.
> . . . While the law may be sometimes hard for the individual, it is best for the race, because it insures the survival of the fittest in every department.

Accumulation of wealth by the few can lead to a "reign of harmony" and "reconciliation of the rich and the poor" as long as the wealthy use their riches "as a matter of duty" in the ways "best calculated to produce the most beneficial results for the community":

> The laws of accumulation will be left free; the laws of distribution free. Individualism will continue, but the millionaire will be but a trustee for the poor; intrusted for a season with a great part of the increased wealth of the community, but administering it for the community far better than it could or would have done for itself.

Andrew Carnegie was the living embodiment of a folklore of individualism, which maintained that private property was a natural element of the social order, obtained by industry and thrift and demonstrating the moral superiority of its possessors. As Russell Conwell, a famous public speaker of the time, put it in his inspirational piece "Acres of Diamonds," "Godliness is in league with riches." Or, as the Episcopal bishop William Lawrence said, "In the long run it is only to the man of morality that wealth comes." By contrast, poverty was the result of laziness, waste, or lack of ability—desirable only because it taught the need for hard work and saving. This philosophy was not merely a rationalization of wealth by the wealthy, although it was certainly that. It was also the faith of millions, including the great middle class and a large number of workers.

The Results of Individualism

Individualism also had its seamy side. The apologist for wealth had much to apologize for. In 1900, when profits of the Carnegie Steel Company were more than $20 million for the year (most of it going to Andrew Carnegie himself), the average *annual* wage for steel workers was about $600. The justice of this division of society's income was not self-evident, and it threatened the polarization of social classes that Marx had predicted. Yet the more extreme adherents of the philosophy of laissez-faire went merrily on their way, apparently unaware of the potentially explosive situation they were creating.

At one time, when the New York Central Railroad canceled a fast extra-fare train between New York and Chicago, a public outcry was raised. Interviewed by a newspaper reporter, William Vanderbilt, the company's president and majority stockholder, exploded, "The public be damned. I am working for my stockholders. If the public want the train why don't they pay for it?" The statement raised a storm of protest; Vanderbilt decided it was time to diversify his interests and sold $30 million of his Central stock.

It was a great age for the speculator, the promoter, and the freebooter. In 1869 Jay Gould and Jim Fisk, financial speculators who had learned their trade through apparently illegal watering of Erie Railroad stock, attempted to corner the free gold supply in the New York money market. Tying up the federal government's supply in the New York subtreasury by bringing President Grant's brother-in-law into the plot, they drove the price of gold to great heights. Their Washington connections brought advance warning of government action to break the corner, and they sold out in time to make large profits. When a financial panic ensued, they even allowed their own brokers to be bankrupted. This Black Friday of September 24, 1869, was only the most spectacular of the speculative games that unsettled the economy from time to time.

The builders of monopoly were also at work. The new industrial economy was particularly vulnerable to competitive price wars. In the railroad industry, for instance, capital costs were high, and rate cutting could bring returns down to well below total costs while still covering operating expenses. Rate wars could bankrupt the weaker lines, but, since railroad property could be used only for operating trains, defeated companies would merely reorganize on a stronger financial basis and return to the business wars better able to survive than the lines that had won out the first time. It is little wonder that railroad companies merged, arranged agreements on rates and division of traffic, bought stock interests in one another, and formed "communities of interest."

Similar factors were at work in other industries as well: steel, agricultural equipment, sugar refining, oil refining and distribution, and public utilities. Giant trusts were formed to bring stability into industries made chaotic by the very competition that the theorists had claimed was the basis of economic order. In combining, financiers sometimes lost sight of economic benefits to company, stockholders, or public when large fees for legal and financial services beckoned. When J. P. Morgan began building large steel companies out of small ones in the 1890s, he discovered that issuing securities in amounts larger than the real value of the merged properties could bring high rewards. Capitalizing "good will" and potential monopoly profits could put money into the hands of bankers and lawyers. When Andrew Carnegie threatened to wreck the scheme by sharp competition, Morgan was forced to buy him out at Carnegie's price. The United States Steel Corporation was born, with stocks and bonds sold to the public and distributed to the promoters at prices equal to about twice the real value of the properties. The company's monopoly position enabled it ultimately to carry through, but the public paid through high prices for steel. Shortly after the Carnegie-Morgan deal was closed, the two men met on an ocean voyage. Carnegie is reported to have said, "I made one mistake, Pierpont, when I sold out to you. I should have asked you $100 million more than I did." To which Morgan replied, "I should have paid it."

This kind of free-wheeling individualism engendered an inevitable reaction. In 1877 the United States came close to revolution as a result of depression and industrial discontent. Layoffs and wage reductions on the railroads triggered local strikes that spread to other lines all over the country. Violence and fighting broke out, and much railroad property was destroyed. Barely a decade later, the Haymarket Square riot erupted in Chicago. A strike at the great McCormick Reaper Works, in which the eight-hour day and union membership were major issues, was followed by a general strike throughout the city. Over fifty thousand workers left their jobs. Agitation by anarchists, who wanted to end capitalism and all government by destructive revolution, was especially strong, and after a riot in front of the McCormick Works in which a number of workers were injured, the tiny anarchist newspaper called for "revenge" for the "massacre." A meeting called the next evening at Haymarket Square attracted a large, peaceful crowd, which had largely dispersed when police moved in to break it up. A bomb was thrown. Seven policemen were killed, and sixty-eight more were wounded, many by crossfire from their fellows. Eight anarchist leaders were arrested and tried for murder as accessories before the fact. Found guilty in a supercharged atmosphere of fear and hate, four were executed, one committed suicide in jail, and three were given long prison terms. No one ever found out who threw the bomb.

Again in the 1890s economic conflict bred violence. The hard times of that decade were called the "great depression"—until the 1930s. Unemployment was high, and basic industries such as steel, railroads, and agricultural equipment were hard hit. Fighting broke out in the summer of 1892 at Andrew Carnegie's Homestead steel plant near Pittsburgh. Wage cuts, refusal of the company to recognize a union or to bargain with the men, and importation of several hundred strikebreakers led to a pitched battle between workers and management forces. Twenty men were killed and perhaps fifty wounded. Henry Frick, manager of the plant, later was shot and stabbed in his office by an agitator. He survived. The National Guard finally restored order, but the strike was broken.

Near Chicago, where George Pullman had paternalistically established a "model town" next to his railroad-car factory, hard times resulted in layoffs and evictions, and the workers walked out. A sympathy boycott of

Pullman cars by the American Railway Union, led by Eugene Debs, tied up the nation's transportation system, and serious fighting occurred in Chicago. An injunction against the strike was obtained by the attorney general of the United States, himself a former railroad lawyer, and President Cleveland called out national troops in spite of protests from Governor Altgeld that they were not needed. In the face of this power the strike failed and Debs was jailed, to emerge a fully convinced socialist.

The conservative leaders of business, however, seemed to learn nothing and to forget nothing. When a strike in the anthracite coal mines in 1902 threatened to leave big-city consumers freezing through a long winter, George F. Baer, head of the employers' association that refused the union's offer to submit the dispute to arbitration, wrote to a complaining stockholder:

> Dear Mr. Clark: I have your letter of the 16th. I do not know who you are. I see that you are a religious man; but you are evidently biased in favor of the right of the workingman to control a business in which he has no other interest than to secure fair wages. I beg of you not to be discouraged. The rights and interests of the laboring man will be protected and cared for—not by agitators—but by the Christian gentlemen to whom God has given control of the property rights of the country. Pray earnestly that the right may triumph, always remembering that the Lord God omnipotent still reigns and that this reign is one of law and order, not violence and crime.

This bald statement of the divine right of capital so aroused public opinion that the federal government finally interposed itself between the two fighting parties of capital and labor. President Theodore Roosevelt threatened to seize the mines unless management agreed to arbitrate the dispute. For the first time, intervention by the federal government was on the side of labor rather than capital.

The Limitations of Individualism

The philosophy, law, and folklore of rugged individualism was on a collision course with labor. Its refusal to deal with problems of depression and unemployment, monopoly and concentrated economic power, and income distribution and economic justice was bringing criticism and attack. Perhaps sound in theory, it did not deal with the great issues that Marxism had raised about capitalism or with the social problems that were encountered along the path of economic development. When lack of solutions to these problems resulted in upheavals and violence, public opinion began to turn the other way. Reiteration of old theories and slogans was not enough. Economics, social theory, and public policy would have to come to terms with reality, and particularly with the reality of economic conflict.

SEVEN

NEOCLASSICAL ECONOMICS

Léon Walras (1837–1910) developed a mathematical theory of general equilibrium that was a major contribution to today's economics.

Economists, for the most part, did not accept the extreme position of the philosophy of individualism. They were concerned with social problems, and the influence of Benthamite utilitarianism made them willing to support government intervention in economic affairs if clear social benefits could be demonstrated. Nevertheless, most economists remained within the framework of the individualist philosophy, accepting government action only in limited amounts for limited goals. The emphasis on laissez-faire remained, and economic theory reflected that point of view.

It reflected something else, too: the Marxist critique of capitalism. In part consciously and in part unconsciously, the economists of 1870 to 1900 developed new theoretical formulations that served to refute the Marxist propositions about capitalism.

Marginal Utility and Individual Welfare

In the early 1870s three economists, unaware of each other's ideas, developed a new theory of value to replace the old labor theory. An Englishman, a Frenchman, and an Austrian each wrote in a different language, yet their theories were remarkably similar—another example of that often-observed phenomenon in the development of science, the independent and simultaneous discovery of a new principle. Within ten years the new ideas had swept triumphantly through the economics profession and were hailed as a great breakthrough by all but a few diehards who clung obstinately to the old classical system. To compound the coincidence, the discovery came only a few years after Marx had published his attack on capitalism, using the labor theory of value as a base for his exploitation theory.

Later, it turned out that the new ideas were not so new after all. The basic principles had been stated by an Italian mathematician a century and a half before, and during the preceding fifty years had been published by a German engineer, a French public-utilities expert, and several rather obscure English economists. Even Aristotle had used the idea in his treatise on ethics, and related concepts had been discussed by Catholic theologians in the sixteenth and seventeenth centuries. All of these writings had been ignored until Marx attacked the private-enterprise system. When that happened the labor theory of value had to go, and economists had to give serious attention to problems of income distribution and business cycles. A new approach to economics was born.

The new principle was a simple one: the value of a product or service is due not to the labor embodied in it but to the usefulness of the last unit purchased. That, in essence, was the famous *principle of marginal utility.*

Karl Menger (1840–1921), the Austrian codiscoverer, best stated the basic principle. He pointed out that the rational consumer, faced with a large number of alternatives on which to spend income, will seek to maximize satisfaction. This will be achieved when the consumer has allocated spending so that the last (or marginal) amount spent on one commodity gives no more and no less satisfaction—or welfare, or utility—than the last amount spent on anything else. If it is possible to shift spending from one commodity to another and thereby raise the total satisfaction obtained, the rational consumer will do so, until utility "at the margin" is equalized. In this fashion the demand for any one commodity by any one consumer is determined. Menger pictured the consumer as a person who continually weighed the relative advantages of this or that course of action and always chose the one that gave the greatest increment in satisfaction.

William Stanley Jevons (1835–1882), the English codiscoverer, emphasized another aspect of the principle by showing that utility at the margin diminishes: The more one has of a commodity, the less satisfaction one gets from consuming another unit and the less one is willing to pay for it. This means that plentiful commodities will be cheap, because an additional unit is not worth much to the buyer, even though the commodity itself may be essential to sustain life—such as water or bread. Scarce commodities, on the other hand, will be expensive, because no one has much of them and one more unit will bring a great deal of satisfaction to the buyer—such as diamonds or mink coats.

Léon Walras (1837–1910), the Frenchman who published the same principle in the early 1870s, had a still different emphasis. He explained how the entire economic system, including production of capital equipment and raw materials, was keyed to the consumer's spending decisions. The economy was a seamless web of intricate relationships between prices and quantities purchased in which any change in the consumer's allocation of expenditures was felt throughout the entire system in tiny adjustments of production and prices. Especially in a competitive economy, the whole system automatically adjusted to match production to demand.

Thus, if consumers' preferences were to shift, so that people bought more beef and less lamb, the price of beef would rise and the price of lamb would fall. The rise in the price of beef would increase profits in beef production, stimulating increased output to match the rising demand for beef. Conversely, the lower price for lamb would bring reduced profits there, and output of lamb would fall. The resources released from raising sheep would shift to raising cattle.

The adjustment would not stop there. The increased supplies of beef coming onto the market would start to bring its price down again, and profits to producers would decrease. Meanwhile, the reduced supplies of lamb would bring its price up toward its former level, and profits would start recovering. Ultimately a new market equilibrium would be reached in which prices of beef and lamb generated equal profits at the margin for the producers of meat, while consumers were equating satisfactions at the margin from consuming beef and lamb.

Now generalize this two-commodity example to a multicommodity economy. One arrives at a general equilibrium involving all buyers and sellers, all consumers and producers, and all inputs and outputs. Walras developed this vision as a complex mathematical model in which he was able to specify the exact conditions under which it might be achieved: everyone acting on the basis of individual self-interest; perfectly competitive markets; and complete flexibility in shifting resources from one use to another.

These assumptions gave the theory a highly abstract and metaphysical air. Economic theory tended to focus increasingly on an imaginary exchange economy that was seen as a model of the basic forces operating in the real world, abstracting from the many real-world events that obscured the operation of those forces.

Nevertheless, three basic ideas were established as key elements of neoclassical economics. One was the equimarginal principle: consumers allocate their expenditures to equalize benefits per unit of expenditure at the margin, and producers use their resources to equalize profits per unit of capital at the margin. The second was the principle of diminishing marginal utility: satisfactions diminish at the margin as consumption of a good rises. This paralleled the older classical idea of diminishing returns in production: increases in output diminish in amount as a variable factor of production is added to a fixed factor, as, for example, adding labor to a given acreage of land. Finally, these ideas led to the concept of a general equilibrium in which production matched the preferences of consumers, and the highest possible level of consumer benefits would be achieved, given the existing resources and technology.

The new economics of marginal utility and general equilibrium found the source of economic values on the demand side of the market, in the preferences of consumers. The old labor theory of value had focused on the supply side of the market and had explained value and price in terms of costs of production, which were reduced ultimately to costs measured in labor time. It was an English economist, Alfred Marshall (1842–1924), who reconciled these two approaches. He insisted that market price—that is, economic value—was determined by both supply and demand, which interact with each other in much the same way as Adam Smith described the operation of competitive markets. Marshall demonstrated that in the long run prices in competitive markets would tend toward the lowest possible costs of production at which the amounts desired by consumers would be provided. But although Marshall brought costs of production back into the picture, he and most other economists accepted the broader approach of Menger and Walras: the basic pattern of production was determined by the myriad independent decisions of millions of individual consumers.

One of the most important conclusions drawn from this line of thinking was that a system of free markets tended to maximize individual benefits. Since it was assumed that consumers would try to maximize their satisfactions, and since production was patterned after consumer wants, it followed that the result would be benefit maximizing. The analysis also showed that costs of production were pushed to the lowest possible level by the forces of competition. The whole economy, in a sense, was a pleasure-maximizing machine in which the difference between consumer benefits and production costs was increased to the highest level possible—if the economy was allowed to operate without constraints.

These ideas shifted the whole focus of economics away from the great issue of social classes and their economic interests, which had been emphasized by Ricardo and Marx, and centered economic theory upon the individual. The principles of income distribution on which Ricardo had based his analysis of the progress of industrialism and on which Marx had rested his theory of the breakdown of capitalism were replaced by the individual consumer as the major determinant of economic activity and economic progress. The whole economic system was conceived as revolving around individual consumers and their needs.

Economics was transformed into a discipline consistent with the social philosophy developed by Herbert Spencer and William Graham Sumner. That philosophy, of course, reflected the freewheeling individualism that was remaking the face of the world. The economists and their highly abstract theories were part of the same social and intellectual development that brought forth the legal theories of Stephen Field and the folklore of the self-made individual.

Economic Justice: Income Distribution

This is not to say that the economists who used marginal analysis ignored the problem of income distribution. Taking up the Marxist challenge, these new theologians of industrial society developed a theory proving that all factors of production—whether labor, land, or capital—earned a return exactly equal to their contribution to the value of output. No one could exploit anyone else, there was no unearned surplus to be appropriated by the owners of capital, and full justice must prevail in the distribution of income. The worker received what he earned, no more and no less.

The new analysis of income distribution was called the *theory of marginal productivity*. It originated with an American, John Bates Clark, in his *Distribution of Wealth: A Theory of Wages, Interest and Profit* (1899). Like the theory of marginal utility, it was based on the last, or marginal, unit, and its fundamental conclusion was very simple: workers would be paid a wage equal to the value of the last unit of output they produced. Consider, for example, a plant that manufactures only one product. This plant will pay wages equal to those established in the competitive labor market. The manager will add to the work force as long as the added output per worker can be sold for more than the wage paid—that is, as long as profits rise because additional revenues exceed additional costs. The manager will stop hiring workers when increased output will not bring in enough additional revenue to cover the wage that must be paid. The plant's demand for labor is determined, therefore, by the level at which wages equal the value of a worker's output at the margin. If an employer tried to pay a wage less than this value, the worker could, of course, get a job elsewhere with a competitive firm. It was a wonderful theory. The worker would get no more and no less than his or her contribution to society. If the worker's productivity was high, the wage would be high; if the worker was lazy or incompetent, earnings would be low.

The same theory was applied to the boss, to profits earned on capital, and to the rent from land. Each of these elements in the production process was subject to the same economic law. No one could be exploited, because everyone got what he or she deserved. The economists even revived a theorem devised by a Swiss mathematician more than a hundred years before, which proved that there could be no surplus value unaccounted for by these payments to the various factors of production. Marxism was dead.

The validity of the theory of marginal productivity depended on the existence of that theoretical nirvana, perfect competition. It also required that all factors of production be fully and freely substitutable for one another, and that there be no change in costs of production per unit of output as the level of production rose or fell. But these highly restrictive assumptions did not bother many economists, who by this time were lost in the theoretical glories of a perfectly competitive economy.*

Prosperity and Depression: Business Cycles

Wherever large-scale industrialization appeared, the economic system was subjected to alternating periods of prosperity and depression, often marked by a "crisis" in finance and business confidence. These breakdowns occurred with varying degrees of severity but with an apparent regularity that

---

*It should be noted, however, that some economists never accepted the theory of marginal productivity. This dissident group included Alfred Marshall, the dominant figure in English economics from 1890 to the post–World War I period.

required explanation. During the nineteenth century, financial crises followed by depressed economic conditions occurred in England in 1815, 1825, 1836, 1847, 1857, 1866, 1873, 1882, 1890, and 1900. In the United States crises were somewhat less frequent, perhaps because of the presence of an extensive land frontier, but they were still numerous, occurring in 1819, 1837, 1854, 1857, 1873, 1883, and 1893. Furthermore, the world economy experienced three "great depressions" during the "hungry forties," the 1870s, and the 1890s.

At first the problem was ignored. Both the classical economists of the first half of the century and the neoclassical group that appeared after 1870 accepted the general propositions of Say's Law of Markets, according to which there should be no periodic economic breakdowns and the economy should continue to operate at uninterrupted high levels of output and employment. Those few who did investigate business cycles looked for causes outside the system of production and distribution, for Say's Law taught that demand was created by production and that, in the aggregate, the two could never get out of phase with one another.

Beginning in the 1860s British and French statisticians, rather than economists, first verified the periodic and cyclical nature of economic fluctuations. They identified several cycles of about ten years' duration and speculated on possible causes. Stanley Jevons in England was one of the few economists who gave much attention to the problem, and he attributed the causes of "great irregular fluctuations" to variations in agriculture, excessive investment or speculation, wars and political disturbances, or "other fortuitous occurrences which we cannot calculate upon, or allow for." Later Jevons developed a theory even more favorable to the adherents of Say's Law and the existing scheme of things. After finding a statistical correlation between cycles of sunspots and business fluctuations, he wrote in 1884:

> It seems probable that commercial crises are connected with a periodic variation of weather affecting all parts of the earth, and probably arising from increased waves of heat received from the sun at average intervals of ten years and a fraction.

But business cycles were creating problems for government, too, and hardheaded administrators responsible for policy needed facts. Government men sat down to analyze the data. In 1886 Carroll Wright, in his first annual report as United States commissioner of labor, identified business investment as the most important fluctuating element in the economy. Natural events, wars, and speculation were not the cause of crises: the culprit was overinvestment in capital equipment. Bad times came when opportunities for investment were inadequate. This emphasis on the process of investment was reiterated a few years later by Sir Hubert Llewellyn Smith, Wright's English counterpart as commissioner of labour in the Board of Trade, who reported to Parliament in 1895 that economic instability was concentrated in a few industries, such as machinery and other metals-producing industries, shipbuilding, construction, and mining, all of which were subject to "violent oscillation" in investment. Other sectors of the economy were relatively stable, and fluctuations there reflected the larger changes taking place in unstable industries.

These investigations by government agencies did not have much effect on economists, however, who continued to pursue the clues given them by Say's Law. In its best and most complete formulation that law utilized the rate of interest as the automatic stabilizer of the economy, the factor that ensured that savings would be directed into investment and prevent any break in the even flow of spending. But since breaks were obviously occurring, and since the rate of interest was part of the monetary system, it was logical to look to that sector of the economy for the causes of difficulty: There could be problems in the monetary system even though production and distribution were sound.

By the last decade of the nineteenth century, many economists began to agree that business cycles were caused by unwarranted expansion of the money supply. Easy credit would bring interest rates down and thereby stimulate excessive investment and speculation. Once the economy had overexpanded a crisis was inevitable, since the normal operation of the system could not support the unnecessary production capacity and credit created during the wave of optimism. After a crisis began, the economy would simply have to suffer until the high prices and unwise expansion were brought back to normal.

The preventive for this unfortunate sequence of events was to manage the monetary system properly. Limiting the expansion of credit to the legitimate needs of business through effective action by the central bank could prevent the process from starting or could stop it while the ensuing readjustment period might still be short and shallow. Stability in the monetary and credit system could bring stability to the economy as a whole.

This theory was spelled out by the Englishman Walter Bagehot as early as 1873 in *Lombard Street*, a classic work on the money markets. It was taught at Harvard around the turn of the century by Oliver M. W. Sprague, one of whose students was the young Franklin D. Roosevelt (who learned the lesson well but was later critical enough to reject it as the basis of policy). It was the theoretical basis for the establishment of the Federal Reserve System in this country in 1914. President Herbert Hoover had this theory in mind when he said, shortly after the 1929 stock market crash, "The fundamental business of the country—that is, production and distribution— is sound." He didn't mention the monetary and credit system, which obviously was not sound and which he tried to strengthen by loans to banks and railroads (whose bonds were owned heavily by the large banks) and by trying to cut federal expenditures. But Hoover's policies pointed up the bias inherent in Say's Law of Markets and in the theory of business cycles it spawned. Production and distribution were *not* sound in 1929, although the theory denied that causes and remedies could be found and applied in those areas.

The Nature and Significance of Economic Science

Neoclassical economics extended Adam Smith's original formulation of how a private enterprise economy functions. Start with the behavioral assumption that individuals seek to maximize their benefits. One line of deductive reasoning concludes that if all individuals do that, the benefits to society as a whole will be maximized (Menger). A second line of reasoning analyzed demand, supply, and price in individual markets, showing how production responds to consumer demand. In the process, producers are shown to produce goods at the lowest possible cost consistent with a continuing supply at levels desired by consumers (Jevons and Marshall). A third line showed how all portions of the market system were tied together in a seamless web, creating a benefit-maximizing and cost-minimizing general equilibrium (Walras). Marginal productivity theory answered socialist critics by arguing that there was no exploitation of labor, that each person received a reward equal to the value of his or her contribution to total output. And economic stability could be assured by proper management of the monetary system.

The theory was also extended by theories of imperfect competition and monopoly in the writing of Joan Robinson (English, 1903–1983), Edward H. Chamberlain (American, 1899–1967), Heinrich von Stackleberg (German, 1905–1946) and others, who dropped the assumption of perfect competition. The results of this work showed that when the number of firms in an industry is not large enough for perfect competition to exist, the resultant market price is higher and output is less than in perfectly competitive markets, even when firms make only normal profits. In industries dominated by a few large firms (oligopoly, meaning few sellers), practices of price fixing and market sharing tended to replace competition or rivalry, resulting not only in high prices and limited output, but also high profits and a tendency to hamper innovation and development of new technologies. These findings used the same techniques and concepts developed by the earlier neoclassical theorists of perfect competition and brought a healthy dose of reality into the discipline.

The neoclassical economists began using mathematics and mathematical logic as important tools of theoretic analysis. Rigorous formal argument that could be stated in algebraic equations or illustrated by geometric diagrams was leading to a new, more accurate mode of professional discourse.

Mathematics had not been a significant analytical tool for the classical economists, with two exceptions. Antoine Augustin Cournot (1801–1877), a Frenchman trained in mathematics and employed as a university administrator, wrote *Researches Into the Mathematical Theory of Wealth* (1838), in which economic relationships were presented as algebraic equations. For example, the proposition that more of a commodity will be sold at a lower price than at a higher price becomes $D = F(p)$, that is, demand is a function of price, in the language of mathematics. F can then be analyzed as an algebraic equation that specifies the factors that determine the shape and slope of the demand curve. An English engineer who dabbled in economics, H. C. Fleeming Jenkin (1833–1885), then developed Cournot's concept of the demand function, and the related concept of the supply function (S = F (p), with a different F) into a geometric diagram of the determination of price in competitive markets that is still in use today. His paper, "The Graphic Representation of the Laws of Supply and Demand" (1870), written during a controversy over the characteristics of prices in competitive markets, showed that an equilibrium price was one at which supply and demand were equal. Sound familiar?

Not much more was done with mathematics as an analytic tool until the rise of neoclassical economics. Although William Stanley Jevons did not use mathematics in his *Theory of Political Economy* (1871), he was convinced of its importance. He wrote in a letter, "I wish especially to become a good mathematician, without which nothing . . . can be thoroughly done." Jevon's contemporary, Leon Walrus, took a more effective mathematical approach in his *Elements of Pure Economics* (1874), which is full of complex geometric diagrams and systems of algebraic equations. Although Carl Menger's *Principles of Economics* (1871) had only a few arithmetic tables to illustrate diminishing marginal utility, Alfred Marshall's *Principles of Economics* (1890) provided rigorous proofs of economic propositions in footnotes using geometric diagrams and in an algebraic mathematical appendix. Two Austrian economists, Rudolf Auspitz and Richard Lieben, published *Researches on the Theory of Price* (1889), which analyzed the determination of market prices in geometric diagrams, followed by mathematical appendices that repeated the argument using the differential calculus. Vilfredo Pareto, who followed Walras in the economics chair at the University of Lausanne in 1893, developed his predecessor's theory of general equilibrium in a more rigorous mathematical model in his *Manual of Political Economy* (Italian edition, 1906; expanded French edition, 1909). Several economists after the Second World War developed a more sophisticated general equilibrium model based on Pareto but using mathematical concepts and techniques not available in his day.

Meanwhile, in England, Frances Y. Edgeworth's *Mathematical Psychics* (1881) argued that the use of mathematics can eliminate "loose indefinite relations" in theory, while developing an "economical calculus" of exact meanings. Edgeworth went on to develop algebraic formulations and geometric diagrams to show how demand curves were generated from individual preferences, and how freely negotiated contracts benefited both parties to the agreement.

In the United States, Irving Fisher's *Mathematical Investigations in the Theory of Value and Prices* (1892) was a masterly exposition of general equilibrium theory, stated in mathematical form. It emphasized the interrelatedness of economic phenomena: a change in one variable results in changes in all other variables until a new equilibrium is established. Thus, a change in the price of one commodity ripples through the entire system of prices as consumers readjust the amounts they buy, and all other prices in the system change, even if only slightly.

These beginnings, and others like them around the turn of the century, were given greater impetus by the publication of *Principia Mathematica* (3 volumes, 1910–1913) by two English philosopher-mathematicians, Alfred North Whitehead (1861–1947) and Bertrand Russell (1872–1970). The title of the book invited comparison with Isaac Newton's great 1687 treatise on *Philosophiae Naturalis Principia Mathematica* (Mathematical Principles of Natural Philosophy). Whitehead and Russell knew they had something big. Both men were working on problems in logic when they decided to work together on the logic of arithmetic. They began by defining a few basic concepts in meaningful and unambiguous terms, then moving by logical steps to more complex concepts. They used this purely deductive method to derive and explain all the basic propositions of arithmetic—in three volumes of intricate logic and mathematical equations. It was not a book that ordinary people could fully grasp, but we can understand its larger implications.

Whitehead and Russell derived propositions and conclusions step by step from initial assumptions through purely logical analysis—from initial cause to final effect by pure logic. This deductive method had been widely used before, but there had always been problems created by the different meanings implied by words. Whitehead and Russell solved this problem by using mathematical symbols ($+$, $-$, $\div$, $\times$, $=$) as verbs and other mathematical symbols (1, 2, 3, or a, b, c) as nouns. Sentences looked like $1 + 1 = 2$ or $a^2 + b^2 = c^2$. Highly complex statements using mathematical logic could derive rigorously correct conclusions from initial assumptions in this type of formal system. It seemed as if the ancient Aristotelian ideal of perfect deduction from initial premises was at last possible. By implication, the deductive method could be applied to any phenomenon, not just arithmetic. This was the road to truth. It was as if God the Creator was a great mathematician who had created a world in which everything had an inner formal logic, and Whitehead and Russell had discovered the Tree of Knowledge.

But alas, it was not to be. In 1931 Kurt Gödel, a German mathematician who later joined the Institute for Advanced Study at Princeton, detected a serious flaw in the mathematical logic of formal systems, known as Gödel's Undecidability Theorem. Briefly, this theorem states that a long chain of deductive logic will contain one or more propositions that cannot be proven to be true or to be false. Pure logic was not enough. Even if the undecidable proposition were known to be true, it could not be proven within the system of logic itself. Acceptance of such propositions must come from outside the system, either through casual empiricism (real-world examples), faith, or assumption. If God the Creator was a mathematician, Gödel showed that God had left room for both doubt and faith.

There is a further limitation on the use of formal systems of logic in economics. When one argues, for instance, "If A, then B" about real-world relationships, the result must be expressed as a probability. Economic data are only samples of all the possible instances. We never have all cases of A or B. Since we have only a sample, we know that the probability of "If A, then B" is something less than 100 percent. So when we have a long series of logical statements, such as "If A, then B; if B, then C; . . . if Y, then Z" the probability of "If A, then Z" becomes very small. Consider this: if there is a high probability that each of the "if . . . then" statements is correct (say, 90 percent), by the time one reaches the twelfth statement, the probability that "If A, then M" is correct is less than 30 percent. If we go all the way to "If A, then Z," that statement will be correct only about 5 percent of the time, given the 90 percent probability of each statement. The formal logic may be correct, but when it is applied to the real world, the results may be quite unreliable.

Despite Gödel's undecidability theorem and the difficulties of applying systems of formal mathematical logic to real-world economic problems, the use of formal systems of logic in economic theory spread rapidly during the 1920s and 1930s. This development in high theory was strongly influenced by a 1932 volume, *An Essay on the Nature and Significance of Economic Science*, by Lionel Robbins (1898–1984), an English economist who spent most of his academic career at the London School of Economics. Robbins argued that there was a body of economic knowledge free from value judgments. This scientific economics was derived by logical deduction from obviously correct basic assumptions. The fundamental problem of economics was the obvious "fact" of scarcity: people had unlimited wants, but the means of satisfying those wants were limited in supply. This led to Robbin's definition of economics as the "science that studies the relationship between ends and means that have alternative uses," a statement that even today is found in one form or another in the first chapter of almost every introductory economics textbook in the English-speaking world. Robbins argued that general propositions could be developed only by logical deduction from correct premises. Empirical studies were of very limited value, because the conclusions were valid only for the time and place from which the data were drawn. On the other hand, general propositions derived by logical analysis from correct assumptions could be applied to any situation, in any time and place.

Robbins sought to purge economics of value judgments. For example, arguments that a more egalitarian distribution of income was somehow "better" than the existing one were unscientific. How could one prove that taking a dollar from a rich man and giving it to a poor widow would reduce the rich man's satisfactions by less than it would add to the widow's? Robbins wanted careful logic, not value judgments or ethical and moral standards.

The method of logical deduction from correct assumptions championed by Robbins derived much of its rigor from its simple theoretical structure. The boundaries of economic activity were clearly defined in the institutional structure of a system of self-adjusting markets. There were no complications derived from complex social institutions such as family, religion, or state, which were rarely mentioned by the neoclassical economists. The driving force was also simple: the acquisitive nature of human beings, which was assumed to be a universal constraint. This gave the results of theoretical analysis an aura of universal validity and applicability. Like Newtonian physics, it was a science of finite space in which inexorable natural forces worked out a stable equilibrium.

Critics, however, were quick to point out faults. The new methodology was criticized as being essentially static, like Newtonian physics, and not well adapted to analysis of an economy in constant flux and disequilibrium. It assumed the existence of a universal human nature—acquisitive and economic—that was attacked as a distortion. There was no room for changes in the institutional structure of the economy in a method that assumed *ceteris paribus*, that is, "everything else remains the same." And there was no way to determine how much of a change would occur from one position of equilibrium to another. In brief, critics argued that the analytical concepts were limited, unrealistic, and not quantified.

This criticism led to the final element in the methodology of neoclassical economics: empirical studies to verify or disprove the results of theoretic analysis. Theory would provide a hypothesis, which would then be tested by empirical studies. For example, the conclusion that a higher price for automobiles would result in reduced purchases of gasoline could be verified or disproved by statistical studies relating automobile prices with demand for gasoline. This required that theoretical concepts would have to be at least potentially testable.

One of the fundamental problems of empirical research is how to make meaningful statements about the world when information is imperfect and is available from only part of the reality under investigation. Data may also be contaminated by observational error. Any phenomenon may have multiple causes that need to be disentangled. Yet the scholar is expected to extract from imperfect data and complex situations reasonable explanations that apply not only to the specific case, but also to the general class of phenomena under study. Advances in statistical methods enabled economists to attack these problems, and a new subfield in economics was born: *Econometrics*, in which statistical methods are applied to analysis of economic data.

The method was complete. Theoretical analysis, refined by mathematical logic, would provide testable propositions. Statistical studies would then verify or correct the hypotheses, leading to more highly refined propositions that were a closer approximation to reality. In this way economic science could move toward greater understanding of the world, just as the physical sciences do. This method continues today to dominate the economics profession.

The Ideology of Capitalism

In spite of its scientific method, neoclassical economics had strong ideological implications. The theoretical model assumed the existence of a structure of economic institutions based on individuals functioning in an environment of self-adjusting markets. It pictured a private-enterprise economy that produced what consumers wanted and, therefore, maximized welfare, distributed products justly, and normally operated at full-employment levels. Economic growth through saving and capital accumulation was the source of progress. The model was essentially the same as Adam Smith's, modernized to eliminate the labor theory of value and to bring it into conformity with the philosophy of individualism and newer ideas about scientific method.

Unlike the social Darwinism of Spencer, Sumner, Field, and Carnegie, however, neoclassical economics was not a rigorous laissez-faire theory. One major exception was in the area of monetary policy, where responsibility for maintaining economic stability through proper management of the money supply was assigned to government acting through the central bank. But even in this area, policy discretion was to be limited: the criterion for monetary policy was that it limit expansion of credit to the legitimate needs of business—that is, to the needs of production and distribution. Both of those aspects of the economy were to be governed by the free play of market forces unhampered by government intervention. In the last analysis, the free market largely indicated what little monetary intervention was allowed.

Other types of intervention were approved by most neoclassical economists. One was the effort to preserve competition by what, in this country, came to be called "antitrust" laws. Since their theories were based on the assumption of perfect competition in all markets, these economists were at least consistent when they argued for regulation of "natural" monopolies and for laws to prevent restraint of trade. Their commitment to competition and their support of antimonopoly legislation were not complete, however. Some economists argued that private monopolies, unsustained by government restrictions on competition, would inevitably fall from their positions of power because of efforts of other business firms to get a share of the excessive profits. Others wanted to move slowly for fear that antitrust action might reduce the advantages to be obtained from mass production. In spite of these relatively mild dissents, however, a fairly consistent emphasis on the advantages of competition was developed and has been sustained to this day.

Still other concessions to government intervention were made. For example, in a paper given in 1886 before the Economic Section of the British Association for the Advancement of Science, Henry Sidgwick, a prominent English economist, listed a number of "economic exceptions to laissez faire." They included actions based on moral considerations such as sanitary regulations, control of narcotics and intoxicants, and restrictions on gambling; efforts to improve the productivity of individuals by education; measures that require total public participation for effectiveness, such as public health measures and flood control; and provision of services whose benefits are general and for which the individual cannot be charged, such as lighthouses on rocky shores or certain types of scientific research. Not one of these exceptions seems especially significant to the modern mind, accustomed to almost a hundred years of growing government activity, but they do point to the fact that much of neoclassical economics represented accommodations to existing needs, and that it was not the simple paean to individualism and laissez-faire its critics sometimes made it out to be. Many neoclassical economists could look upon their discipline as a scientific and rational path to reform. Benthamite liberalism remained alive.

The new economics, however, had strong ideological implications. It was a complete answer to Marx. Where the classical economists had used the labor theory of value to justify private property, Marx had used it as the basis for his theory of exploitation. Once Marx had written his devastating attack on capitalism, it was inevitable that the ideology of the existing order jettison the labor theory of value, and it was the necessity of doing so that helps explain both the "discovery" of a "new" theory of value and its rapid sweep to acceptance.

Viewed in this light, the development of the new economics of the 1870s and later must give us pause. It suggests that ideas are not accepted because they are "right" and rejected because they are "wrong," but that they are accepted when they are useful and rejected when their usefulness ends. In this case, the labor theory of value was part of the accepted canon of economic ideas as long as it could be used as part of the ideology of capitalism. When Marx destroyed its usefulness for that purpose, the theory was discarded and replaced by the theory of marginal utility, which could support the theory of free markets and be used to belabor the Marxists.

Indeed, the new theory made refutation of Marx unnecessary, for it enabled the theory of private-enterprise capitalism to be rebuilt on a new basis. As the Austrian economist Eugen Böhm-Bawerk (1851–1914) pointed out in 1884, the entire Marxist analysis became irrelevant. This disciple of Karl Menger spent much of his career attacking Marxism in great detail, but he always felt that the best single argument was that the labor theory of value was just plain wrong. In England, Philip Wicksteed (1844–1927) came to the same conclusion at about the same time; he wrote that the entire Marxist analysis was invalid because it was based on labor instead of utility. The consensus of orthodox economists of the late nineteenth and early twentieth centuries was perhaps most succinctly stated by another Austrian, Friedrich von Wieser (1851–1926), who rejected the Marxist theory of surplus value as follows:

> This argument is not conclusive, if for no other reason than simply because it takes the ground of the labor-theory, which cannot be maintained for the developed conditions of national economy.

The ideology of capitalism had survived its first great crisis and had been reconstructed on new grounds.

EIGHT
THE HUMAN
FAMILY

*Thorstein Veblen (1857–1929)
emphasized the importance of
changing economic institutions.*

With the emergence of Marxism, the great debate over the economic system centered around the issue of socialism versus capitalism. The orthodox response based on the extremes of Darwinian individualism and the moderation of neoclassical economics served to further divide the antagonists. But the pattern of social thought is never simple. There are more than two or three possible responses in any ideological debate, and the issue of the proper organization of economic life brought forth a wide variety of ideas that opened up other dimensions of the issue. It was not just a question of socialized property and planning at one end of the scale versus private property and competitive enterprise at the other, with a variety of compromises forming a continuum between the two extremes. Other approaches, other formulations of the issue, and other solutions were offered.

One large middle ground involved the human race and its needs as a social unit. Marx had looked on the social system as being divided into antagonistic social classes, with social conflict as the source of change. Orthodox economists, on the other hand, saw society as a mass of individual units brought into an uneasy equilibrium by the forces of the market. Yet a third group of economic thinkers considered people and society as a single interrelated unit, with the individual motivated by self-interest, by feelings of brotherhood, by curiosity, by ethical values, and by social and economic status. This complex view of the nature of people and society was developed in a variety of ways by different writers who, as a group, advocated a society in which human welfare was consciously sought as the chief objective of social policy. These thinkers were the architects of the philosophy of the welfare state. Pragmatic yet visionary, critical yet hopeful, they built many of the ideas on which the mixed economies of Western Europe and North

99

America are based. Their influence on public policy far exceeded that of the socialists or the orthodox neoclassical economists.

These critics of the market economy felt that its materialism—making a profit and accumulating wealth—was antagonistic to traditional humane and community values. Ideas of brotherhood and community, of individual responsibility for others, had little place in a market economy dominated by the principle of *caveat emptor*. At the same time they pointed to the problems created for people and communities by unemployment, business cycles, financial crises, conflict between capital and labor, unsafe workplaces, child labor, and the continuing replication of poverty from one generation to the next. They called for government intervention in economic affairs to stabilize the process of production, modify the distribution of wealth, and protect people from the often destructive effects of the marketplace.

Papal Economics

Pope Leo XIII (1810–1903) tried to find, in the abstract principles of social justice, a middle ground between the warring factions of capital and labor. In a famous encyclical of 1891 he defined the social problems of the age as essentially moral rather than economic and called for their solution on the basis of justice animated by charity. It was not a solution that could be measured by benefits and costs in the marketplace, and it was by no means "practical," but that was the whole point: morality and justice are not market phenomena but stand above worldly considerations of profit and loss, wages and costs. Leo XIII called for consideration of economic issues in an entirely new dimension.

The pope, who was born Gioacchino Vincenzo Pecci, had devoted his entire life to the service of the Roman Catholic Church. He was educated as a Jesuit, became a priest in 1837, and held a variety of administrative posts in the papal government, rising rapidly to become an archbishop in 1846 and a cardinal in 1853. He was elected pope in 1878, at a time when the nationalism of the nineteenth century was causing severe problems for the relationship between church and state in every European country, and when industrialization was creating new social classes whose relationship to the church was not yet clearly defined. Leo XIII held the papacy for a quarter of a century, and it was in large part through his efforts that the Catholic Church adapted itself to the new political and economic order.

In a series of encyclicals issued between 1878 and 1901, Leo XIII sought to analyze the problems of modern society and their remedies, the nature of the state and its relationship to the individual and the church, and the fundamental economic problems of the age. One of his first encyclicals condemned socialism and upheld the right of private property, continuing a traditional position of the church. By 1891, however, Leo XIII was prepared to take a position much more critical of the existing order. Problems of church and state had largely been settled by compromise in France, Germany, Belgium, Switzerland, and Austria-Hungary, so that attention could be given to the struggles between capital and labor and between capitalist and socialist that were threatening to tear apart the fabric of the European social order. In *Rerum Novarum,* sometimes called *On the Condition of Labor,* he argued that "a remedy must be found . . . for the misery and wretchedness which press so heavily at this moment on the large majority of the very poor." He continued with an indictment of laissez-faire policies:

> Working men have been given over, isolated and defenseless, to the callousness of employers and the greed of unrestrained competition. The evil has been increased by rapacious usury . . . still practiced by avaricious and grasping men. And to this must be added the custom of working by contract, and the concentration of so many branches of trade in the hands of a few individuals, so that a small number of very rich men have been able to lay upon the masses of the poor a yoke little better than slavery itself.

This passage, hardly distinguishable from the writings of avowed socialists, was followed, however, by a condemnation of socialism and a plea for private property as a natural right of the individual.

Leo XIII viewed the proper form of society as one in which the interest of the community as a whole transcended that of the individual and in which economic relationships were motivated by goodwill and concern for the interests of others rather than by pure profit-seeking acquisitiveness. Building on Catholic social thought that went back to Thomas Aquinas in the thirteenth century and to others before him, Leo XIII saw larger community interests at stake than those of the market. He criticized the rugged individualism of the market economy and called for a return to human and community values.

By placing the interests of the community above those of the marketplace Leo XIII assigned an important function to the state: it *ought to intervene* in economic affairs whenever the welfare and preservation of society as a whole might be endangered, but always with justice and fairness. It was quite proper for the state to limit hours of work, establish minimum wages, prohibit child labor, and provide other welfare legislation wherever required for the protection of society and its members. Labor unions were also proper, as long as they did not restrict membership and pursue selfish goals. Indeed, Leo XIII argued for the organization of a Catholic labor union to ensure that the labor movement gave proper consideration to ethical values. Viewed from the twenty-first century, these papal pronouncements seem mild indeed, but at the turn of the century they were not, especially as they came from the leader of a religion that has generally supported conservatism in political and economic affairs.

The tradition of Leo XIII was continued by later popes, by the Catholic trade union movement, and by liberal theologians in the church. Pope Pius XI commemorated the fortieth anniversary of *Rerum Novarum* in 1931 with another encyclical, *Quadragesimo Anno (Reconstructing the Social Order),* which applied the same principles to problems of the depression and the rise of fascism and communism in Europe. It tried to find a middle ground between those warring factions in a humanitarian concern for human welfare. In 1961 Pope John XXIII issued *Mater et Magistra (Christianity and Social Progress)* to restate the idea that individuals and community were one and to emphasize that both individual freedoms and individual welfare had to be reconciled in a society that stressed community values and social justice. Although these papal encyclicals did not propose specific economic policies or reforms, they helped create a climate of opinion that gave high priority to equity in economic life.

Mater et Magistra, however, widened the scope of papal concerns. While suggesting a wider role for government intervention to promote social justice, it also called for reduction of global inequities between the advanced and the less developed countries. Pope Paul VI followed in 1967 with *Populorum Progression (The Progress of Peoples)*, which argued for aid to the economically backward areas of the world, greater restrictions on private property, and greater openness to a variety of economic systems. Following along these lines, Pope John Paul II issued *Laborem Exercens (On Human Work)* in 1981, the ninetieth anniversary of *Rerum Novarum,* which was a philosophical and theological reflection on the role of work in forming the person and carrying on God's work. This encyclical criticized Marxist socialism but spoke highly of participatory socialism.

Then, on the hundredth anniversary of *Rerum Novarum* in 1991, just two years after the collapse of the Soviet Union, Pope John Paul II spoke once more on economic matters. In *Centissiumus Annus (The Hundredth Year)* capitalism was highly praised as "the most efficient instrument for utilizing resources and effectively responding to needs." However, "there are many human needs which find no place on the market." While he praised the efficiency of free markets, John Paul II called for action to repair the injustices of capitalism. He left room for both supporters of the status quo and supporters of reform.

This tradition in Roman Catholic theology had important repercussions in the 1970s and 1980s. In Latin America a "liberation theology" developed in opposition to right-wing dictatorships and their supporters in big business and the economic elite. A 1971 volume, *A Theology of Liberation,* written by Gustavo Gutierrez, a Peruvian priest, was the leading statement of liberation theology: social justice for all, land redistribution, extension of social services, greater equality of income, and popular control of both government and the economy. These goals often meant active participation in politics by priests and church officials, including political coalitions with socialist and communist parties—a strategy strongly opposed by the politically conservative Pope John Paul II in the 1980s, who prohibited priests from engaging in political activity. (One Jesuit priest remarked, "Except himself.") Nevertheless, liberation theology became an important force in Latin America, and a similar movement developed in Asia.

In the United States, the Roman Catholic bishops issued a pastoral letter in 1984 that dealt with economic affairs. It called for sweeping measures to help the poor: reduction of unemployment to 3 or 4 percent, including direct government action to create jobs; major changes in the welfare system to promote work incentives; joint action by government, business, and unions to help the chronically unemployed and others on the margin of poverty; and changes in labor laws to help workers organize unions. The bishops criticized the "consumerist mentality" that prevailed in the United States, and advocated measures to discourage high levels of consumption while encouraging investment and savings. They also advocated "private and public endeavors that promote the economic rights of all persons." The basic theme was that poverty would not disappear simply with economic growth. Elimination of poverty was a strong ethical goal, and would require conscious social action.

English Philosophers of the Welfare State

In England John A. Hobson, the Fabian socialists, and Richard H. Tawney led the fight for a positive liberalism designed to cure the social ills of an industrial society. They defined government's role as one fostering those social relationships and institutions that emphasize humanistic goals. The state should remove hindrances to the good life and promote conditions that enable the individual to do and enjoy the things worth doing and enjoying.

Under the influence of these ideas England witnessed a quarter century of reform, including legislation for factory safety (1891, 1895), limited working hours for women and children (1895), the beginnings of slum clearance (1890), wider powers for labor unions (1890–1900), compensation to workers for injuries suffered on the job and child-welfare legislation (1906), old-age pensions (1908), the beginnings of town planning and redevelopment (1909), and disability and sickness insurance (1911). The major components of the modern welfare state were being brought together.

John A. Hobson (1858–1940) was one of the chief exponents of the ideas behind this social legislation. He was denied a university post because of his unorthodox views, but from his pen flowed an unending stream of books and articles that shamed his orthodox contemporaries by their insight and critical acuity. An early work, *The Physiology of Industry*, analyzed the causes of depressions and found them in inadequate consumer spending. *The Evolution of Modern Capitalism* criticized the industrial order for its monopolies, unequal income distribution, and depressions. *Imperialism* attacked the selfish expansion of the European states; its argument was later incorporated by Lenin into the communist ideology. *Incentives in the New Industrial Order* proclaimed that socialism could work because it would utilize a broad spectrum of motivations, not just those of big-business capitalism. *Work and Wealth*, however, was Hobson's most important work. In it he argued for a concept of the good life in which government would be responsible for a more equitable distribution of income and for social controls to ensure full employment and high wages and to promote health, education, and recreation. Hobson believed that government action could end poverty, unemployment, and insecurity, and could establish a society in which human happiness prevailed. Utopian, yes—but this was the vision that lay behind English social legislation. Hobson did not originate it, but he was its best spokesman.

Hobson's ideals were similar to those of the Fabian Society, organized in 1883 by a group of English intellectuals whose ambitious goal was "reorganizing society in accordance with the highest moral possibilities" through a democratic socialist regime designed to promote "the greatest happiness of the greatest number." It was a small but very influential group; among the early members were the dramatist George Bernard Shaw, Sidney Webb, Graham Wallas, and Annie Besant. They were joined later by the novelist H. G. Wells and Beatrice Webb. The *Fabian Essays*, published in 1889 under Shaw's editorial leadership, advocated a gradual extension of state intervention in economic affairs to improve working conditions, replace monopoly with government ownership, and promote a more egalitarian distribution of income.

The society was named after the Roman general Fabius Maximus, "the delayer," who fought Hannibal, the Carthaginian commander, with what would now be called guerrilla tactics. The name signified the society's political philosophy and plan of action. In opposition to the Marxists, the Fabians viewed the state not as an instrument of class warfare that had to be destroyed, but as a means of social control that should be captured and used to promote social welfare. To this end they advocated formation of a labor party with a socialist program and were among the groups that did successfully form such a party in 1906. They also sought to use local governments, which had been greatly strengthened by legislation of the late 1880s and early 1890s, to achieve their goals. The tactics of the Fabians involved political action within the framework of democratic, parliamentary government. They worked to institute their reforms by convincing the general public of the correctness of their views and by publicizing their stand in a series of research reports and popular pamphlets.

Beatrice Webb (1858–1943) and her husband Sidney Webb (1859–1943) provided much of the intellectual leadership of the Fabians. Their *History of Trade Unionism* (1894, with four extended and revised later editions) showed how labor unions survived and grew despite past defeats and how they could become an important force for improving the condition of working people. The latter theme was expounded more fully in *Industrial Democracy* (1897). This was followed by the *History of English Local Government* (1906–1929) in nine huge volumes that chronicled the evolution of government provision for the poor by the local parish in medieval and modern times, to the nineteenth-century policies of *laissez-faire,* and finally to the twentieth-century revival of local government interest in social legislation. The theme running through all of these books is that one function of government is to provide a framework within which people can satisfy their individual social and economic needs. Socialism—collective ownership of the means of production—could fulfill that function better than private profit and private enterprise capitalism, according to the Webbs. Their final publication, *Soviet Communism: A New Civilization?* (two volumes, 1935) was a rosy and optimistic picture of the Soviet Union published in the same year as the first round of Stalin's political purges. The Webbs were not the only misguided ones at the time.

The Fabian socialists enjoyed considerable success. Their work helped push the welfare legislation of pre-1914 England through Parliament, and they helped organize the Labour party. Although they failed in their attempts to use local governments for social reform and to establish government ownership of large-scale industries (coal, steel, electric power, finance, and railroads), their ideas and tactics lived on in the Labour party and came to fruition after World War II, when the Fabian Society had a resurgence of activity and influence. Much English welfare legislation and the post–World War II socialization of transport, coal mining, and other basic industries can be traced back to the influence of the Fabians.

A different sort of influence was wielded by Richard H. Tawney (1880–1963), a scholar whose field of research was English economic history of the sixteenth century—a period considerably removed from the hurly-burly of political and economic issues of the twentieth century. But Tawney was a man of both ages. His masterly treatise *The Agrarian Problem in the 16th Century* (1912) broke new ground in historical theory by analyzing the breakdown of the old agricultural, feudal order and the emergence of the modern market economy and society. Then, looking at modern society with the eyes of both an outraged reformer and an objective scholar, Tawney wrote three of the most important books of his time.

The first was *The Acquisitive Society* (1920). Tawney compared the functional society of the Middle Ages, in which each individual had his place, his duties, and his rewards, with the modern industrial world, in which productive effort gains relatively little reward while the promoter, speculator, and *rentier* collect large sums of unearned income. Modern society should be reorganized, argued Tawney, so that rewards are received by those who expend work and effort, by those who perform the tasks that society needs if it is to function for the welfare of all. "It is foolish to maintain property rights for which no service is performed," said Tawney, "for payment without service is waste." Society, he argued, should be reformed along the functional lines of a socialist society.

Then came the most influential of all of Tawney's works, *Religion and the Rise of Capitalism* (1926). Going back to his academic field of the sixteenth century, Tawney took up the scholarly debate begun by the Germans Werner Sombart and Max Weber over whether the Protestant Reformation created the intellectual climate that made possible the rise of modern capitalism. Tawney agreed that the two were related, and that each influenced the other. But the major thrust of his argument was that the business activities of modern society were completely amoral. Ever since the Protestant ethic of hard work and worldly success had become an end in itself, without reference to broader or higher values, business had been carried on without moral principles. It was almost as if modern men and women were continually reenacting the Faust legend, selling their souls for material prosperity while relegating ethical values to a quickly forgotten two hours on Sunday. Tawney described the modern world as "the smiling illusion of progress won from the mastery of the material environment by a race too selfish and superficial to determine the purpose to which its triumphs shall be applied."

This plea for values going beyond material wealth was followed by *Equality* (1931), which argued persuasively for a society that would provide an egalitarian distribution of wealth through "the pooling of surplus resources by means of taxation, and the use of the funds thus obtained to make accessible to all, irrespective of their income, occupation or social position, the conditions of civilization which, in the absence of such measures, can be enjoyed only by the rich." Such egalitarianism would, in turn, support and sustain the democratic political framework that made it possible.

The foremost scholar of an obscure historical field, Tawney used his detailed knowledge of the subject to cast new light on his own times. He developed a broad-ranging philosophy that raised basic criticisms of the economic life of his era. Tawney's solutions to the problems he described were socialistic because he believed that only through socialism could human values receive proper development.

Thorstein Veblen and John R. Commons

The idea of the democratic welfare state developed in the United States on much more pragmatic grounds than in England. The American approach developed through the work of a small group of economists who investigated the economic problems of business cycles, labor relations, monopoly and big business, and social welfare, and through political leaders from the progressive era to the New Deal. The basic theme of both groups was that modern industrial society faced serious problems, and that the power of government should be used to protect both the social fabric and individuals within it from the often destructive forces of the market. The Americans sought workable solutions to specific problems within the traditional framework of their society, in contrast to the socialist philosophy that prevailed in England.

If any one writer were to be singled out as the most influential exponent of the philosophy underlying the American development, it would be Thorstein Veblen (1857–1929). Coming out of the rural midwestern society that produced the Populist movement and William Jennings Bryan, this son of a Norwegian immigrant studied philosophy at Johns Hopkins and Yale and economics at Cornell. He made a career out of failure, never rising above the rank of assistant professor in a teaching career at Chicago, Stanford, and Missouri. Even when he lectured at the New School for Social Research in New York City during the early 1920s, his salary was paid in part by contributions from his former students. But Veblen's books made him famous, and his ideas earned him the respect of his fellow economists. He was elected to the presidency of the American Economic Association in 1924 but declined the honor with the cynical comment that the position was not offered when it might have done him some good professionally.

There are innumerable stories about Veblen. He left the University of Chicago in 1906 under a cloud created partly by his unorthodox ideas and partly by his having taken a trans-Atlantic trip with a prominent Chicago married woman. His extramarital escapades continued during his three years at Stanford, where the administration and several faculty members are said to have heaved great sighs of relief when he left.

Veblen did not enjoy teaching. When he went to the University of Missouri in 1911, his reputation preceded him. Students flocked to register for his classes, but they were met by a man who mumbled into his beard and who, on the first day of classes, filled the blackboards with a long list of readings on which they were to be examined in a week. This brought the class down to manageable size—about a dozen students. Moreover, Veblen did not give grades above C, in order to discourage those hoping to be selected for Phi Beta Kappa.

Veblen shone in his books. In *The Theory of the Leisure Class* (1899), one of the most influential books of the last hundred years, Veblen criticized the materialistic criteria of success in a pecuniary culture. Since the survival of individuals and families depended on income, money and wealth became the standard by which all actions were judged. The wealthy spent their money conspicuously to prove their claims to success, and those with lesser incomes emulated the wealthy and their way of life: if the boss took a month-long vacation to Bermuda on his yacht, the secretary scrimped for years to take a one-week cruise to the Caribbean. Since leisure time was the greatest indication of success—showing that one did not have to work at all—the wealthy had many servants, did not allow wives or children to work, and spent their time seeking pleasure. "Conspicuous leisure," "conspicuous consumption," and "pecuniary emulation" were inherent in the market economy, and all led to a vast waste of resources, productive effort, and time. Veblen did not state his views on what alternative value systems might be desirable, but he clearly rejected those of the pecuniary culture.

Veblen's next book, *The Theory of Business Enterprise* (1904), carried the argument further, with an analysis of the production side of the market. He distinguished between production for use and production for profit, pointing out that businesses often prevented achievement of the former by pursuing the latter. The drive for profit led to restriction of output through monopoly. It held back technological advances, as business firms sought to protect their existing capital investment. It led to depressions and cutbacks in production, due to excessive extensions of credit and financial manipulations. It promoted separation of ownership and control in business, as efforts were made to control greater amounts of wealth with existing capital. It led to military expenditures and war through business control of political power. The single-minded pursuit of profit, in other words, prevented full realization of the gains that could be achieved by machine technology. Just as consumer attitudes led to waste in a pecuniary society, so also did the basic patterns of business behavior.

These two books, and Veblen's other writings, focused as much on economic and social change as they did on descriptions of the pecuniary society. The business and leisure classes might dominate a society, said Veblen, but change was inevitable. Technology had a life of its own, and scientists, engineers, and others were continually seeking better methods of production and more efficient systems of organization, irrespective of profits. On the other hand, business leaders and owners of wealth were "vested interests" who resisted change because it might upset their comfortable positions. A great conflict was therefore inherent between the march of technology and the conservatism of the existing order, between the interests of the community at large and those of the wealthy powers-that-be. A cultural lag must inevitably develop between the needs of a society created by changing conditions and the established institutions supported by the leisure-class elite. Veblen saw this conflict polarizing around the two extremes of a technologically dominated socialism based on central planning and devoted to community welfare and useful production on the one hand, and a military authoritarianism designed to protect the existing structure of power and wealth on the other. He felt that the latter would triumph, as business managers sought to protect their own interests through state support of monopolistic controls combined with militarism and colonialism to create and preserve prosperity. Perhaps Veblen was influenced in his day by the parallels between militaristic Germany and the colonialism, big-navy ideology, and strong presidency of Theodore Roosevelt. But whatever the source, as early as 1904 he had predicted the rise of fascism and the emergence of the corporate state—institutions that did indeed appear in the 1920s and 1930s in Germany, Japan, and Italy.

Veblen's viewpoint could not be ignored: fundamental forces of change were at work, he argued, requiring adaptations in social, economic, and political institutions that would inevitably be opposed by those who had achieved wealth and success. Veblen may not have originated this point of view, but he gave it a solid theoretical foundation in his concepts of the relation between change and vested interests. Allied with his critique of the pecuniary society and the business system, these concepts gave direction as well as viewpoint to movements for economic and social reform.

Veblen's books were widely read by the general public. In addition to these popular works, however, Veblen also presented to professional economists a devastating critique of neoclassical economics in a series of articles and book reviews in professional journals. Economics was old-fashioned, he argued, in its preoccupation with static equilibrium. Its assumption of the hedonistic psychology of the economic individual was a narrow interpretation of human nature. It ignored society as a whole in its concentration on the isolated individual. The importance of economic institutions and the processes of institutional change were excluded from analysis. Its conclusions were almost wholly theoretical and were interlaced with ideological justification of the existing order. This critique was, in fact, largely responsible for the development of empirical studies to supplement and refine theoretical analysis, which became a major feature of economics after Veblen.

Veblen's influence was widespread not only upon the public, but also within the discipline of economics. His pupils and followers investigated in detail the issues he emphasized. Wesley Mitchell studied business cycles and founded the National Bureau of Economic Research. Adolf Berle and Gardner Means wrote on the separation of ownership and control in the large corporation. Means and Walton Hamilton analyzed the pricing policies of big business. Clarence Ayres looked at the impact of changing technology on economic institutions. Robert and Helen Lynd studied the structure of community power in books such as *Middletown* and *Middletown in Transition,* and C. Wright Mills did the same on a national scale in *The Power Elite.* Even literary criticism was affected: Vernon Parrington applied Veblenian ideas in his monumental *Main Currents in American Thought.*

Paralleling Veblen's work and influence was that of John R. Commons (1862–1945). Where Veblen had articulated the basic approach and viewpoint of the twentieth-century reform movement, Commons and his followers pioneered specific measures and legislation. Commons was also a midwesterner who studied at Johns Hopkins University in the 1880s, when it was the foremost American graduate school. His teaching career took him first to Wesleyan, then to Oberlin, Indiana, and Syracuse. While at Syracuse he published a study that argued that the growth of the state paralleled the development of the institution of private property, as society sought to control the economic power that accompanied accumulation of property. Such ideas, plus Commons's desire to add a course in labor problems to the curriculum, impelled the university's conservative administration to abolish his position. For the next four years, he worked with the United States Industrial Commission studying labor unions and labor-management relations and with the National Civic Federation promoting conciliation between labor and management.

In 1904 Commons returned to academia with a position at the University of Wisconsin. He spent almost as much time on leave from the university to serve on government commissions as he did on the campus. His major interests were public utility regulation and labor problems. He helped draft Wisconsin's public utility law of 1907 and wrote extensively in favor of compensation to workers for injuries suffered on the job, unemployment insurance, and peaceful collective bargaining. In 1911 he helped set up the Wisconsin Industrial Commission, which sought to develop mediation and conciliation in labor disputes. In 1914 he served on a similar national commission in Washington and in 1915 wrote a report calling for a national labor board to promote settlement of labor disputes through collective bargaining. He then turned to unemployment insurance and began the movement that led to enactment of a law in Wisconsin in 1932 and nationally a few years later. Realizing that unemployment insurance could not work effectively without economic stabilization, Commons entered that area and in the 1920s became president of the National Monetary Association, which sought programs to achieve stability of credit and prices.

All of these programs and policies later became major parts of the public economy of the United States: public utility regulation as part of a regulatory system for businesses "affected with the public interest"; collective bargaining and mediation to settle disputes between labor and management on a voluntary basis; promotion of economic stability at high levels of output and employment; and social legislation (unemployment insurance, workers' compensation, and old-age insurance) to mitigate the chief harmful effects of the industrial system. Much of the New Deal legislation of the 1930s lay within the framework pioneered by Commons.

Underlying Commons's ideas was the concept of the economy as a web of relationships among people who had diverging or conflicting interests but who also had an interest in resolving those conflicts in order to keep the system functioning effectively. The development of modern industrial society may have created important social problems of monopoly, business cycles, labor-management conflict, and others, but everyone, Commons argued, could agree that all would benefit if those problems could be resolved. This approach led to a view of government as mediator between conflicting economic interests and between economic forces and the individual. Commons and other liberal reformers saw conflicts of interest, which had to be resolved with fairness to both sides, between business and the public, between labor and management, and in broader terms, between the free operation of market forces and individual welfare. This view of conflict differed sharply from those maintained by the other two chief ideological positions—from the neoclassical economists, who saw harmony emerging in all areas out of the equilibrating forces of the market, and from the Marxists, who argued that class conflict would inevitably tear the social order apart. Commons accepted both of these concepts but went beyond them; he argued that market forces could reconcile some but not all of the conflicting interests of the modern world, and that a complex industrial society continually created new conflicts whose equitable resolution required government action.

The New Deal

The reforming, social welfare philosophy expressed by Veblen and the policies pioneered by Commons and his associates came to fruition during the 1930s under the New Deal administrations of Franklin D. Roosevelt. It is true that old ideas began to change before the thirties: witness the welfare legislation of New York and Wisconsin, the conservation movement prior to World War I, and the gradual acceptance by government of the use of monetary policy to promote economic stability. Crusaders and critics from the

Populists onward had been forging the social philosophy of the New Deal. But the years from 1929 to 1933 were a great watershed in American social thought, and the legislation of the five years after 1933 created a framework within which the American economy continued to function more than a half-century later.

The most important aspect of the New Deal philosophy was the belief that society as a whole, functioning through government, must protect itself and its members against the disruptive forces inherent in an industrial, market-oriented economy. This represented a great shift away from the philosophy that the self-adjusting market should be given free sway and that people, resources, and wealth should be treated essentially as commodities.

The New Deal emphasized five main types of direct intervention in economic affairs. First was its assumption of responsibility for maintaining high levels of employment, although the unemployment of the Great Depression was not conquered until World War II. The most effective method developed by the New Deal was to use the federal budget to ensure an adequate level of total spending; the budget deficits of the thirties sought to supplement inadequate private spending with public spending. This concept was embodied in the Employment Act of 1946 and institutionalized in the President's Council of Economic Advisers. More direct methods to counter the unemployment of the 1930s were also used, including direct relief payments, construction of public works, and job programs for the unemployed (Work Projects Administration) and for youth (Civilian Conservation Corps).

The second type of intervention was legislation establishing collective bargaining as a means of settling labor-management disputes. Since the 1890s the American Federation of Labor had sought gains for labor primarily through collective bargaining rather than radical political action or socialism. The Socialist party and a radical union, the Industrial Workers of the World, were strong prior to World War I, but they were largely destroyed by repressive measures taken by the federal and state governments and courts during the war and immediately thereafter—a dismal chapter in the history of civil rights in the United States—leaving collective bargaining as the only practical alternative for workers. Although the bulk of business opinion, typified by the National Association of Manufacturers, was opposed to unions and collective bargaining, an important segment of the business community, led by some leaders of major corporations, saw in collective bargaining the answer to continued class conflict. Out of this meeting of minds of labor leaders and some leaders of the corporate community, together with the stresses created by the Great Depression and the election of Franklin D. Roosevelt, came the National Labor Relations Act (1935), which made collective bargaining the national policy. Although modified by additional legislation after World War II, the policy remained as one of the cornerstones of the nation's economic constitution.

A third type of intervention in economic affairs involved the relationship between government and business. The New Deal moved toward programs for control of markets and prices by business enterprise under government supervision, tailored to the needs of specific sectors of the economy. This policy was pioneered earlier in railroad transportation. Supervised by the Interstate Commerce Commission (established in 1887) in the period between the great depression of the 1890s and World War I, the large railroad corporations developed control of railroad rates, division of markets, and dampening of competition designed to maintain profits and the security of the existing firms. In the 1920s the idea of "business self-government" spread broadly through the business community via the growth of trade associations. Under the New Deal it was embodied in the National Recovery Administration (NRA), a great effort to promote economic recovery through "codes of fair practice" designed to limit competition and maintain prices at profitable levels. This experiment failed, and was one of the most heavily criticized of the New Deal programs. But similar efforts succeeded in other sectors of the economy. Cooperation between the federal and state governments and the major oil companies established a system of production controls and price stabilization in the oil business that lasted until the early 1970s, when the Arab-dominated Organization of Petroleum Exporting Countries (OPEC) took over control of production and prices from the great international oil corporations. The New Deal also tried to establish controls over output and prices in the bituminous coal industry, supervised by a federal commission, but the effort failed until the United Mine Workers Union was able to establish such a system during World War II as part of its wage bargaining with the major companies. A system of regional monopolies supervised by state and federal regulatory agencies was established in electric power production. The communications industries were treated in similar fashion. Legislation regulating banks, the securities exchanges, and other financial institutions restricted competition between firms in different sectors of the financial markets and hindered entry of new firms into each sector. In agriculture, a system of price supports and marketing agreements protected farm enterprises from the effects of market forces, and created a lush environment for the growth of large farms at the expense of the small family farm. Although many conservative critics attacked the New Deal as antibusiness, the administration was engaged in building a new symbiosis between big business and big government around the philosophy of business control of markets under government supervision. In areas such as energy, communications, finance, and agriculture, the New Deal moved away from reliance on free-market adjustment toward market management. Much of this aspect of the New Deal was eliminated in the 1980s and 1990s in a program of "deregulation" of industry, but much remains.

The fourth main type of government intervention in economic affairs was regional land-use planning based on water resources. Typified by the Tennessee Valley Authority, this type of planning was the outgrowth of a number of pre–New Deal policies—reclamation, waterway development, forest conservation, city planning, and the controversy over electric power development. Today we take for granted the desirability of unified development of water resources and related land uses. The debates now center on issues of conservation, pollution, and the use of exhaustible resources in a growing economy.

Efforts to protect people from the hazards of life in the market economy represented the fifth type of government intervention into economic affairs during the New Deal years. This included old-age and survivors insurance and unemployment compensation (Social Security Act, 1935) and minimum-wage legislation, prohibition of child labor, and limitations on hours of work (Fair Labor Standards Act, 1938). The New Deal shied away from medical insurance, however, and legislation to assure medical care for the elderly (Medicare) and the needy (Medicaid) did not come until 1965. Even as this is written the idea of universal medical insurance has been unable to overcome the "vested interests" of the health services industry.

The growth of government responsibility for economic affairs during the 1930s was supported by a new view of the individual's place in society. The older proposition—that the benefit-maximizing individual would contribute most to society as a whole, and the corollary that the unsuccessful ought to bear the cost burden themselves—was not tenable in a modern industrial society, particularly one plagued by a depression that crushed not only the unemployed, but even intelligent, hardworking business people. In its place arose the belief that society had a responsibility for the welfare of each person, partly because the individual contributed to society by working, by raising a family, and by participating generally in the activities of the social order, and partly because the problems of a complex society were often too great to be solved by the individual. It was felt that people functioned more effectively, both in their own interests and as contributors to society, in a secure environment. One goal of New Deal policy was to create sufficient economic security in order to release greater individual energies that would, in the long run, more than compensate for the costs involved. In practice this meant the passage of a range of "welfare" measures—unemployment insurance, social security, workers' compensation, and federal grants-in-aid in health and education—which have achieved general acceptance today. Of course, such measures are not simply humanitarian commitments. They also help stabilize consumer demand.

Another major tenet of New Deal social philosophy was that the community had social responsibilities beyond mere profit making. In the pre–New Deal era, profit and success were their own justification; wealth reflected not only hard work and ability, but also the fact that the search for wealth resulted in meeting the needs of others, "as if by an invisible hand." By contrast, the New Deal stressed that the market economy often ran roughshod over human and social values, and that individual gain was not always synonymous with social good. Success and profit were not enough; business had to justify itself on other grounds. Nowhere was this requirement spelled out in detail, but New Deal legislation implied that it included a reasonably stable economy, broadly effective labor-management relations, reasonable prices, and straightforward financial activities.

Two further aspects of the changes of the 1930s had great significance for America and the world. First, reform and welfare programs greatly strengthened the nation's economic and social order. Through labor unions and collective bargaining workers were able to achieve both higher standards of living and a new feeling of dignity and importance. Farmers were protected from some of the insecurity found in their highly unstable sector of the economy. Middle-income families were assisted in becoming homeowners, and their savings were protected. Some of the more objectionable practices of big business were prohibited, and government regulation of other business activities was expanded. The risks of old age and unemployment were ameliorated, and a beginning was made on a system of welfare payments to aid the poor. Although some groups were hardly affected, including most blacks, migrant workers, and the rural poor, and low-wage workers did not benefit significantly, the economic interests of many Americans were advanced—and their commitment to the existing order of things was strengthened. The New Deal, as America's answer to the challenge of change, was reform rather than revolution.

In a second respect, the legacy of the New Deal was less favorable. It set in motion a shift toward an American version of the corporate state that most Americans have been loath to recognize. As the federal government became the instrument of reform, and federal expenditures were increased to meet social needs, political power tended to shift from the states to Washington. Within Washington, the executive branch of the government gained power at the expense of Congress, partly because the president took the initiative in promoting legislation, and partly because the enlarged federal expenditures were managed by the executive branch. This subtle shift did not go unnoticed at the time. Indeed, it was a favorite theme of New Deal critics, but its implications did not become clear until World War II and thereafter, when the military and national security activities of the executive branch came to dominate national policy. This came about, in part, because of the huge amount of military-related spending, and the national preoccupation with the "Cold War" and related international commitments. The New Deal reforms brought with them a growth in the power of the national government and its executive branch that later resulted in even greater power for the military.

This shift in the locus of power was validated by fundamental changes in constitutional law. A series of Supreme Court decisions made between 1937 and 1939, upholding the chief New Deal legislation, greatly expanded the powers of the federal government. Prior to 1930 the federal government could engage only in those activities specifically designated by the Constitution. By 1940 it was empowered to take action to "promote the general welfare." A constitution of limits was replaced by a constitution of largely open powers for the national government.

Nevertheless, the New Deal greatly strengthened the essential elements of the private-enterprise economy. It preserved the individual's right to spend or save as one pleased, to choose an occupation, and to make business decisions. Although the New Deal restructured much of the country's social and economic framework, its methods never included detailed planning or controls. Nor did it encroach upon personal decision making—one of the basic tenets of American individualism. Furthermore, it left untouched the fundamental structure of economic power in an economy dominated increasingly by large corporations, and it did little to shift the distribution of income and wealth.

The 1930s saw some basic changes in the economic institutions of the United States and a fundamental shift in economic philosophy. The ideal of laissez-faire gave way to an interventionist, welfare-oriented economic philosophy. Yet the basic structure of a private-enterprise economy with private accumulation of wealth was retained. In this respect developments in the United States were similar to those occurring in all of the advanced industrial nations. During the 1930s there was strong political and ideological conflict between the advocates of an expanded role of government and the protagonists of the older ideas and policies. Yet the decades following World War II were to see a growing symbiosis between corporate economic power in the private sector and the expanded economic, political, and military power of the national government.

Creative Destruction and Fictitious Commodities

Two noted economists probed the fundamental problems that underlay these humanistic concerns about the modern economy. Joseph Schumpeter (1883–1950), whom we shall meet again in a later chapter, was a strong supporter of private-enterprise capitalism and the policy of laissez-faire. Nevertheless, he pointed out that the process of economic development and technological change could be as destructive of the old as it was creative of the new. The benefits were greater than the costs, he argued, but in the process of economic growth and expansion old products, technologies, organizations, and leaders were displaced by the new. Capitalism continually revitalized itself in this way, remained dynamic, and moved to higher levels of production even though the process was uneven and sometimes erratic—this was Schumpeter's answer to Marx's contention that capitalism would lose its dynamism. But the process was not without costs to people and communities. Technological change brought new jobs and industries, but eliminated older jobs and factories. Economic growth was uneven, interrupted by recessions, depressions, unemployment and insecurity. According to Schumpeter this "creative destruction" brought forth demands for government intervention to ameliorate the unavoidable negative effects of the dynamism of capitalism.

As we pointed out in an earlier chapter, Adam Smith recognized the potential destructive effects of market forces in his role as commissioner of customs in Scotland. Herbert Spencer, William Graham Sumner, and other social Darwinists approved of this aspect of private enterprise as "survival of the fittest." Yet, as was said about the Industrial Revolution in England, "the mills of Manchester grind exceedingly small." And one of Schumpeter's contemporaries, the Protestant theologian Reinhold Niebuhr (1892–1971), contrasted concern for others with the morality of the market in *Moral Man and Immoral Society: A Study of Ethics and Politics* (1932).

Karl Polanyi (1886–1964), an economic historian and socialist contemporary of Schumpeter, identified a second source of humanistic concerns about the modern economy. A major theme of his book *The Great Transformation* (1944) was that land, labor, and capital were dealt with in the market economy as if they were commodities. Market forces allocated them to uses dictated by the profit motive. Yet they are not produced primarily for sale, as are other commodities. Labor is a fundamental human activity that is part of life, and is carried on for broader purposes than sale for profit. It cannot be separated from life itself. Land, in his view, is another name for nature, whose form can be changed by human effort but that cannot be produced. Capital comprises both the tools used in production and the knowledge with which they are used and applied. Together, these three—land, labor, and capital—are part of a social process through which useful things are produced, enabling the lives of people and communities to be carried on. They perform important functions, but none are produced primarily for sale.

Yet the self-regulating market economy used these "fictitious commodities" as if they were the same as other commodities. The marketplace, and the profit that drives it, becomes the arbiter of human fate, the natural environment, and the social order. Furthermore, the moral and ethical values by which the social system functions go far beyond those of the marketplace, which is driven by profit in an ethical milieu of *caveat emptor*.

It was inevitable, argued Polanyi, that government, as the political arm of the social order, would intervene in the market economy to protect people, resources, capital, and humane values from the sometimes destructive effects of pure market forces. Here was a socialist (Karl Polanyi) agreeing with a defender of laissez-faire capitalism (Joseph Schumpeter) on one of the basic ills of a private-enterprise market economy.

NINE

WOMEN AND
THE ECONOMY

Jane Addams (1860–1935), a
social reformer and pacifist,
founded the settlement house
movement in the United States.

Before the late nineteenth century the role of women in the development of
economic thought was limited by the almost total domination of the field by
men. Women were not trained in economics, did not hold professorships in
the universities, and did not publish in the scholarly journals that were beginning to appear. Nevertheless, there were a number of women who had
an impact on economic thought and policy, if not in the narrower area of
economic theory, and whose contributions helped change the world in
which we live. We have already seen the contributions of a few women to
the development of economics: the influence of Harriet Taylor on John Stuart Mill, the role of Rosa Luxemburg in the Marxist debates over revolutionary strategy, the ideas of Beatrice Webb and the Fabian Society, and Joan
Robinson's contribution to the neoclassical discussion of imperfect competition. We will return to Joan Robinson in a later chapter.

Economic Orthodoxy

Jane Marcet (1769–1858) was a popularizer of economics in the first half of
the nineteenth century in England. Her *Conversations on Political Economy*
(1816) was an explanation of classical economics written for young people.
Even today her treatise is a useful guide to orthodox economics as it existed
prior to the publication of Ricardo's *Principles*. In a later book entitled *Rich
and Poor* (1851) Marcet showed her ideological bias. Written in simple language and directed specifically at the "lower classes," its theme was that
"the rich are their friends, not their foes." Harriet Martineau was another
English popularizer (1802–1876) whose *Illustrations of Political Economy*

(1832–1834) consisted of fictional stories illustrating the laissez-faire theories of classical economics.

Later in the nineteenth century, Mary Paley Marshall (1850–1944) became the first professionally trained woman economist in England and the first woman to obtain a degree from Cambridge University. She taught extension courses in economics there and wrote *The Economics of Industry* (1879) jointly with Alfred Marshall, whom she had married in 1877. It was a popular textbook until superseded by her husband's *Principles of Economics* in 1890. Except for occasional lecturing and tutoring at the college for women at Cambridge, Mary Paley Marshall retired from professional life, making a home for her husband and helping him with his writing. After his death in 1924 she became the librarian of the Marshall Library at Cambridge. One biographer commented that she might have become an economist of high repute had it not been for the "suffocating influence" of her famous husband. Economics in her day was truly a man's world.

The Feminists

Mary Wollstonecraft (1759–1797) is widely recognized as initiating the modern women's rights movement in the English-speaking world. Her father was an alcoholic from whom she sought to protect her abused mother, a gesture repeated later in life when she helped her sister leave an abusive husband. At nineteen she left home to make her own way, suffering years of poverty as a companion, schoolteacher, governess, translator, and editor. A novel, *Mary, a Fiction* (1788), was based on her own life. In 1790 she published *A Vindication of the Rights of Man* in response to Edmund Burke's conservative *Reflections on the French Revolution* of the same year. Two years later *A Vindication of the Rights of Women* made her both famous and infamous.

This seminal book argued that women were an oppressed group, both legally and economically. It set forth the chief doctrines of the later women's movement: complete equality of the sexes, voting rights for women, and equal opportunities in education, jobs, and the professions. Her analysis of how the legal system reduced women to the status of nonpersons became a theme of much feminist writing and agitation as the women's movement grew.

Wollstonecraft went to Paris in 1792 to observe the French Revolution firsthand. There she met Gilbert Imlay, an American lumber merchant, and bore him a daughter. In 1795 she visited Scandinavia with Imlay, claiming to be his wife. When he deserted her, she failed in an attempt to take her own life. After she recovered, she returned to England and took up residence with William Godwin (1756–1836), a leading radical of the time. Novelist and political theorist, his *Enquiry Concerning Human Justice* (1793) argued that all government, law, marriage, and indeed, all organized social institutions were obstacles to human happiness. Nevertheless, he and Mary married when she became pregnant. Mary died at the age of thirty-eight, shortly after the birth of their daughter. The daughter, Mary Godwin, later married the poet Percy Bysshe Shelley, and, as Mary Shelley, wrote the famous novel *Frankenstein* in 1818.

Harriet Taylor, who had made such an important impact on John Stuart Mill in his support of measures designed to alleviate the conditions of the poor, was also a strong advocate of equal legal treatment of women, as can be seen in her work, *The Enfranchisement of Women* (1851). Barbara Smith Bodichon (1827–1891), now almost forgotten, also argued for women's property rights in *The Most Important Laws Concerning Women* (1854). She was perhaps the first to point out the crowding of women workers in low-wage jobs in *Women and Work* (1857). Later in the century an American, Helen Stuart Campbell (1839–1918) wrote three widely read books dealing with poverty and the place of women in the American economy: *The Problem of the Poor* (1882), *Prisoners of Poverty* (1887), and *Women Wage Earners* (1893). They revealed the seamy side of the great expansion of the American economy that followed the Civil War.

Millicent Fawcett (1847–1929), like Mary Paley Marshall, was the wife of an economist at England's Cambridge University. Her husband, Henry Fawcett (1833–1884), went into economics rather than law after he was blinded in a shooting accident as a young man. As a classical economist, the intellectual ferment associated with neoclassical economics passed him by, but as a member of Parliament he advocated liberal economic reforms that were often opposed to the conservative teachings of classical orthodoxy. His wife, with no formal education in economics, became her husband's full-time secretary after their marriage in 1867 and collaborated with him on his writings, including his *Pauperism and Its Remedies* (1871). Fawcett also authored two popular introductory economics textbooks of her own and was instrumental in the founding of Newham Hall in Cambridge, which was incorporated into Cambridge University in 1874 as its first women's college.

Millicent Fawcett had joined a women's suffrage group in 1867 and entered the suffrage movement full time after her husband's death in 1884. From 1897 to 1918 she was president of the National Union of Women's Societies and the recognized leader of the drive for voting rights for women in England. She also contributed to a significant economic analysis of the place of women in the economy. While serving as president of the National Union she chaired a study group to investigate the employment of women and women's wages. She reported these findings in two important papers, "The Position of Women in Economic Life" (1917) and "Equal Pay for Equal Work" (1918).

Three propositions emerged from Fawcett's papers: Women were crowded into a few occupations, women were excluded from the higher-paying jobs, and women were paid less than men. Francis Y. Edgeworth, one of the leading British economic theorists and an important contributor to neoclassical theory, turned these findings into an analysis of how the crowding of a minority group into a few occupations led to low wages there and in turn to higher wages elsewhere. Edgeworth also explained why the system was self-perpetuating. Edgeworth's paper, "Equal Pay to Men and Women for Equal Work" (1922), was largely ignored by the economics profession in the years after World War I, but his analysis was revived and extended in the 1970s by an American economist, Barbara Bergmann (1927–), whose work documented a record of employment discrimination against women. The analysis of "crowding" of minorities into low-wage occupations and its effect was also applied to the study of the urban ghettos of post–World War II America.

After Parliament voted women the right to vote in 1918, Fawcett continued to campaign for women's legal rights. These were ultimately granted in 1928, just a year before she died.

A different line of argument was developed by Charlotte Perkins Gilman (1860–1935), who also was not a trained economist. Born in Hartford, Connecticut, and married at twenty-three after a troubled childhood, she fell into a serious depression and was treated by a highly respected neurologist who prescribed for her the then-fashionable treatment of complete rest as a remedy for psychological problems. The experience led to her first great success as a writer, the short story, "The Yellow Wallpaper" (1892), in which a young woman suffering from depression is driven mad by her husband, a doctor who has forced upon her the complete rest cure. The story made her famous, and it remains today one of the best-known short stories of the modern era.

Gilman was greatly influenced by Edward Bellamy's utopian novel, *Looking Backward* (1888), which pictured an ideal socialist society in the year 2000. Bellamy's novel was outsold in the nineteenth century only by Harriet Beecher Stowe's *Uncle Tom's Cabin* (Stowe was Gilman's great-aunt). Gilman took up the cause of the National party, which had been formed to advocate Bellamy's ideas, with a whirlwind of writings, speeches, and political organizing. Bellamy's utopia had postulated the idea of full equality of men and women. This led Gilman to study the place of women in the economy of her day. In *Women and Economics* (1898, reprinted in 1970) Perkins argued that "the relationship between men and women was essentially an economic one." Men were free to work in the economic and political world because women stayed home to raise children and provide the man with a refuge from his struggles outside the home. In return women received food, clothing, and shelter as their reward. Male-female relationships were seen as an economic contract in which only one individual, the male, was able to contribute to the progress of the economy and society. The potential contribution of the female half of the population was aborted because women, confined to the home and excluded from the world of affairs, had no opportunity to develop their full potential and contribute to social and economic advancement. The male-dominated economic, political, and social order was poorer because it *was* male dominated.

Perkins extended this argument to working women. Long hours and low pay kept them from developing fully. This was equally true of most working men. Women in the home and working men and women were in similarly repressed situations. This left the world of affairs to be dominated by the more affluent men who could construct a social order that benefited themselves and their kind.

Gilman developed these arguments at greater length in four other works: *Concerning Children* (1900), *The Home: Its Work and Influence* (1903), *Human Work* (1904), and *The Man-Made World* (1911). These argued that women needed to be economically independent of men so that they might choose between home and children, a career, or a combination of the two. The publications made Charlotte Perkins Gilman one of the best-known leaders of the women's rights movement in pre–World War I America.

From 1909 through 1916 Gilman published a women's magazine, *Forerunner*, in which she wrote every word of every issue. She also wrote four utopian novels that ran as serials. Three were peopled by men and women, but the last, *Herland* (1915, published as a book in 1979), described a community with only women and children and no men. How could that be? The answer: parthenogenesis, a process known to biologists as reproduction by means of unfertilized eggs. In this utopia Gilman imagined that scientific advances had made parthenogenesis possible for humans. There were no families in *Herland*, only individuals and the community. The children were raised by the community as a whole and were trained to become cooperative and caring adults. Women had genuine autonomy as individuals, and they participated in the community as equals. The profit motive was replaced by an understanding that what helps the community benefits the individual and vice versa.

Gilman's magazine did not survive the First World War. She wrote little of consequence after that and experienced periods of depression once more. She and her second husband, both suffering from cancer, committed suicide together in 1935.

On the Left

Mary Marcy (1877–1922) was another writer who did not have formal training in economics. Born in Belleville, Illinois, and orphaned as a child, as a young adult she supported her younger brother and sister by working as a telephone switchboard operator. She taught herself shorthand and later worked as a stenographer. She was interested in social and political issues from an early age: during the 1896 presidential campaign she was fired by her employer, a manufacturer of American flags, for wearing a William Jennings Bryan campaign button. Hearing about this incident, Clarence Darrow, the famous lawyer, obtained a job for her in the office of the president of the University of Chicago, where she was able to take classes tuition free. She married Leslie H. Marcy in 1901, and the two lived for a time in Kansas City. They joined the Socialist party in 1903, and Mary soon became a leading figure in the party's radical wing. She wrote a series of muckraking exposés entitled "Letters of a Pork Packer's Stenographer" for the *International Socialist Review* (ISR) in 1904, which won her instant notoriety among leftist socialists. After testifying before a grand jury investigating monopolistic practices in the meat-packing industry, she was blacklisted and found work with a social welfare agency. From this experience came a second series of articles in the ISR, "Out of the Dump," which documented living conditions among the poor.

At this point Mary Marcy's career took a leap forward. Charles H. Kerr, publisher of the ISR, chose her as the paper's editor, with instructions to turn it into "a fighting magazine of socialism . . . of, by and for the working class." Her first effort was a series of articles for workers explaining the Marxist concepts of value, price, and surplus value. As *Shop Talks on Economics,* they were published as a pamphlet by the left-wing Industrial Workers of the World. Over two million copies were sold at ten cents each, and they were translated into seven foreign languages. This effort was followed by a series of editorials and special articles on a wide variety of topics, all from a Marxist-socialist point of view. The magazine's circulation rose spectacularly.

Under Marcy's leadership the ISR published articles by most of the left-wing American socialists and Marxists, and by a number of European Marxists. It also published Marcy's own poetry, stories, and pieces for children, as well as poems and articles by Carl Sandberg and stories by Jack London. Some of the more conservative socialist leaders criticized and condemned the ISR under Marcy's editorship because of its Marxist orientation.

Marcy singled out and stressed some of the same humanitarian themes found in Marx's earlier writings (not available in English translation at the time, and Marcy could not read German). She presented the socialist movement as primarily a means of human expression, helping liberate creative energies, promoting workers' self-development, and freeing workers from the constraints and exploitation of capitalism. Here is the concluding paragraph from Marcy's "Letters of a Pork Packer's Stenographer":

> It is not riches I want, nor power, nor yet fame! It is to make work a means, and not the end of living; to have a little play among the toil; to watch the sun rise in the freshness of the morning; to see the spreading of leaves, and the growing of flowers; to progress a little, instead of losing a little; to be able to pause, amid our hurry-ever, to rest and dream awhile!

Marcy saw socialism as a grassroots movement of working people reacting to their own experiences and developing the ideas, leadership, strategy, and tactics that would transform the social order. This was also one of Marx's important themes. Marcy saw little point to the sectarian squabbles among the leaders of the American left, and she opposed the Leninist concept of a dictatorship of the proletariat led by a narrow political party. In the preface to a biography of Eugene V. Debs, the American socialist leader, she wrote:

Leaders will never be able to carry the workers into the Promised Land. Men do not wage the great class struggle in the study, or in the editorial rooms. Methods of class warfare do not come from the brains of the isolated scholar, but from the brains and experiences of the fighters. The workers are the fighters and thinkers of the revolutionary movements.

The ISR took a strong stand against American participation in the First World War. Marcy wrote a series of strongly worded articles between 1914 and 1917 urging workers to oppose the war, arguing that the real enemy was not the armies of other countries, also made up of working people, but the capitalist class of their own country. She called for a refusal to register for the draft, for work slowdowns, and even for a general strike. The United States government suppressed the ISR in 1918. Out of work, the Marcys mortgaged their home to provide bail money for William (Big Bill) Hayward, president of the Industrial Workers of the World, who had publicly opposed the war and was in jail awaiting trial for treason. Hayward jumped bail and went to Russia; the Marcys lost their home.

It was a period of turmoil for the American left. In 1920 the U.S. attorney general, A. Mitchel Palmer, launched the notorious "Palmer raids" to deport aliens and radicals. Shortly afterward, a nationwide steel strike occurred with leftist leadership. It failed miserably. The formation of two rival communist parties in 1921 created wide division and disunity on the left. The Marcys opposed the formation of a revolutionary political party. Letters from Haywood also brought disturbing news. The Bolsheviks in Russia under Lenin's leadership were turning toward authoritarian rule. Dispirited, depressed, and in failing health, Mary Marcy committed suicide in 1922. She was forty-five years of age.

Reformers

Jane Addams (1860–1935), the great social reformer and pacifist, also lacked professional training. Born in Cedarville, Illinois, she was raised in a comfortable household by her widowed father, a state senator and an abolitionist friend of Abraham Lincoln. She wanted to study medicine, but a spinal illness that left her slightly deformed forced her to give up medical studies. After college she traveled to Europe with a college friend, Ellen Starr (1859–1940), who became her longtime associate and collaborator. They visited Toynbee Hall, a pioneering settlement house in London serving the needs of the poor. Returning to Chicago, the two young women founded Hull House in 1889, a settlement house in one of the city's worst slums. Financed by private donations, Hull House provided a wide variety of services for the poor: a medical clinic, classes for immigrants, assistance for unmarried pregnant girls, and a wide variety of health, educational, cultural, and recreational activities. Hull House became a model for similar settlement houses in other cities as well as a training ground for hands-on social reform activists. The two women lobbied for child labor laws, factory legislation, and programs to alleviate poverty. However, when the Illinois legislature passed several laws along those lines, they were overturned by the courts.

Addams was more politically active than her friend Starr. At the 1912 convention of the new Progressive party she seconded the nomination of Theodore Roosevelt for president and later campaigned in favor of the social welfare planks in the party platform. Between 1911 and 1914 she served as vice-president of the National American Suffrage Association. After the First World War she founded the women's International League for Peace and Freedom and served as its president until her death in 1935. Addams was co-recipient of the Nobel Peace Prize in 1931. A prolific writer, she published numerous books on poverty and other social problems, including *Twenty Years at Hull House* (1910) and *The Second Twenty Years at Hull House* (1930). Ironically, she was denounced as "un-American" by the American Legion and was described as part of "a movement to destroy civilization and Christianity" by the Daughters of the American Revolution.

Ellen Starr stayed out of the limelight, unlike her colleague, although she also was an activist for child labor laws and general labor issues. Eventually she joined the socialist party, but in 1930 she retired to a Catholic convent after suffering a crippling illness.

Frances Perkins (1880–1965) continued the tradition of women concerned with the poor, women in the economy, and social reform. She was born in Boston, attended Mount Holyoke College, worked in settlement houses, taught, and earned a graduate degree in political science at Columbia University. She witnessed the Triangle Shirtwaist fire in 1911 in New York City where 146 women factory workers died. Motivated by the event, she began to work for safer working conditions, limited hours for working women, and other forms of labor legislation. In these endeavors she was opposed by labor union leaders in New York City, who did not want protective labor laws for women. They felt that such laws would encourage women to enter the labor market and take jobs away from men who had families to support. From these encounters Frances Perkins developed a lifelong distrust of labor unions. Nevertheless, as Industrial Commissioner of New York State from 1926 to 1932 she won passage of a landmark series of labor laws. In 1932 she became secretary of labor under President Franklin D. Roosevelt, a post she held until 1945. She was the first woman member of a federal government cabinet. She helped develop important New Deal legislation, including the Social Security Act (1935), which included provisions for unemployment insurance as well as old-age benefits. She was also instrumental in putting together the Fair Labor Standards Act (1938), which established a minimum wage and maximum hours. The National Labor Relations Act (1935) was also passed while Perkins was secretary of labor. It established a national policy of fostering collective bargaining between labor unions and management by protecting the right to organize and requiring employers and unions to bargain in good faith. Perkins supported this measure, despite her distrust of unions. Her life work was devoted to building a protective framework of laws and customs in which working people could enjoy more fully the benefits of a prosperous and growing economy.

Other women also helped change the world we live in: Rose Schneiderman (1884–1972) was one of these. Born in Poland, she emigrated to the United States in 1892. In her early teens she went to work sewing caps and helped organize a New York local of the United Cloth and Cap Makers Union. In 1904 she was elected to the national union's executive board, the highest position yet held by a woman in a national labor organization. In 1905 she joined the Women's Trade Union League (WTLU), a national organization that strived to improve job conditions of working women. She rose in the WTLU and served as its president for twenty-four years, stepping down in 1950. She helped organize the garment workers union prior to the First World War, worked for women's right to vote, lectured widely, and worked actively to improve working conditions. Her official positions included membership on the Labor Advisory Board (the only woman) of the New Deal's National Recovery Administration (1933–1935) and secretary of labor in New York State between 1937 and 1943.

On the Right

Ayn Rand (1905–1982) was a novelist and philosopher whose highly controversial advocacy of unfettered individualism and pure laissez-faire capitalism was widely influential in the 1960s and 1970s. She was born Alice Rosenman in Russia, where she experienced firsthand the violence of the Russian revolution as a teenager, and where later she graduated from the University of Leningrad. She emigrated to the United States, the "country of the individual," and became a citizen in 1931.

Four novels contain the heart of her social and economic philosophy. The first, *We the Living* (1936), set in Russia immediately after the Bolshevik seizure of power, tells how three young people are trapped and destroyed by the authoritarian regime. The second, *Anthem* (1938), is a short novel about a heroic dissenter in a futuristic collectivized state who breaks away to create a new world of free individuals. Her next work, *The Fountainhead* (1943), was a best-seller. It is the story of an idealistic, uncompromising architect—a creative individual who stands up against the ignorant common herd and admits to no constraints on his actions, defying both accepted morality (he rapes the woman he is attracted to) and the law (he blows up the housing project he designed because it was changed by bureaucrats pressured by public opinion). At his trial he defends the right of the creative individual to pursue his own needs and desires without constraint. In 1949 the novel was made into a popular movie starring Gary Cooper, with Rand writing the script. Her last novel, *Atlas Shrugged* (1957), is a turgid and dense book that denounces government interference with the rights of individuals who ought to be completely free to act in their own "rational self interest." It glorifies completely unrestrained laissez-faire capitalism as the ideal economic system. Rand argued that free-market transactions enable both buyer and seller to satisfy their needs and desires, and thus it is the only economic system in which the individual is completely free from constraint. In the novel she describes how the construction of a transcontinental railroad not only satisfies the need of a ruthless capitalist for wealth and power, but also benefits the nation as a whole. The capitalist who builds the railroad feels no qualms about using any means, including murder, to remove obstacles to his goal.

Rand's later works present the social philosophy of "Objectivism," which she developed in her novels. *For the New Intellectual* (1961) is a collection of the philosophical passages from her four earlier novels, such as the architect's plea for complete freedom of the individual in *The Fountainhead*. Her other volumes include *The Virtue of Selfishness* (1964) and *Capitalism: The Unknown Ideal* (1967), which largely repeat the message of *Atlas Shrugged*. Rand's philosophy emphasizes the necessity of complete freedom for the creative individual, exemplified by the protagonists of her novels, who overcome or ignore the obstacles created by "the state" and the uncomprehending common herd. Like Friedrich Nietzsche's supermen, their will to power and self-satisfaction is their only guide. Rand's hero in *Anthem*, for example, exults, "It is my will that chooses, and the choice of my will is the only edict that I must respect." Law and morality don't matter, and self-aggrandizement is the highest moral value. As Rand put it, "One puts oneself above all and crushes everything in one's way to get the best for oneself." Such people are "beyond good and evil," to use Nietzsche's words.

Rand was far from being a feminist. The men in her novels often act brutally toward their women, who seem to be attracted to men who act that way. Rand's women are there to meet the needs and demands of the men. It seems strange to find that in Rand's individualistic and libertarian philosophy she assigns women the role of homemaker and wife to satisfy the needs of men, much as Adolf Hitler's Third Reich assigned women the same role to meet the needs of the state.

Nevertheless, Rand's ideas were important in the rise of conservative political ideologies in the Cold War era. At the grassroots level they appealed to many young libertarians, and they influenced some important political figures, including Margaret Thatcher and Michael Fraser, conservative prime ministers of England and Australia in the 1980s. In the United States, Alan Greenspan (1926–), a close friend and disciple of Rand's, was chairman of President Richard Nixon's council of Economic Advisors in 1972 and is the current chairman of the Board of Governors of the Federal Reserve System. He wrote three chapters in Rand's *Capitalism: The Unknown Ideal*. George Gilder (born 1939), one of the popularizers of "supply side" economics in the 1980s, listed Rand as one of the shapers of his early views.

* * * * * *

Women made important contributions to the evolving debates over the merits and shortcomings of modern capitalism. They included advocates of revolution like Rosa Luxemburg and radical socialists like Mary Marcy. Some were feminists who fought for women's rights like Mary Wollstonecraft, Millicent Fawcett, and Charlotte Perkins Gilman. Some were hands-on social reformers who worked for a more humane social system, like Jane Addams, Rose Schneiderman, and Frances Perkins. Some, like Ayn Rand, spoke up for fundamentalist, private enterprise capitalism. They were not trained economists or economic theorists, but they were reacting to the world as they saw and experienced it. Together they were representative of the entire gamut of opinion about modern capitalism. Today, the impact that women economists have made upon society and the discipline of economics is a positive one. In positions of government, for example, a first was effected when President Clinton appointed Laura Tyson as chairperson of the Council of Economic Advisors in 1993–95. In the world of research and academics women are appearing in greater numbers. The future looks bright. The world should not be surprised when an entirely new approach to a monumental work like the *Wealth of Nations* is produced by a feminine hand.

TEN

THE KEYNESIAN
REVOLUTION

*John Maynard Keynes
(1883–1946) was the economist
whose macroeconomic theory
reshaped modern economics.*

In 1936 the whole direction and emphasis of modern economics was transformed by the appearance of a single book. Its forbidding title was *The General Theory of Employment, Interest, and Money,* and it was written by the most controversial English economist of the time, John Maynard Keynes (pronounced "canes"). It dealt with crucial problems of employment and unemployment at a time when the world economy was in the grip of the most disastrous and widespread depression it had ever experienced. Although many people had given up hope of ever rebuilding worldwide prosperity and a viable economic system, this book offered a theoretical analysis diagnosing the patient as seriously ill but not beyond hope and prescribing remedies that could restore its health. Keynes and his suggested policies immediately became the center of controversy among professional economists and politicians. Although damned by left-wing radicals and right-wing conservatives alike, Keynesian economics nevertheless swept aside almost all opposition among economists to establish a new orthodoxy within the profession. Together with Smith's *Wealth of Nations* and Marx's *Capital, The General Theory of Employment* stands as one of three key books in the development of economics.

John Maynard Keynes

The man responsible for this revolution in social thought occupied a unique position in English public life. A member of the social and intellectual elite that had come to dominate public affairs in England, his unorthodox criticism of accepted economic policies seemed to fly in the face of all that the reigning leaders believed. Keynes was a critic of the Establishment from within the Establishment itself.

Keynes was born in 1883 in Cambridge, England, the son of a prominent economist and logician, John Neville Keynes. He was educated at Eton and Cambridge, where he studied philosophy and economics. A favorite and brilliant pupil of Alfred Marshall, he absorbed the essentials of neoclassical economics and always accepted its analysis of production and distribution. His special field was monetary economics. He worked with the government on problems of Indian finance, and at the Treasury, in addition to lecturing at Cambridge. During the years before World War I, he became a member of the Bloomsbury set of artists and writers, which included such intellectuals as Lytton Strachey, E. M. Forster, Virginia Woolf, and Roger Fry. Typical of this group's attitude were Strachey's biographies debunking leading figures of the era in his *Eminent Victorians*—brilliant and critical but generally accepting the sense and order of the existing social system. This attitude was also typical of Keynes. Himself a product of a comfortable social class that considered itself born to rule because of its intelligence, training, and dedication, he nevertheless sought always to achieve better ways of doing things within the framework of the old verities. By all accounts, Keynes was a brilliant snob with a most engaging personality, but he also had an analytical mind that could immediately probe to the essentials of a problem, perceiving its broader ramifications as well as its connections with other issues. If there had to be an intellectual elite, it was fortunate that a man like Keynes was part of it.

Keynes worked at the Treasury during World War I, making quite a name for himself as a financial expert, and in 1919 he was the Treasury's chief representative at the Versailles peace conference. With an intuitive understanding of world politics and a detailed knowledge of international finance, he knew that a stable peace depended on a magnanimous settlement and a realistic reparations burden for Germany. While statesmen argued over boundaries, frontiers, and national prestige, Keynes realized that the economic problems of Europe were more important than the political. When the adopted peace treaty demanded huge reparations and ignored economic realities, Keynes resigned and returned home to write a slashing attack on the peace settlement and the men who developed it. In one of the most prophetic works of the age, *The Economic Consequences of the Peace*, he forecast the breakdown of the agreements and much of the economic turmoil that would follow. The book was a sensation, but it largely destroyed Keynes's official contacts with government for a decade.

Keynes went back to lecturing at Cambridge, became an executive of two insurance companies and several investment firms, speculated heavily in foreign exchange, stocks, and commodities to amass a substantial fortune, became active in the Liberal party, wrote extensively in *The Nation* and other journals, patronized art, music, and ballet, and married Lydia Lopokova, one of the great dancers of the Diaghilev Ballet. He lost his wealth in the stock market crash of 1929, borrowed to start over again, and made another fortune in the 1930s.

Keynes was critical of British economic policy, particularly the unwise effort to return to the gold standard in the mid-1920s—from this controversy would come his most important contribution to economics. Keynes attacked the policy primarily on the ground that its goal of achieving international economic stability was incorrect, that internal economic welfare was far more important. Stable prices and high levels of employment were more desirable than stability in the value of the pound on the foreign exchanges, he argued, pointing out that a return to the gold standard at the prewar exchange rate would seriously diminish British exports and cause domestic wages, prices, employment, and output to fall, just as they had a hundred years before, at the close of the Napoleonic wars, because of similar policies. Thus, in *A Tract on Monetary Reform* (1923), Keynes advocated a managed monetary system in place of the automatism of the gold standard. But fiscal fundamentalism proved too strong: England went back to the gold standard, and disaster struck—unemployment, falling prices, and a nationwide general strike. Economic stagnation prevailed in England throughout the rest of the twenties, once again fulfilling Keynes's prophecy.

One reason few listened to Keynes in 1923 and 1924 was that he had not developed a successful theoretical defense of his position. In order to demonstrate the deflationary effects of the government's monetary policy, he would have had to analyze the interconnections between the gold standard and the domestic level of employment, and to prove that the orthodox economic analysis of those relationships, which applied Say's Law of Markets, was wrong. He was unable to do so at the time, but his keen mind saw that a thorough revision of the theory of employment and its relationship to monetary theory had to be developed. Keynes devoted the next twelve years to that task.

His next effort, a two-volume *Treatise On Money*, published in 1930 just after the stock market crash, did not do the job. In many ways Keynes's most scholarly book, it presented the basic framework of his new theory but left enough theoretical points unresolved to arouse more professional criticism than acceptance. Nevertheless, his point of view was important. The main argument of the book rested on the distinction between investment and savings and the different goals that motivated them. Say's Law insisted that the two had to be equal, but Keynes argued that they need not be. When savings exceeded investment, economic activity would decline; if the opposite were true, economic activity would increase. The remedies were those that Keynes had previously recommended—a managed monetary system to help maintain equality between savings and investment and hence to promote economic stability, supplemented by public works expenditures to mitigate the effects of whatever depression and unemployment might occur.

At the time the *Treatise* was published, economists as well as government officials were unaware of the seriousness of the depression, public opinion did not yet recognize the need for drastic remedies, and most people expected the market contraction to be brief. Keynes did not share these views but returned to his writing to attempt another frontal attack on the accepted economic ideas.

The Climate of Opinion in the Mid-1930s

The product of this phase of Keynes's labor was *The General Theory of Employment, Interest, and Money.* This book made an immediate sensation, not because it proposed a theory radically different from that in the *Treatise,* but because, by the time of its publication in 1936, a path had been prepared for it. First, Keynes's previous publications had familiarized economists and policymakers with his general point of view. Second, several other important economists had also broken through the orthodoxy of Say's Law of Markets to arrive at related conclusions. And third, the climate of opinion had shifted, particularly during the early years of the Great Depression, toward greater acceptance of ideas that tied the level of prosperity to total spending.

One vitally important element of the later Keynesian analysis was developed by a Russian economist with strong Marxist leanings, Michel Tugan-Baranowsky (1865–1919), who argued that a regular flow of savings comes into capital markets from consumers with relatively fixed incomes; that the investment process is, by contrast, highly volatile; and that the resultant disparities between the flow of savings and the flow of investment are at the root of the business cycle. These disparities could not be overcome by changes in the rate of interest, he declared, because many people who saved were motivated by reasons other than the rate of return they earned.

A more important breakthrough was made by an eccentric Swedish economist, Knut Wicksell (1851–1926), who once spent a term in jail for violating a law that prohibited public advocacy of birth control and planned parenthood. Nevertheless, Wicksell was a brilliant scholar whose work made it possible for the next generation of Swedish economists and for Keynes to develop the contemporary theory of national income.

According to the orthodox theory of full employment embodied in Say's Law of Markets, any money saved would find its way to investment through the money markets. If there was a tendency for savings to exceed investments, a decline in the rate of interest would quickly right matters; if investment were to outrun the supply of savings, the rate of interest would rise and reestablish equality. If this equality of savings and investment occurred at relatively high levels of prices and wages that left some labor unemployed, wages would fall—bringing the price level down with them—until all resources were productively employed.

Wicksell noticed, however, that the actual course of events did not substantiate the theory. On the contrary, in depressions, when loans and investment were at low levels and hoarding of cash was widespread, interest rates were high, and it was almost impossible to borrow. On the other hand, at the peak of a boom when investment was high and cash balances were low, interest rates were also relatively low. This was diametrically opposed to the theory, so Wicksell attempted a reconstruction. He postulated that there was a natural rate of interest consistent with full employment and with equality between savings and investment. However, the market rate of interest could differ from this natural rate for a variety of reasons, and when it did the economy would either expand or contract. The essential point was that the natural equilibrium was brought about not by changes in the rate of interest but by changes in the *level of economic activity*—that is, by increases or decreases in output and employment.

This was the great reformulation that ultimately led to the Keynesian revolution. Wicksell's concept of natural and market rates of interest was soon dropped, even by his brilliant followers among the Swedish economists, who included Gunnar Myrdal, Bertil Ohlin, and Dag Hammarskjöld, later a secretary general of the United Nations. But his fundamental concept of changes in the level of total spending as the equilibrating mechanism of the economy was retained and built into the economics of national income as we know it today.

Closer to Keynes than Wicksell was D. H. Robertson, one of Keynes's younger colleagues at Cambridge. In 1926 Robertson published a short book on the business cycle that stressed the importance of the relationship between savings and the demand for capital goods. The banks had a dual function, he pointed out: to provide the proper amount of working capital for business and to provide an amount of cash to the public consistent with the existing price level. The equilibrium was a precarious one, he argued, and the economy's efforts to achieve it resulted in the fluctuations of the business cycle. Here again was an analysis that emphasized the kind of variables with which Keynes was working and which familiarized economists with related ideas.

These theoretical inquiries were supplemented during the 1920s by statistical studies of national income, spending, saving, and investment that contributed significantly to the later development of Keynesian economics by providing it with a solid empirical foundation. In the United States the studies were carried on largely by the National Bureau of Economic Research under the direction of Simon Kuznets, in England by Arthur Bowley, and in Sweden at the University of Stockholm. Much of the support for these studies came from various foundations supported by the Rockefeller family.

The path for a new economics was prepared by a shifting climate of opinion, as well as by developments in theory and statistics. In the United States in the 1920s, for example, William T. Foster and Waddill Catchings wrote a series of three widely read books that emphasized the need for high levels of consumer spending if production were to continue at a high level. They developed the concept of the circular flow of spending and argued that purchasing power must continually flow from producer to consumer and back to producer in order to sustain prosperity. Profits and savings had to be immediately spent, or the circular flow would be interrupted, output would fall, and large-scale unemployment would occur. The basic argument that consumption must be stimulated to keep pace with production stood in direct opposition to the orthodox precept that production created its own demand.

This view was supplemented by the work of the so-called "monetary cranks," a group of writers who developed all sorts of monetary schemes designed to promote spending as a means of achieving full prosperity. They advocated several types of "funny money," as their detractors called it, such as money backed by reserves of commodities instead of gold, so that its quantity would be based on the level of production, and "stamped money"—stamped with a date—which would gradually lose its value as time went on, a scheme designed to induce people to spend money rapidly. They also advocated a requirement that banks hold reserves equal to their deposits, instead of fractional reserves, to prevent banks from creating money by their lending power and thereby stimulating overexpansion of the economy. These and similar ideas were spread widely during the 1920s by such people as the Nobel prize–winning scientist Frederick Soddy, a persuasive English ex–army officer named Clifford Douglas, the German businessman Silivio Gesell, and even the prestigious Yale University economist Irving Fisher. Most economists laughed at these ideas, although the orthodox emphasis on the supply of and demand for money was partly responsible for them. Nevertheless, these concepts had wide popular appeal. In the United States, for example, the Stable Money Association was formed to publicize Irving Fisher's ideas. Its members included bankers, railroad presidents, and even a former member of the Board of Governors of the Federal Reserve System.

All of these ideas reflected a fundamental change taking place in the economy. After more than a hundred years of economic growth and industrialization, the economic center of gravity was shifting from the investor to the consumer. In the days when industrialization was just beginning, the most important source of economic growth was capital investment in industries that largely supplied other industries—steel, coal, machinery, railroads. The classical economics of Ricardo and his followers had reflected that reality of the economic scene and had built a theory of economic growth largely upon the investment process and the concept that the purpose of saving was investment. But as industrialization proceeded, incomes rose and the spending and saving patterns of consumers became more important. Higher incomes enabled consumers to spend greater sums on durable goods such as houses and home furnishings, automobiles, and electrical equipment. Installment plan methods of financing these purchases were developed. Savings began to flow into insurance policies and mortgage payments. The entire economy was transformed as consumer-oriented industries became the bellwethers of prosperity and economic growth. It was a slow process, which started in the United States in the years before World War I and developed more recently in Western Europe, but it transformed industry, finance, and public policy. In economics, it made the former emphasis on the investment process increasingly obsolete and made the idea of automatic investment of savings (Say's Law) less and less applicable to the real world.

The Great Depression of the 1930s forced many people to recognize the changes and the consequent irrelevance of the old ideas. The very magnitude of the disaster would itself have been enough to evoke a reconsideration: in the major industrial nations more than one out of four workers were out of jobs; the banks of the world closed their doors in a disastrous wave of failures; business firms were bankrupted; farmers lost their land; and the entire economic system appeared to be grinding to a halt as incomes fell and spending declined. The commonsense explanation for the debacle seemed to be a huge decline in spending and the commonsense remedy seemed to be a large increase in spending.

In most industrial countries, including the United States, this commonsense view led to large government expenditures on public works, financed by borrowing, to ease some of the hardships of depression and unemployment. But the policy's justification was humanitarian and pragmatic, not based on economic analysis. Orthodox economic theory continued to call for tightening of the belt until "business confidence" could be restored, protection of the monetary system by fiscal restraint, and restoration of profits by wage reductions. The time was ripe for change.

The General Theory of Employment

Keynes announced the revolution in economic theory in his book's emphatic one-paragraph first chapter:

> I have called this book the *General Theory of Employment, Interest, and Money,* placing the emphasis on the prefix general. The object of such a title is to contrast the character of my arguments and conclusions with those of the classical theory of the subject, upon which I was brought up and which dominates the economic thought, both practical and theoretical, of the governing and academic classes of this generation, as it has for a hundred years past. Moreover, the characteristics of the special case assumed by the classical theory happen not to be those of the economic society in which we actually live, with the result that its teaching is misleading and disastrous if we attempt to apply it to the facts of experience.

The book is an analysis of the causes of unemployment, written for the economic theorist and couched in the most esoteric language of the discipline. Indeed, Keynes created a new vocabulary within which the factors causing unemployment could be analyzed: the propensity to consume, the inducement to invest, the marginal efficiency of capital, liquidity preference, and the multiplier. Together with the money supply, these variables determined the level of output and employment and had a major influence on the level of prices. Behind the esoteric terminology, however, lay the same simple principles that had been imperfectly developed in the earlier *Treatise on Money.*

Keynes first reiterated that unless savings were channeled back into the stream of spending, total spending would fall, creating unemployment and stagnation. Then he added something new—the concept of equilibrium at less than full employment. A fall in total spending caused by reduced investment would reduce incomes, which in turn would cause savings to decline until the desire to save was brought into balance with the desire to invest. At that point savings withdrawn from the income stream would be equaled by offsetting investment expenditures, and the decline in total spending would be halted. This "equilibrium" might well be established at a depression level, however, and unless there was a change in the relevant variables, the economy could stagnate indefinitely. Furthermore, the extent of the decline could be estimated fairly accurately by using the "multiplier"—the relationship between any change in consumption or investment and the level of total spending.

These basic relationships were then analyzed further, particularly the factors that determined the inducement to invest. Keynes argued that the amount of investment expenditure depended on the expected rate of return on new investment and the rate of interest. The former was the expected gain and the latter was the cost. If at any time the rate of interest could be lowered, and if there were no changes in business expectations of profit, the amount of new investment would be increased and would, in turn, have a multiplied effect on total spending. For this reason Keynes advocated easy money and low interest rates as one means of reducing unemployment. The rate of interest, in turn, depended on the quantity of money and the desire to hold it in cash or bank accounts. For example, if the desire to hold liquid assets remained unchanged while the quantity of money was increased, the rate of interest would fall, investment spending would rise, there would be a multiplied increase in total spending, and output and employment would increase. Here again, an easy money policy would help reduce unemployment.

Keynes's theory is illustrated on the next page. Employment depends on total spending, the components of which, in the private sector, are consumer spending and business investment. The level of investment spending depends on the rate of interest and the expected rate of return on new investment. For example, if business firms expect to earn 10 percent on new investment and are able to borrow at 8 percent, investment spending will increase until the expected return falls or the rate of interest rises, or both, to bring the two rates into equality. As for the rate of interest, it depends on the desire to hold cash and the quantity of money available. When the amount of money that people or institutions want to hold differs from the amount available, the rate of interest will either rise or fall until the two quantities are the same.

As an example of these relationships, let the central bank expand the reserves of the banking system, which causes banks to increase their loans, thereby increasing the supply of money. With no increase in the desire to hold cash, the increased supply of money will bring interest rates down. A reduced rate of interest will stimulate additional investment (as long as the expected rate of return on new investment does not change). More

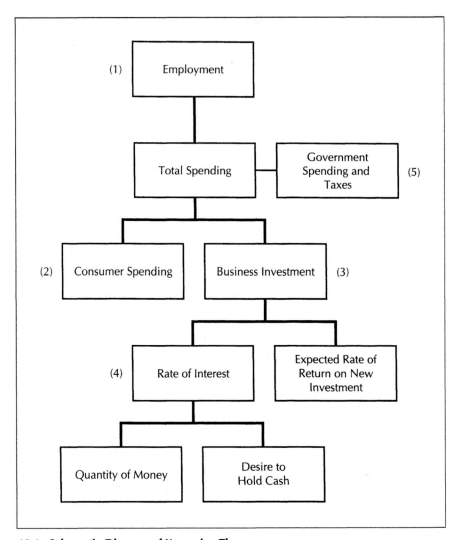

10-1. Schematic Diagram of Keynesian Theory

FUNDAMENTAL RELATIONSHIPS

1. In a private-enterprise economy, employment depends on the total amount spent for consumption and investment.
2. Consumer spending is essentially passive. It moves up or down as incomes rise and fall.
3. Business investment, however, may fluctuate widely in response to (a) changes in rate of interest, and (b) the expected rate of return on new investment.
4. Rates of interest, in turn, depend on (a) the quantity of money, which can be controlled by the monetary authorities, and (b) the desire of people and business firms to hold cash.
5. In addition, an economic stabilization policy may require direct government action to raise or lower total spending through changes in government expenditures or tax receipts.

investment will then increase the national income by a calculated amount, because of the continued respending of the original increase in the circular flow of spending through the economy.

Keynes did not put all of his trust in monetary policy. He felt that the extremely depressed situation of the mid-1930s necessitated a large program of public works financed by borrowing. Such a program would add directly to employment, and the multiplied effect of the increased government spending would expand incomes, spending, and employment still further. Keynes had developed this emphasis on deficit financing in several pamphlets and letters prior to the publication of the *General Theory*—including an open letter to President Roosevelt printed in the *New York Times* in 1933—and it became a major element in the Keynesian prescriptions for ending the depression.

The analysis carried implications for long-range social policy as well as for the immediate problem of ending the depression. Keynes worried about the ability of a mature economy, which generated large amounts of savings annually, to sustain the high levels of investment necessary for maintenance of full employment. Thrift was not always a virtue, and high levels of spending might be more necessary than savings in an advanced, developed economy. So Keynes advocated a more egalitarian distribution of income, including restrictions on unearned income, as a means of achieving better economic health in the long run, since the rich tended to save a larger proportion of their income than did the poor.

The basic ideas expounded in the *General Theory* stood in direct opposition to the old theory that the rate of interest determined equality between savings and investment and that wage reductions would lead to full employment. Orthodox economists argued that wage reductions would lead to higher profits, increased output, and increased employment. Keynes responded that lower wages would bring lower demand for goods, with exactly the opposite effects. In terms of the events of the 1930s and the climate of political opinion, the new theory was far more realistic than the old. Right or wrong, it at least offered some hope that proper policies could cure the ills of the economy, and it laid down the general lines that those policies should follow.

The Meaning of Keynesian Economics

The *General Theory* received a mixed reception. To judge by the reviews in scholarly journals, the older generation of economists missed its significance or did not fully understand its intricate theoretical complexities. But younger economists seized upon it avidly, seeking both to fathom its difficulties and to spread its gospel. In particular, a group of young economists in the United States government used its ideas to justify the already existing policy of public works, deficit spending, and easy money. They were aided by two somewhat older men, Gerhard Colm, a German refugee then in the Bureau of the Budget whose experience in Germany had given him an understanding of the need for expansionary economic policies, and Alvin Hansen, a Harvard professor who became the chief American exponent of the Keynesian point of view. Hansen produced a series of books and articles publicizing the new ideas, while Colm and others worked quietly and anonymously within the government to build effective policies. But conservatives, young and old, reacted with horror against the ideas that seemed to be destroying the verities of hard money, savings, and fiscal restraint: "Keynesian economics" came to be a term of opprobrium in their circles.

Keynes, meanwhile, was *hors de combat*. Illness and a heart attack temporarily retired him within a year after the publication of the *General Theory*, and by the time he recovered, World War II had begun. During the war Keynes acted as an advisor to the British Treasury and helped negotiate major loans from the United States. During the war he helped formulate the Bretton Woods plan for the International Monetary Fund to help stabilize the world economy and avoid some of the pitfalls of the twenties. Knighted for his efforts, he died in 1946 at the age of sixty-two, recognized for what he was, the greatest economist of his time, overshadowed—perhaps—only by Adam Smith among economists of all time.

Keynes had almost single-handedly developed the rationale for the basic economic policies of the second half of the twentieth century in the nations of Western Europe and North America. Keynesian economic policies using *monetary management* and an active *fiscal policy* (that is, government spending and taxing policies) were expected to maintain economic stability and promote economic growth. Yet most economists assumed that with the devil of unemployment exorcised from the body economic, the self-adjusting market mechanism could be relied upon to allocate resources. The benefit-maximizing consumer and the profit-maximizing producer, meeting in the competitive marketplace, would bring about a pattern of production that matched the wants of consumers. By and large, their argument ran, the free economy could be relied upon to allocate resources to the best advantage, assisted by laws to maintain competition and to resolve social conflicts. Although the overall level of economic activity had to be managed by government in the interest of the nation as a whole, the economy nevertheless could be left free to respond to the decisions of individual consumers and producers. The promise of Keynesian economics was that individual freedom and social order were consistent with each other within the framework of prosperity for all. As we shall see, however, the promise was far from reality.

ELEVEN
ECONOMIC
P-LANNING

Joseph Stalin (1879–1953) was the Soviet leader under whom the Soviet system of central planning was developed.

While Keynes was leading the way toward new policies designed to preserve and revitalize the market economy, a new challenge to capitalism was arising. During the 1920s and 1930s socialist leaders in the Soviet Union devised methods of large-scale economic planning that brought rapid rates of economic growth and transformed a backward, rural economy into an industrial giant. The social costs of the program were high, but its basic goals were achieved.

Many Western economists argued at first that a planned economy must fail, but others examined the theory of planning in greater detail—explored its rationale and its operating techniques—and concluded that a workable system was quite feasible. A number of underdeveloped, formerly colonial nations experimented with a range of socialist and quasi-socialist, planned and semiplanned economies. Both theory and practice have shown that economic planning can work effectively to achieve certain types of goals, such as rapid industrial development, massive allocation of resources to military purposes, or exploration of space.

In more recent years, however, serious problems surfaced in economic systems based on central planning through bureaucratic organization and controls. The chief difficulties include inefficient matching of consumer needs with production decisions, prices that do not correspond with production costs, and the development of a new elite of economic bureaucrats and managers. These problems ultimately led to the breakdown of the Soviet and Eastern European economies and to a move in China to a form of "market socialism" that involves a mix of private enterprise and government ownership.

Planning in the Soviet Union

The Soviet Union adopted a system of central economic planning in the 1920s. Immediately after the Russian Revolution (1917–1921), it seemed that the economy of the new Soviet state would gradually grind to a halt. Revolution, counterrevolution, and war destroyed most of the industry that had not been lost to foreign countries as the result of the peace settlement in eastern Europe. The new government was not prepared to manage factories, and the former owners could hardly be expected to operate in a regime dedicated to their elimination. The peasants seized the large agricultural estates and consumed most of the reduced output instead of marketing it to supply the cities. When the government sent soldiers to seize grain, a peasant revolt threatened. And with the old bureaucracy gone, tax collection failed, the government resorted to printing presses to obtain money, and inflation further complicated the economic chaos that developed.

Drastic measures were called for. The government shifted to a "New Economic Policy" that represented a retreat from full nationalization of trade and industry. Light industry and retail trade were returned to private ownership, but the government retained the "commanding heights" of the economy—heavy industry, power, transportation, banking, and much wholesale trade. The economy responded well. Output rose to its prewar levels in most industries by 1928. Reconstruction was rapid, and the government gained valuable experience in planning the nationalized industries. The first great crisis was over.

But new problems were at hand. Russia was still the most backward country in Europe. Its peasant agriculture was primitive by modern standards, much of the population was illiterate, and a large part of its "industrial" production was carried on by handicraft methods. Yet here was a nation faithful to a Marxist ideology that postulated that socialism would naturally evolve in highly industrialized economies in which the industrial working class comprised a majority of the population. Compounding the problem was the fact that world revolution had failed and the fear that the USSR might be attacked at any time by the antagonistic capitalist countries that surrounded it.

V. I. Lenin (1870–1924) had laid down the basic lines on which these problems could be resolved. He had led the Bolshevik revolution to a successful conclusion after convincing his followers that Russia could bypass the capitalist industrial era and move directly from an agricultural, semi-feudal society into the socialist era. The instrument of transition was to be rapid and large-scale industrialization, building the working-class society in which socialism could flourish. The necessary social basis for the transition to an urban, industrial society would be an alliance between workers and peasants (but not the well-to-do peasants, the "kulaks") under a workers' dictatorship. Lenin died before his strategy could be translated into specific policies, and in the late 1920s a great public debate took place among Soviet economists and political leaders over methods of planning and rates of growth. Until it was ended by Stalinist authoritarianism in 1930 with the first of the purge trials, this debate produced some extremely revealing discussions of economic development policy.

One approach (called by Stalin the "right deviation") was advocated by the moderates, led by Nikolai Bukharin (1888–1938), the Communist party's leading Marxist theoretician. He had in 1920 coauthored a famous treatise on economics that announced that the economic laws of capitalism no longer applied to the new Soviet state, which therefore had tremendous freedom to experiment with planning and other policies. By the late 1920s, however, he had shifted his position, arguing that the nation's rate of economic growth was limited by the amount of agricultural surplus that could be produced to feed the cities and to export in exchange for machinery. Industry had to grow, but two of its chief tasks were production of agricultural machinery and production of consumer goods for sale to the peasants as an inducement for them to market their products. Bukharin was concerned about the loyalty of the peasantry to the regime—and well he might have been—and was willing to restrict industrial development to the level made possible by expansion of agricultural production on a voluntary basis. This policy was based on the belief that fundamental economic relationships—such as those between industry and agriculture, heavy industry and consumer goods—determined the rate of economic development, and that it was dangerous for planners to try to expand beyond the pace inherent in those relationships. Bukharin also tied his policies to foreign affairs. World revolution had to be temporarily postponed, he argued, because the first attempt had not succeeded. Moreover, the regime had to build firm support at home to resist the unfriendly capitalist powers. This meant gaining the allegiance of the peasants by not pushing them too hard.

A second approach, opposing that of the moderates, was put forward by the "left wing" of the Communist party, led by Leon Trotsky (1879–1940), Lenin's right-hand man during the revolution. The chief economist of this faction was Evgeni Preobrazhenski, who had been coauthor with Bukharin of the 1920 treatise but who now opposed him. The development strategy proposed by this group was to press the economy to the utmost to attain the maximum possible rate of industrialization at all costs, squeezing living standards in order to free resources for industrial development and using the power of the state to extract the maximum surplus from agriculture for food, raw materials, and export. Agriculture was to be transformed by mechanization and by the formation of large collective farms. The left wing scorned the balanced planning advocated by Bukharin in favor of rapid industrialization, even at the cost of economic dislocation. Like Bukharin, the left also related its policies to the international situation, arguing that the Soviet state could never be secure in a capitalist world; that the Soviet Union could best protect itself by fostering world revolution; and that the best way to foster revolution was to demonstrate the superior productivity of socialism through impressive economic growth, which would also bring the working classes of other nations to Russia's support and further hinder a capitalist attack.

The great industrialization debate clearly involved the gravest of issues for the USSR, and the wily Joseph Stalin (1879–1953) used it as a stepping-stone to full power. He took an intermediate position at first, supporting rapid industrialization and "taut" planning as advocated by the left but siding with the right against collectivization of agriculture, in order to conciliate the peasantry. On the issue of world revolution, he aligned himself with Bukharin and the right, and on the basis of this alliance was able to defeat Trotsky in a contest for power and drive him into exile. Then, in an amazing political turnabout, he suddenly advocated the left's agricultural policy, accelerated the rate of capital accumulation beyond even that faction's expectations, and used the support he thereby gained to purge Bukharin and his followers. The debate was resolved by the establishment of ambitious development goals and a method of economic planning to achieve them, with Stalinist authoritarianism as a major driving force behind the whole system.

Stalin stated the USSR's basic goals in 1928. They included "the final victory of socialism in our country," "an adequate industrial base for defense," and economic growth "to overtake and outstrip the advanced capitalist countries." The goals were essentially political and ideological in nature, although economic means would be used to achieve them. "Maximum capital investment in industry" to achieve a "fast rate of industrial development" was the path to be followed, said Stalin, and this required "a state of tension in our plans."

The planning technique in general was not complicated, although the development of administrative details required much experimentation. The desired expansion of the economy was determined by top government leaders, who selected targets that would press the economy to its limits. A few key industries, such as coal, power, steel, and machinery, were selected as "leading links" and given top priority. The rest of the economy was tied to the target industries by a system of "balanced estimates," which determined the inputs and outputs of all sectors of the economy needed to achieve the goals for the leading links, and through them, for the economy as a whole. Production plans for individual enterprises were calculated on the basis of these industry-wide balances and supplemented by corresponding plans for finance and labor.

The ambitious goals and taut planning required that strong incentives be developed to draw forth the best efforts of the Russian people. Here the Soviet growth strategy ran into difficulty because restrictions on output of consumer goods held back any significant increase in living standards. Any effort to increase production of consumer goods meant that less effort was available for expansion of industry; every ton of steel used for refrigerators meant one less ton of steel for electrical generators; every labor hour spent for construction of housing meant one less labor hour for building a power dam. For a time this problem was avoided by reducing unemployment, drawing women into the labor force, and shifting workers from agriculture to industry. Some incentive was provided by raising wages and salaries periodically, but with production of consumer goods held down, increased wages only drove prices up. Widening the differences between wage rates for jobs of differing skills also helped, but this practice was limited by its inconsistency with the egalitarian principles of socialism and by the fact that it brought lower standards of living to lower-income groups, who could afford to buy only a small share of the limited quantity of consumer goods. "Socialist" incentives were also tried—honors, medals, publicity, and various special benefits awarded to workers who exceeded production norms. But, in the end, the regime was forced to use compulsory methods, however reluctant it may have been to do so. Political goals required political incentives.

This was particularly true in agriculture. The shift from individual farms to collectives in the early 1930s aroused sharp resistance from the peasants and was the major cause of the terrible famine of 1933. The collective farms, however, facilitated agricultural mechanization, substantially increased output, and enabled the regime to apply planning to agriculture and ensure that the entire increase in output went to the state rather than to farmers. Compulsory deliveries of farm products at low prices were instituted, and restrictions were placed on the use of private farm plots. But these measures gave little incentive to individual peasants to improve farming methods, and production stagnated after the initial increase in output.

Compulsory and restrictive measures became necessary for industrial workers as well. Regulations designed to reduce labor mobility were introduced in the late 1930s and, when World War II began, were extended to prohibit a worker from quitting his job without permission from the plant manager. Legal penalties were imposed for tardiness, unexcused absence, consistent failure to fulfill work norms, and other economic "crimes." Perhaps justified under wartime conditions, these negative incentives for labor continued in force until the early 1950s.

The power of the state rather than economic incentives was used to ensure plan fulfillment. The Stalinist system of authority became as much a part of Soviet economic development strategy as the industrialization drive and taut planning. At the same time, of course, concentration camps—the Gulag, or "country within the country"—had appeared as part of the Soviet scene. Although their purposes were more political than economic, they further darkened the already gray picture.

The system couldn't continue indefinitely. After Stalin's death, his successors attempted to gain the support of the people by eliminating much of the repression and by producing more consumer goods to raise living standards. Inevitably, the rate of economic growth slowed down as the hard-driving Stalinist pattern of authority was eased. Agriculture remained stagnant and backward: after an initial increase in farm output in the 1953–1958 period, obtained by opening huge areas of new land in central Asia and by providing greater incentives to the farmers, production levels stopped rising. Moreover, two major crop failures in 1972–1973 and 1975 required large purchases of grain from abroad. Industrial expansion also began to level off, despite administrative reorganizations, greater flexibility for plant managers, improved systems of rewards and incentives, and other efforts to sustain high rates of growth. Major inefficiencies in resource allocation became apparent, and the formerly rapid rate of economic growth first faltered and then ended.

As the rate of growth of the Soviet economy slowed down after the death of Stalin in 1953—Soviet economists call this the "era of stagnation"—deficiencies in the system of planning, which had been glossed over while the economy was growing rapidly, became increasingly obvious. The chief problems were these:

1. Planning emphasized quantity of output and often ignored quality.

2. The mix of output was determined by the planning bureaucracy rather than the desires and wants of consumers. It was "planners' sovereignty" rather than "consumer sovereignty."

3. Costs of production became increasingly out of line with selling prices, as planners sought stability and continuity in the price system rather than economically efficient prices.

4. Inadequate provision was made for the cost of capital, leading to overly capital-intensive methods of production.

5. There was little incentive to apply new technologies, contributing significantly to the slowdown in economic growth.

6. Incentives for plant managers to do more than merely meet prescribed output targets were largely lacking.

7. Similarly, incentives for workers to do more than meet prescribed minimum output norms were meager.

These and other deficiencies in the system of planning resulted in an inadequate supply and poor quality of many consumer goods, high prices for some goods and long lines in stores for others, and considerable grumbling about special privileges for Communist party members and the managerial bureaucracy. This discontent, in turn, led to reduced work effort and job inefficiency, while efforts to allay the discontent by increased production of consumer goods diverted resources from investment and military production, thereby compounding the planners' economic problems.

Despite its inefficiencies, the Stalinist system of economic planning was remarkably successful in achieving its goals. Overall economic growth was rapid between 1928 and 1937, with an average annual increase in gross national product of 8.3 percent. Growth slowed to an annual average of 2.4 percent between 1937 and 1950, showing the effects of World War II, but increased to an annual average of 7.1 percent between 1950 and 1958.* Rapid industrialization was achieved, an urban working class was created, and the nation was transformed into a modern industrial society. Much of this economic growth can be attributed to growth of the work force and development of formerly unused natural resources. Credit the system of central economic planning and administration with bringing these resources into use.

One of the largest development projects centered on Magnitogorsk (translated "magnetic mountain") in the southern Ural mountains on the boundary between Europe and Asia. Magnitogorsk was a mountain of high-grade iron ore that became the basis of a huge complex of enterprises—iron and steel, chemicals, machinery, and transportation equipment. Coal was shipped by rail from the Kuznetsk coal fields in central Asia to the south Urals industrial complex, a distance of some fifteen hundred miles, and iron ore was shipped back to Kuznetsk to supply steel mills there. These industrial areas became the chief base for Soviet arms production during World War II, when much of western Russia, including the Ukraine, was occupied by German armies.

Ironically (pun intended), the high-grade iron ore of Magnitogorsk was largely used up during World War II, lower-grade ore had to be brought in from elsewhere, and the entire south Urals–Kuznetsk industrial complex became a high-cost, subsidized operation by the mid-1960s. Subsidies enabled managements of the plants to continue operating without the modernization that could have cut costs. Failure to invest for modernization and reorganization was an important cause of the Soviet economic collapse.

But reflect for a moment on the events of World War II. The crucial battles of the war, according to military historians, were fought at Stalingrad, Leningrad, and Moscow, where the German armies were stopped in the terrible winter of 1942–1943, and these were followed by an almost continuous series of tank, air, artillery, and infantry battles on the plains of western Russia from July 1943 to August 1944. The German armies lost some five million men in those battles and were driven back to where they had started in June, 1941. Russian casualties were double those of the Germans. The great bulk of the tanks, aircraft, and artillery that made these Soviet campaigns possible came from the south Urals industrial complex based on Magnitogorsk, with some from other Soviet industrial centers and some as military aid from Britain and the United States. The defeat of Germany in World War II was due in large part to the Soviet industrialization push from 1928 to 1939, driven by a system of authoritarian economic planning. The Magnitogorsk–Kuznetsk industrial complex and Stalinist economic planning are both

---

*All estimates of Soviet economic growth are approximations. There are enormous difficulties in the calculations. The estimates given here are the most accurate known to the author. The source is Stanley H. Cohn, *Economic Development in the Soviet Union* (Lexington, Mass.: D.C. Heath & Co., 1969), Chapter 7. Even Cohn's estimates are probably overstated, however, for they were partly based on data published by the U.S. Central Intelligence Agency, which, in retrospect, were remarkably inaccurate.

obsolete today, but we should be thankful for the role they played in World War II.*

Efforts were made during the 1960s to modify the system of central planning. Enterprise managers were given greater flexibility in making decisions, and greater emphasis was placed on profits and losses in evaluating enterprise management. Some small successes were achieved, but the basic problem remained: centralized planning was not working effectively. Driving a relatively backward economy hard from the top may have been necessary to bring modernization and rapid economic growth, but an advanced economy with a more sophisticated technology and an educated urban population required a driving force that stressed individual motivation more and central direction less.

Reforms along these lines were accelerated in the early 1980s with the selection of Mikhail Gorbachev as the new Soviet leader. He represented a younger generation disenchanted with the era of stagnation, and he was supported by military leaders who clearly understood that national power required a strong economic base. A program of economic reforms—"perestroika," or restructuring—was begun in 1985. It involved a large shift from bureaucratic economic controls to greater reliance on individual incentives and market forces; greater freedom for individuals, families, and workers' cooperatives to provide consumer goods and services; wider opportunities for enterprise managers to plan and operate producing units, as well as reduced authority for higher planning authorities; profits rather than assigned production targets as goals; elimination of subsidies for inefficient operations; tying of wages and bonuses to worker productivity and enterprise earnings; and greater participation of workers in selection of supervisors and managers. All of this was designed to make top management accountable for the operation of enterprises and to promote increased efficiency and productivity. Strategic-planning goals continued to be the responsibility of the central government, but implementation of the plans relied more heavily on the management of individual enterprises responding to signals from the marketplace. It was a move away from authoritarian central planning.

Instead of stability, however, Gorbachev's program led to chaos. The Soviet empire broke apart as its constituent elements became independent: the three Baltic countries, Belarus, Ukraine, the trans-Caucasian countries, and the largely Islamic areas of central Asia. All of them had been members of the USSR (Union of Soviet Socialist Republics, or Soviet Union). The Russian SSR became part of the Confederation of Independent States (CIS); it is now usually called Russia.

Internal political upheaval continued in the now truncated Russia. The breakdown of the economy drove Gorbachev from power. He was replaced by Boris Yeltsin, who advocated a rapid transformation from central planning to a market economy and from public to private enterprise. There was

---

*One pundit commented, "Whatever may be said about Stalin, if it weren't for the Soviet industrialization drive we might all be speaking German today."

talk, however naive, of "democratic" Russia, of a peaceful transition from autocracy to popular government, of Russian constitutionalism. A decade later the basic institutions of government are a catastrophe, corruption is the economic norm.

The former managers privatized the enterprises as their own private property. Assets and income flowed into the hands of a few. A massive shift from government ownership to private ownership took place, but it was not a shift to the textbook economics of the west. A predatory capitalism emerged in the Russian sphere. Yeltsin is gone, succeeded by Putin, a career officer in the secret police, who favors order over democracy.

The Theory of Market Socialism

While the Soviet Union in the 1920s and 1930s was forging a system of planning based largely on political goals, economists in other countries debated whether planning as a purely economic system could be efficient. They had limited experience with public ownership and knew little about planned economies. Even the traditional socialist literature had little to say on the topic. Moreover, most orthodox economists were so imbued with the beauties of the theory of the self-adjusting private-enterprise economy that they tended to dismiss economic planning as impractical.

One of the leaders in the attack on planning was Ludwig von Mises (1881–1973), an Austrian neoclassical economist who argued that socialism and planning could not provide a rational basis for economic decision making. Writing in 1920 at the height of the Soviet Union's early difficulties, he pointed out that public ownership of the means of production precluded the establishment of a market for capital. Without such a market there could be no price for capital, no rate of interest to express relative scarcities, and hence no rational basis for determining how much capital should be accumulated and how it should be used. These decisions could be made by planners, he said, but they would not be rational ones that used the resources of the nation efficiently.

Interestingly enough, Mises's arguments had previously been refuted by an Italian economist, Enrico Barone (1859–1924), who showed that accounting prices established by planners could substitute for prices set in competitive markets, at least in theory. However, followers of Mises continued the attack, dismissing Barone's theoretical solution as impractical because it would require literally millions of decisions based on a vast amount of information about consumer preferences, which plainly was not available to any planning board. Even if the information were available, solutions would be obsolete by the time they were calculated—computers were not known in the 1920s, of course.

This argument was answered by two economists who approached the subject from widely different viewpoints. One was a conservative American neoclassicist, Fred M. Taylor (1855–1932), whose presidential address to the

American Economic Association in 1928 demonstrated that Barone's solution could be expeditiously achieved by a trial-and-error process. Consumers could be left free to spend their incomes in any way they liked, according to Taylor, while planners simply established prices that cleared the markets—that is, precluded shortages and gluts—and that equaled costs of production. Production decisions would be determined by the quantities that could be sold at those prices. Once a balance had been achieved, the planners could be reasonably sure that resources were being allocated rationally. Taylor was simply applying the principles of neoclassical economic theory to the planning process.

The second answer was published in 1936–1937 by the socialist Oskar Lange (1904–1965), a Polish economist trained at the University of Chicago who was to become an important participant in Poland's planned economy after World War II. In a much more elaborate analysis than Taylor's, he showed that a planning board could simulate the market process by means of a trial-and-error method of setting prices together with a profit-maximizing rule for decisions by individual plant managers. The result would be maximization of consumer benefits along the lines of the competitive private-enterprise economy. Furthermore, the restrictions of monopoly could be eliminated and full employment ensured by planning the level of investment. Lange and Taylor showed that socialism based on market forces and consumer sovereignty was theoretically feasible. To this the English economist Arthur Pigou added that the private-enterprise economy did not always work well, as attested by the disparity between its description in economic theory and its actual operation. The theoretical argument was won by those who argued in favor of planning, provided that it is based on market forces and not planners' choices.

The critics then shifted ground. Taking their cue from the Soviet Union and the European dictatorships of the 1930s, they argued that planning may be workable in an economic sense but only at the expense of personal and political freedom. The foremost statement of this position was made by Friedrich von Hayek (1899–1992), another Austrian economist, in *The Road to Serfdom* (1944). This influential book argued that once government intervention in the free market begins, it must inevitably lead to socialism, and that socialist planning leads inevitably to loss of freedom. There was no stopping place along the path to oppression, according to Hayek.

Others were quick to answer Hayek. American John Maurice Clark (1884–1963), in *Alternative to Serfdom* (1948), argued that democratic legal and political institutions were quite compatible with government intervention in economic affairs and with public ownership based on market principles. Englishwoman Barbara Ward (1914–1981), in *Planning for Freedom* (1965), argued that market socialism not only was compatible with democratic political institutions but also strengthened them, whereas democracy was threatened in a private-enterprise economy by the political power of big business. Market socialism as it was analyzed by Lange and Taylor, in which planning is oriented toward consumer needs and decisions are made within a framework of democratic political institutions and individual freedom, may well be a feasible alternative to either authoritarian socialism or monopoly capitalism.

Market Socialism in Practice

A modified version of market socialism was put into practice in Yugoslavia, along with worker management of publicly owned enterprises and central planning of economic growth and development. Coming into the orbit of the Soviet Union after World War II, Yugoslavia initially emulated Soviet central planning. But in 1948 the Yugoslav leadership decided that the Soviet style of central planning was part of an authoritarian social system antithetical to the humanist goals of socialism. It set out to build a new system based on worker management of enterprises and decentralized economic power as a third alternative to the state collectivism of the Soviet Union and the private enterprise capitalism of the United States.

Social ownership of the means of production was retained, but management was controlled by workers through workers' councils ranging from fifteen to several hundred members, depending on the size of the enterprise. The councils decided basic issues of management policy, such as prices, hiring of top management, distribution of the income of the enterprise, marketing, hours of work, investment, and similar matters. In large enterprises, where the workers' council was too large for effective decision making, a management board was given the power to make decisions, much as the board of directors of an American corporation acts for the stockholders. In small enterprises the entire work force would meet annually to make these decisions, instead of electing a workers' council. Enterprises employing fewer than six persons could be privately owned, leaving a place in the economy for family enterprises.

Selection of the top management was not left entirely to the workers' councils or the management board. The local government (which often meant the Communist party) and the trade association of the industry were involved in the decision, which had to be approved by the workers' councils. In some of the more economically backward areas, such as Macedonia and Montenegro, the selection of management in the more important enterprises was strongly influenced, if not dominated, by the local or republic governments. In the more economically advanced republics, such as Croatia and Slovenia, selection of enterprise management and policies was left largely, if not wholly, in the hands of the workers' councils. The actual practice varied widely among the six republics and two autonomous areas that made up the nation.

The workers of an enterprise were claimants to the income earned after other payments were made. There was a minimum wage required of all enterprises, and a required wage scale and salary differentials. The enterprise had to meet all costs and pay taxes, make interest payments on its debt, and set aside reserves. Net income above those payments was then shared by the workers through bonuses.

As for agriculture, the Soviet system of collective farms was rejected in favor of privately owned farms limited in size to no more than ten hectares (one hectare = 2.471 acres). In addition there were some cooperative farms and state-owned farms.

The market was the coordinating mechanism of Yugoslav market socialism, just as in the American economy, in contrast to the planned balanced estimates of Soviet central planning. The interplay of demand and supply determined market prices. This differed from the theory of market socialism, as described by Lange and Taylor, where a central planning board would set prices at which demand and supply would be equated. The Yugoslav leadership believed that a system of administered prices was too cumbersome, while market-determined prices could achieve the same results more quickly and with fewer disparities between actual prices and those that equate demand and supply.

Market socialism in Yugoslavia was aided by the fact that domestic producers had to compete with imports, while exports competed in world markets. The largely open economy disciplined domestic producers to remain competitive by keeping costs of production down, developing new products and processes, and exploiting whatever economic advantages they might have. The basic policy was to allow enterprises to set their own prices, competing with both domestic and foreign firms.

Central planning in Yugoslavia focused on the aggregate level of investment and the rate of economic growth. The national government set targets for the rate of economic growth and the investment necessary to achieve it. Investment funds came from consumer savings, the retained earnings of enterprises, and taxes collected by the government. These funds were channeled into the banking system, where enterprises could borrow at interest rates set by the central government. The taxes raised to provide investment funds reduced consumer spending and shifted resources from consumer goods industries to investment. The result of these policies was a high rate of investment and economic growth and relatively low rates of consumption. The central planning of investment was another deviation from the theory of market socialism in which only private savings and retained earnings of enterprises would determine the amount of investment and the rate of economic growth.

Market socialism in Yugoslavia used largely free markets to allocate resources to meet consumer demand. Central planning brought high levels of capital accumulation and strong economic growth. Social ownership and workers' management fostered the egalitarian goals of socialism. Nevertheless, the system had problems: workers' management did not fully eliminate conflict on the labor scene, borrowing on international capital markets brought large international debts, inflation was a problem in a growing economy, and poverty was not fully eliminated. Yet the mixture of market socialism, workers' management, and economic planning worked reasonably well—until the nation fell apart in the 1990s in a vicious civil war based on racial, religious, and national differences.

The concept of worker-owned and managed enterprises developed in other countries besides Yugoslavia. In the United States legislation has made a place for them in the economy, and a number operate in a variety of industries. In Israel the kibbutz is a community in which the members own and operate agricultural and industrial enterprises and share in the net revenues. In Spain over a hundred worker-owned and managed enterprises—the Mondragon group, named after the town where it started in the 1930s—is an important part of the economy in the Basque region of the northern part of the country. These are all examples of market socialism, in which the socially owned enterprises function within a larger market economy. None, of course, are on the scale of the now aborted Yugoslav system.

Market socialism did not work well in China, however. After the Communist party, led by Mao Zedong, achieved power in 1949, the state took over all industrial, commercial, and financial enterprises. The Soviet style of central economic planning and management was adopted, emphasizing rapid growth of heavy industry and capital-intensive techniques of production.

In 1955–1956 Chinese agriculture was organized into communes; that is, most production was done on a collective basis, with farmers receiving work points based on the amount of skill, effort, and time required for their tasks, and with income determined by the number of work points accumulated. Collective output, in turn, was sold to state agencies at fixed prices, although individual families also had private plots, from which output could be sold on free markets. This system was changed drastically during the "Great Leap Forward" of 1958–1959, but by 1962 it reverted to the form that had existed before 1958.

The Chinese leadership was dissatisfied with Soviet-style central decision making almost from the beginning. During the Great Leap Forward central planning was largely abandoned in favor of decentralized decision making by individual enterprises. But no system of coordinating inputs and outputs was substituted, and the economy drifted into chaos. This led to a restoration of economic planning based on targets for inputs and outputs, a materials-allocation system, and prices set by the planners. However, a large portion of the planning was decentralized, taken from the central government and given to the provinces and even to the counties. It was a decentralized version of the Soviet system.

In the late 1970s, after the death of Mao Zedong in 1976, China began to move away from bureaucratic planning toward a form of market socialism. Reform in agriculture came first. The collectivized communes were dissolved in stages from 1979 to 1984: land was allocated to individual farm families in exchange for taxes paid in cash and/or crop deliveries at market prices. Farmers had strong incentives to increase output for sale on the free market, and they responded accordingly. Agricultural output increased more rapidly than the rate of growth of population and the mix of output shifted away from grain and toward other crops more in demand on the free market.

Change in industry came later and more slowly. Instead of allocations, markets for inputs and outputs of state-owned enterprises began to be developed. Markets for capital and urban labor forces were rudimentary, however. Enterprise profits rather than quantity of output became the norm for judging the success of management, with wage structures and bonuses revised to encourage productivity gains and more efficient use of labor. Subsidies for inefficient enterprises were reduced, and beginning in 1985–1986 there was a shift from administratively set prices to market prices. These changes were all in the direction of market socialism, in which socially owned enterprises respond to market prices and market demand rather than to administrative goals.

The Chinese government also loosened controls on individual enterprises and cooperatives, and there has been a significant growth of such enterprises in consumer services and handicraft manufacture. Several areas have been set aside for private enterprise in an effort to promote export industries. Business firms from Hong Kong, Japan, Europe, and the United States are thriving there, along with some privately owned Chinese firms. Economic reform in China is moving toward a mixed economy: largely socialized manufacturing, transportation, communication, finance, and retail distribution, coordinated along market socialist lines; mostly independent farms producing for both state procurement agencies and free markets; and some small private enterprise in retailing and small industry.

The Chinese economy has performed extremely well in the past quarter century. It has sustained an average annual rate of growth of output of about 5 to 6 percent. The growth rate of industrial production is estimated at about 10 percent each year. Population growth has been held to about 2 percent annually, while agricultural production has been growing at an annual rate of about 3 percent. Consumption per person has also been rising at a rate of about 3 percent annually. All of this was achieved despite great political turmoil and several critical changes in the organization of the economy.

Growth in China has been quite uneven, however. Rural areas remain poor and backward, except near the large prosperous cities, and the great bulk of the population remains rural rather than urban. Cities are overcrowded and housing conditions are poor. The expanding and modernizing impetus has come largely from the private, market-oriented sector rather than from the socialized sector, which still produces well over half of the total output. At the 1997 Communist Party Congress the leadership announced that a large part of the public sector would be privatized—that word was not used—by selling stock ownership to the public. Exactly how the transition would be accomplished, how much ownership would be retained by the state, was not announced, nor is it clear how much the leadership of the Communist party is willing to sacrifice control and ideology to obtain greater economic efficiency. As the new century begins, privatization has continued to grow although state-owned enterprises, such as iron and steel mills, still account for much heavy industry.

Planning in the Private-Enterprise Economies

Most of the industrial nations of Western Europe and North America, including the United States, also moved toward a greater degree of economic planning after the debacle of the 1930s. Emphasis was on the level of economic activity, in an effort to maintain prosperity and encourage economic growth. However, planning for those goals led slowly into other areas: management of the conflict between business and labor, the direction of investment into sectors of the economy that governments deemed necessary, and stabilization of international financial relationships. The philosophy was that management of aggregate demand would allow the private sector to make its own decisions about consumption and production, but that ideal came to be modified in practice.

The instruments of economic planning were similar everywhere, including the United States. A national "economic budget" would be drawn up each year. It would show the expected amount of spending by consumers, business, and government. This amount would then be compared with the amount necessary to achieve a desired level of employment or rate of economic growth. Any deficit in expected spending below the desired level could then be made up by government spending or by stimulating private spending through reduced taxes, monetary ease, or subsidies to private industry. Too much spending could be eliminated by manipulating the government budget, taxes, or monetary policy to reduce aggregate demand. It was economic planning on the Keynesian model, which sought to control the level of economic activity while leaving the private sector to allocate resources and satisfy consumer demand.

Most countries found it necessary to supplement national economic budgets by programs designed to channel business investment into relatively backward regions, such as southern Italy or southern France. The West German government fostered expansion of export industries, and so did most of the other countries of Western Europe but with somewhat less success. In the United States, large government spending on armaments stimulated rapid economic growth in the southern and southwestern states. All of the advanced industrial countries also expanded the public provision of services such as education and health, increased their welfare spending, and subsidized housing and transportation. In addition, the energy crisis of the early 1970s and subsequent high costs led nearly all the Western industrial nations, including the United States, to set national goals and to coordinate and encourage output of coal, oil, natural gas, atomic energy, and other sources of energy. Democratic governments did not like to admit that they were trying to manage the production and distribution of goods, but they were doing it anyway.

In the United States, one key area in which the federal government moved toward planning was agriculture, starting in the 1930s. The government's role changed from being the main provider of research and development and the main source of information to assuming the role of coordinator. Goals for output are not actually set; rather, projections or expectations of output in the various foodstuffs are indicated, and farmers are encouraged to base their plantings on the government's forecasts. This "indicative planning" of agricultural production is supplemented by acreage controls and price supports designed to stabilize the earnings of farmers. Most of these measures were eliminated recently, leaving farmers at the mercy of falling agricultural prices, but Congress responded by giving those that remained in business large income subsidies.

Another sensitive area was subject to increased intervention by all the Western governments: labor-management relations. Peaceful settlement of disputes between big business and big labor is essential to the smooth operation of the modern economy. For example, a national strike in trucking can bring the American economy to a standstill within a week. In addition, rapidly rising labor costs can seriously damage industries heavily dependent on export sales; this is especially true in Japan and the Western European countries, where prosperity is far more dependent on exports than in the United States. So these countries quickly moved to hold wage agreements within limits imposed by foreign competition. In the Scandinavian countries the unions and employers' associations, under the watchful eye of government, disciplined themselves. Even the United States government began to move into this area of economic planning in the 1960s and 1970s.

A new pattern began to emerge in virtually all of the industrial countries of the West. Government budgets were used to promote high levels of output and employment. Tax systems were used to promote investment and channel it into particular sectors of the economy. Monetary policy sought to stabilize prices. Particularly in Europe, governments intervened to diminish conflict between labor and management. Special programs were devised to promote development in backward areas or to ease the impact of declining industries. This was not authoritarian planning on the Soviet model nor was it market socialism. But it did involve the setting of economic goals and planning how to achieve them.

TWELVE

WORLD WAR II AND THE COLD WAR

John von Neumann (1903–1957) was one of the originators of the mathematical theory of games.

The American economy during the Second World War provided a laboratory experiment for the allocation of scarce resources to competing uses. Resources were directed from peacetime to wartime production—from butter to guns, so to speak. The problem included the financing of wartime spending and control of inflation. Then, after the war ended, the Cold War between the United States and the Soviet Union became not only a contest for world hegemony, but also a battle of ideologies and social philosophies.

The Wartime Economy

After the Japanese assault on Pearl Harbor on December 7, 1941, the United States mobilized for war. The strategy involved a large investment to expand military industries, along with shifting of resources from consumer goods production to producing and equipping armies, navies, and weapons. This involved huge increases in government spending and its financing, the organization and management of a wartime economy, and control of inflation.

There was considerable slack in the economy at the close of 1941. The economy had not yet fully recovered from the Great Depression of the 1930s. In 1940 the unemployment rate was still 14.6 percent of the work force, and in 1941, when rearmament had begun after the fall of France, it remained at 9.9 percent. Industrial production was well below capacity. The slack was eliminated quickly, however, as the economy moved to war production and production capacity expanded rapidly. By the end of 1942 the production of aircraft and ships was poised for an explosive expansion, and production of automobiles for civilian use was halted. Women moved into the labor market in large numbers, and the unemployed found jobs. The unemployment rate was down to 4.7 percent in 1942 and 1.9 percent in 1943. Capacity for military production increased by over fifteen times between 1940 and 1943. Factories added second and third shifts, and workers worked overtime— with a 50 percent wage premium for work beyond the basic forty-hour work week. The average work week in durable goods manufacturing rose from thirty-eight hours in 1940 to forty-seven hours in 1943. Business firms were given large incentives in the form of "cost-plus" contracts that guaranteed a profit if output targets were met and bonuses if targets were exceeded. Meanwhile, down on the farm, crop surpluses vanished along with the depressed farm prices of the 1930s, output increased as idle land was brought into production, and surplus labor was diverted to the armed forces and factory production. Despite food rationing, Americans as a whole ate better during the war than ever before.

There was enough slack in the economy when the United States entered the war for production of civilian goods to increase simultaneously with military production. Incomes rose, triggering increased demand for consumer goods, which was met by increased output. Between 1940 and 1942, for example, employment in consumer goods industries rose by 10 percent. Some of the increase in production of consumer goods went to the armed forces—clothing, for example—but serious shortages on the home front did not appear until later in the war.

Management of the war effort centered in the War Production Board (WPB) established in January 1942, just six weeks after Pearl Harbor. It organized production for the war in cooperation with the War and Navy Departments and had wide powers to control use of scarce materials and civilian production. The basic method of control was contracts with individual business firms, a method well known in the marketplace and within a highly developed body of contract law. Firms with "primary" contracts subcontracted production of parts and other inputs with "secondary" firms, thereby bringing the great bulk of business firms into the production pipeline. Use of contracts guaranteed central control while funding production in a manner well known to private enterprise. The threat of sanctions was always present, however: a firm that sought higher prices or diverted output from the planned uses would discover its allocation of scarce materials would be cut or canceled; a union that sought higher wages than the wage guidelines could find its members drafted into the armed forces.

Prices of civilian goods were controlled by the Office of Price Administration (OPA). In addition to controlling prices, OPA was empowered to ration scarce commodities (sugar, gasoline, shoes, meat), and in some areas it froze rents. Violations of price control by wholesalers and retailers were treated lightly, particularly in the courts, but the system was quite successful nonetheless. Inflation was held in check: consumer prices in 1945 were only 33 percent above the 1940 level.

The United States never developed a comprehensive program to move men and women into war jobs, but the lure of high pay was sufficient. Compulsion was used to meet the needs of the armed forces, however. The Selective Service System required all men aged eighteen to forty-five to register for military service, and during the war years some 10 million were conscripted. Selection was carried out by local draft boards, which proved reluctant to draft men under nineteen or to take fathers; if drafted they were seldom sent to combat units. Women were not drafted, but they could volunteer to serve in a variety of noncombat positions.

The war effort was financed chiefly through government borrowing and tax revenues. From 1942 through 1945 the federal government spent $350 billion ($318 billion for direct war purposes) but took in only $145 billion in taxes. The remainder came from sale of bonds, including an amazing $157 billion of war bonds sold to the general public, which greatly eased the problem of inflation. The remaining $45 billion was absorbed by financial institutions. As for taxes, corporate taxes were raised in an effort to keep profits down to an average of 10 percent, which was only slightly above the level of the late 1930s. By 1943 revenue from corporate taxes was more than six times as large as in 1940. Revenue from the personal income tax increased as well, partly because more people were earning more and partly because of changes in the law. Prior to 1940 only the more affluent 10 percent paid income taxes. By 1945 over 90 percent of all families and individuals paid, and at substantially higher rates than in 1940. Revenues from the personal income tax grew sixfold in the five years from 1941 to 1945.

Despite its success in producing huge amounts of military goods, there was a great deal of confusion and inefficiency in the war effort. After the war the War Records Section of the Bureau of the Budget pointed out that building merchant ships took steel from the Navy, and plants changed to war production when their former product was needed more. Locomotive plants produced tanks, leading to a shortage of rail locomotives. Truck plants shifted to aircraft, leading to shortages of trucks later on. There was a great deal of waste, but this waste stimulated efforts to plan more effectively, which would have an important impact on the discipline of economics after the war.

Economists learned a lot from the wartime experience. Perhaps the most important point was that the economy could be brought to full employment and more rapid economic growth through government spending. Government spending during the 1930s had been too small to break the grip of the Great Depression. But massive wartime spending provided a stimulus that brought both full employment and full use of the capacity to produce, as well as increased investment and an enlarged capacity to produce. For example, in 1940 the nation's steel mills produced 67 million tons while operating at 82 percent capacity. By 1944, after considerable new investment, the industry produced 87 million tons, a 30 percent increase, and was operating at very close to full capacity. The economy as a whole had a greatly expanded capacity to produce when the war ended.

Wartime spending was excessive, however, with respect to prices. Prices rose by about one-third during the war, as incomes rose while consumer goods available for sale were held in check. Rationing and price controls helped hold the line, but probably the strongest brake on prices were the war bond drives that absorbed over $150 billion of the excess purchasing power. In addition, some sectors of the economy were left unregulated, particularly entertainment, gambling, and a variety of illegal activities. Despite the wartime inflation, however, economists could argue that if higher consumer incomes had been allowed to stimulate greater production of consumer goods, there might well have been no inflation of prices at all. Military spending was potentially inflationary because it created incomes but not goods to buy with the income.

There was another, more sobering, lesson to be learned from the wartime economy. During the 1930s there was strong opposition to government spending, particularly deficit spending financed by borrowing. Political opposition came from a large segment of the business and financial community and from conservatives in Congress. That opposition disappeared during the war, however, partly because the war effort was the first priority and partly because of the profits to be made from cost-plus pricing in the military contract system. The lesson learned during the war was that military spending could gain needed political support, but as the 1930s showed, not much else would. This lesson was to play an important role in postwar economic policy, leading to what is now called the Military Keynesianism of the Kennedy-Johnson and Reagan administrations.

World War II also fostered an important trend in economic theory that took on increased momentum after the war: the use of mathematical models to plan optimal use of resources. The innovation was called "activity analysis" or, in a simplified version, "linear programming." The basic idea was drawn from neoclassical economics. If you have a variety of goals, limited resources, and existing technologies or processes to use, optimal results will be obtained when the gains at the margin for each goal are equalized, or conversely, if costs at the margin are minimized. This was a basic problem in wartime production when quantities of aircraft, tanks, guns, ammunition, and other supplies had to be produced and the quantities of any one had to be coordinated with all the others. For example, you don't want to produce guns and not enough ammunition for them. Resources used to produce too many guns means fewer resources to produce enough ammunition to use the guns most efficiently, and vice versa. Balance of benefits at the margin is necessary.

Activity Analysis

Tjalling C. Koopmans (1910–1985), a Dutch-born economist and statistician who came to the United States in 1940, worked out a general solution to this problem in resource allocation in 1942 while working at the Combined Shipping Adjustment Board, a joint American and British effort to use the allied merchant shipping fleets most efficiently. Koopmans devised a system of mathematical analysis that could be applied to other economic activities as well—hence the name "activity analysis" (sometimes "operations research" or "linear programming").

Suppose the activity of a ship moving a given distance in a given time could be described in a mathematical equation. It would then be possible to determine maximum and minimum values for the distance traveled by inserting a variety of constraints such as fuel availability, various speeds, feasibility and safety of routes, skills and size of the crew, weather, and other constraints. A wide variety of useful approximations to real-life situations could be obtained. Koopmans realized that this method could be used in solving many real-world problems, and that proved to be true.

Koopmans was not the first to develop the methodology of mathematical activity analysis. Leonid Kantorovich (1912–1986), a Russian economist working with Soviet planning agencies, published a paper on "Mathematical Methods of Organizing and Planning Production" in 1939, which was quite similar to Koopmans's work, but it was Koopmans who developed the general solution. The two were joint recipients of the Nobel Memorial Prize in Economic Science in 1975.

Input-Output Analysis

During the Cold War several other advances in mathematical economics were developed that were useful in planning the allocation of resources to military uses and national defense. Input-output analysis was one. It is based on the idea that an economy is composed of interdependent sectors in which the production of one sector is an input into other sectors, and vice versa. The various inputs and outputs can be measured, and the system as a whole can be pictured in a checkerboard fashion of rows and columns that show the outputs and inputs.

Table 12.1 is a highly simplified version of an input-output table using only three sectors that produce wheat (agriculture), cloth (manufacturing), and labor (households). The horizontal rows show output, and the vertical columns show input. Row 1 tells us, for example, that out of 100 bushels of wheat, 25 bushels are used in growing the wheat, 20 are used in manufacturing, and 55 are consumed. Column 1 tells us that producing 100 bushels of wheat requires 14 yards of cloth and 80 work years as well as 25 bushels of wheat for seed.

Now, invert the table mathematically. (Don't ask: it's a procedure in linear algebra.) This produces a "structural matrix" of ratios, or proportions—called "input coefficients"—that relate each square of the input-output table to every other square. The military planner is then able to determine where the inputs would come from if production of aircraft, for example, were

Table 12.1
Input–Output

	Agriculture	Manufacturing	Households	Total
Agriculture	25	20	55	100 Bushels
Manufacturing	14	6	30	50 Yards of Cloth
Households	80	180	0	160 Work Years

doubled, as well as how much every other product of the economy would be affected, including other military products.

Input-output analysis was invented by a Russian-born American economist, Wasily Leontief (1906–). He studied at universities in Leningrad and Berlin, worked at Kiel, Germany, as a research economist, and served as an adviser to the Chinese Ministry of Railways in Nanking in 1931, before coming to the United States in that year. He joined the faculty at Harvard University and began working on what was to become input-output analysis. In 1941 he published *The Structure of the American Economy,* which contained actual input-output tables for the entire American economy for the years 1919 and 1929, a corresponding structural matrix, and estimates for 1937 and 1939 based on the matrix. It took almost ten years to develop the final product.

Computers available in 1940 were not capable of making effective use of input-output models. But as faster computers with much larger data-storage capacities were developed, the use of input-output models expanded. The U.S. Bureau of Labor Statistics used Leontief's model of the 1939 American economy to predict postwar production and employment levels. Leontief established the Harvard Economic Research Project for applied use of input-output analysis, research on the method itself, and training of young economists. The U.S. Air Force built an input-output model to use in designing new aircraft and training pilots. In England, Richard Stone of the Department of Applied Economics at Cambridge University used input-output tables to calculate national accounts for the United Nations.

It takes years to prepare an input-output table. An 82-sector table for 1958, prepared by the U.S. Department of Commerce, was not published until 1965. Tables with 360 to 450 sectors have been prepared for 1963, 1967, and 1972, each with a lag of six or seven years to publication. Time lag is a problem: production technologies change, new materials are developed, and the organization of production changes. A ten-year-old input-output model is an imperfect replica of today's production relationships. Nevertheless, by the 1960s input-output models were being used extensively by the Department of Defense to provide workable approximations in helping plan production and supply for the armed forces of the United States. The Nobel Memorial Prize in Economic Science was awarded to Wasily Leontief in 1973 and to Richard Stone in 1984.

Game Theory

John (Janci) von Neumann (1903–1957), a Hungarian-born mathematician, began the development of modern mathematical game theory with a 1928 paper, "On the Theory of Games of Strategy," published in a German mathematics journal. Von Neumann took up the problem of decision making in situations involving two or more players—a poker game, for example—in which any one player's strategy depended partly on chance and partly on the decisions made by others. He argued that almost any event in daily life could be viewed as a game of strategy, including economic decisions of individuals, business firms, and governments. The paper was almost totally ignored by American economists, few of whom read German.

Von Neumann came to the United States in 1930 as a professor at Princeton University. In 1933 he joined the Institute for Advanced Study in Princeton as a permanent member, joining Albert Einstein and Kurt Gödel, the German-born mathematician whom we met earlier in our discussion of mathematical logic. There von Neumann met Oscar Morgenstern (1902–1977), an Austrian-born economist who came to Princeton in 1938. While still in Austria Morgenstern had published a paper on problems in the theory of perfect competition. A mathematician friend pointed out that the problems raised by Morgenstern were similar to those discussed by von Neumann in his 1928 paper, so when Morgenstern got to Princeton, he was eager to meet von Neumann. The two men, one a brilliant mathematician, the other a brilliant economist, began working together. The product was a major treatise, *The Theory of Games and Economic Behavior* (1944), that opened up a wide area for economists to explore: optimum decision theory in situations in which one individual's decision is influenced by decisions made by others. The book dealt chiefly with two-person zero-sum games. Zero-sum games are those in which one player's gain is the other player's loss. The sum of gains plus losses is zero. One conclusion was that a player's best strategy for two-person zero-sum games would minimize the potential losses. The authors were able to prove that this strategy would maximize the potential gains, no matter what strategy the opponent selected. They called it the minimax theorem. This conclusion could be applied to U.S. strategy in the Cold War, which was in essence a zero-sum game. In the 1950s and 1960s U.S. defense strategists used game theory in modeling U.S. alternatives vis-à-vis the Soviet Union in a variety of possible situations.

The more interesting and important part of *The Theory of Games and Economic Behavior* dealt with multiperson, non-zero-sum games. In non-zero-sum games a clearly best single strategy does not emerge. A mixed strategy is better, in which the strategy is changed from time to time so that the opposing party or parties cannot predict the next move. Furthermore, the best mixed strategy is one that is chosen at random from the entire menu of possible strategies. Participants who do not mix their strategies will lose out to those that do, and participants who randomly choose their strategy mix will do the best of all. Another outcome is that more than one player can win in non-zero-sum games, even when there are only two players. With more than two players a variety of combinations and cooperation among the players may be desirable strategies.

Now reflect for a moment on what this means for the economy. Traditional economic theory assumes that the rational individual, seeking to maximize his or her benefits (utility), will make decisions based on the individual's own internal preferences. Given a choice, the individual chooses the action with the largest payoff. Game theory, however, provides a different view of the economy. Because chance plays a part, payoffs can be uncertain—within a given range possibly. And because the decisions made by others can affect one's payoff, one must consider those possibilities in making choices. Choices become dependent on the choices made by others rather than simply being based on one's own preferences. Game theory did not reject the concept of rational choice but made the concept much more realistic and complex.

The Prisoner's Dilemma

The Prisoner's Dilemma illustrates some of the key characteristics of game theory. Two men caught with stolen goods are suspected of burglary, but there is not enough evidence to convict them unless a confession is obtained from one or both. If convicted of burglary they will each get a two-year sentence; if convicted of possession of stolen goods, a lesser crime, they will each get a six-month prison term. If only one confesses he goes free, but the other will get a maximum sentence of five years. The two suspected burglars are kept separate so they can't agree on a story, and each is offered freedom if he confesses and is willing to testify against the other in court. Sounds like a TV show.

The dilemma arises because if one confesses he can have the maximum gain (freedom) if the other does not confess and gets a five-year sentence. If both confess each will get two years. But if neither confesses they can only be convicted of possession of stolen goods, which will mean only six months in jail. It would seem best to keep mum. But if one refuses to confess while the other confesses, he will get the maximum sentence of five years. So what is the best strategy?

The dominating strategy is for each of the suspects to confess to burglary, despite what the other does, for not confessing risks a five-year sentence. A two-year sentence is the worst that a confession could bring. It could also bring freedom, if the other holds out. Indeed, confessing to burglary is the best strategy even if the two suspects were not the burglars but were merely fencing stolen goods. The best strategy is to minimize the maximum sentence.

The Prisoner's Dilemma problem also illustrates the proposition that the outcome can be uncertain. Will one prisoner go free and the other be sentenced to five years, or will both be sentenced to two years? The result will depend in part on chance; both prisoners have to be smart enough and rational enough to make the best choice. This leads to the concept of "limited rationality," in which some participants are better able than others to play the game to their advantage. It's not enough to be "rational." One has to be just as "rational" as everyone else. In economic theory it meant that the concept of economic rationality became more complex and indeterminate than it was before game theory entered the picture.

Game theory had some obvious applications in economics, especially in analyzing the activity of large corporations in industries dominated by a few large firms. Competition tends to disappear in those sectors of the economy, to be replaced by price fixing, market sharing, and price leadership. Game theory proved to be particularly useful in providing a theoretic analysis of those aspects of the modern economy, supplementing the existing empirical studies of those phenomena. Individual cases were provided with a general theoretic framework. Nevertheless, the most important impact on economics was a broader appreciation of such concepts as competition, rational decisions, and utility that lie at the heart of economic theory. Along with it came a much greater concern with chance, uncertainty, and indeterminate outcomes—all of which were highly unsettling to the orthodox mainstream of economic thought. Neither von Neumann nor Morgenstern were awarded the Nobel Memorial Prize in Economic Science.

Macroeconomic Models and Survey Research

Two new research techniques in economics appeared in the post–World War II era. *Macroeconomic models* of the economy were developed as a new tool for economic forecasting. Consisting of hundreds of equations that could be solved simultaneously using the new high-speed computers, these models are used for economic forecasting by both governments and the private sector, predicting such economic variables as total output, consumer spending, changes in the general price level, employment and unemployment, output of major industries, exports and imports, flows of capital—indeed, any variable for which the model has an equation.

Macroeconomic models were originally based on Keynesian theory. They include equations such as $Y = C + S$ (national income equals consumption spending plus savings) and identities such as $S = I$ (savings equal investment). Other equations and identities define the component parts of these simple relationships until a highly complex, multiple-equation model is produced. The theoretic model is then tested and revised using actual economic data, until reliable forecasts are obtained.

Early steps toward development of macroeconomic models were taken by Jan Tinbergen (born 1903), a Dutch economist whose two-volume *Statistical Testing of Business Cycle Theories* (1939) used a system of equations based on data from the American economy for the years 1919–1932 to evaluate theories of business cycles. Laurence Klein (1920–   ) began to experiment with multi-equation econometric models in the late 1940s. Under his direction, the Research Seminar in Quantitative Economics at the University of Michigan produced the first economic forecast from such a model in 1953.

The Michigan model was initially quite simple, with just sixteen equations and four identities, using data for the period 1929–1952, leaving out the war years of 1942–1945. Since then the model has grown to 291 equations and identities. The latest available data are used to make both quarterly and annual forecasts, and the entire model is updated ("reestimated," to use the econometrician's lingo) every five years. The Michigan model, and the economists who use it, produce some of the most accurate of the multitude of economic forecasts that are made every year.

Klein left Michigan in 1954, a victim of the McCarthy era witch-hunts during the Cold War. He continued his work on macroeconomic models soon after at the University of Pennsylvania, where he and his assistants developed an even larger model than the one at Michigan. Klein received the Nobel Award in Economic Science in 1980.

The success of the Michigan model stimulated the development of other large-scale macroeconomic models in the 1960s and 1970s. One model at the Brookings Institution in Washington, D.C., had almost 400 equations but didn't work well and was abandoned in 1972. Models were built not only in the United States, but in many other countries throughout the world, in advanced industrial nations, developing countries, and centrally planned economies, and for systems of world trade. By 1990 there were eleven such models in the United States alone. Macroeconomic models have become important tools in the planning of both government policies and business decisions.

Survey research was the second economic research instrument developed in the years immediately following World War II. An interesting problem arose in 1944 and 1945 when it became clear that Germany and Japan would be defeated. Economists in Washington were worried that consumers would cash in their war bonds as soon as the war ended, spend the money, and set off a rapid inflation before the economy could convert to peacetime production. A Division of Program Surveys was established in the Department of Agriculture to find out. A psychologist, George Katona (1901–1981) was brought in to run the project.

Katona was born in Budapest, Hungary. He was a student at the University of Budapest when the communists seized power and closed the university briefly in 1919. Fleeing to Germany, he continued his studies in psychology, taught, worked in a bank, and wrote for a Berlin newspaper. When the Nazis suppressed the newspaper in 1933 Katona came to the United States and became a citizen. A bout of tuberculosis ended a budding career as an investment advisor, and he turned back to psychology. A pathbreaking book, *Organizing and Memorizing* (1940) showed that organizing material in patterns (gestalts) made it easier to remember and to apply the material to new situations. Another book, *War Without Inflation: The Psychological Approach to Problems of a War Economy* (1942), emphasized the role of consumer behavior in the economy and brought him to the attention of government officials.

Katona and his associates asked a random sample of several thousand consumers representative of the population as a whole about their expectations and their spending plans. Statistical probability analysis was used to evaluate the results. The researchers found that most consumers intended to keep their bonds as a reserve in the event that peace brought lower earnings or unemployment.

Katona went on to almost single-handedly develop survey research as an important tool of empirical research in economics and the other social science disciplines. Today survey research is carried on all over the world by universities, research institutes, governments, and private enterprises.

After the war Katona took his entire survey research group from the Department of Agriculture to the University of Michigan where in 1946 he established a Survey Research Center as part of the University's Institute for Social Research. There he and his colleagues, economist James Morgan and John Lansing, statistician Leslie Kish, and others, continued to develop the theory and practice of survey research, building up a huge bank of data on household income, savings, and expenditures. One of their innovations was the use of "longitudinal" surveys that follow cohorts of households over long periods of time to determine how they are affected by changes in the larger economy. The center continues today as an important source of empirical data for applied research in economics and the other social science disciplines. One of its most important findings is that consumer decisions are based not only on price and income but more importantly on their expectations and their understanding of the larger condition of the economy. Despite fads and changing fashions, consumers are highly rational in managing their affairs in the changing and sometimes chaotic modern world.

The Cold War

Following World War II the United States and the Soviet Union struggled against each other for world hegemony, one capitalist, the other communist. It was a political, diplomatic, economic, and ideological conflict. In a sense it was Adam Smith versus Karl Marx, as well as democracy versus dictatorship.

We can only sketch the chief developments. Western Europe was in the orbit of the United States, helped by the U.S.-sponsored Economic Recovery Program (Marshall Plan, 1947), and with its defense bolstered by the North Atlantic Treaty Organization (NATO, 1949). Eastern Europe, dominated by the Soviet Union, began to recover economically under programs of economic planning, while NATO was countered in 1955 by the Warsaw Treaty Organization, a military alliance of the then USSR and the Soviet-dominated countries of eastern Europe. Germany was divided into the West, allied with NATO, and the communist East Berlin was occupied by American, French, and British troops on one side and Russian on the other. In 1948 the Russians began a blockade of Berlin, trying to drive out the allies, but a massive airlift checkmated that ploy. Then the East German government built the Berlin Wall to halt desertions from East to West. In Asia, Japan became an American ally after its occupation by American troops ended, while China was taken over in 1949 by Marxist revolutionaries under Mao

Zedong (Mao Tse-tung) who drove the corrupt government of Chiang Kai-shek to Taiwan. China supported insurgent guerrillas in Vietnam, Laos, and Cambodia, while the United States promoted formation of the Southeast Asia Treaty Organization (SEATO, 1954) and provided military aid to its members. The newly emerging nations of Asia and Africa also became the scene of Cold War skirmishes as the United States and the Soviet Union competed for their allegiance with economic and military aid. The Soviet Union gained an ally in communist Cuba, while the United States supported several right-wing military dictatorships in Latin America. Some nations, such as India and Yugoslavia, tried to remain neutral. Meanwhile, the intelligence organizations of the United States and the Soviet Union, CIA and KGB, waged a clandestine war of propaganda, espionage, and subversion.

The Cold War turned hot in Asia. Korea had been divided into two independent nations in 1948 by agreement between the United States and the Soviet Union. But invasion of South Korea by North Korea brought U.S. intervention (technically, by the United Nations) and later by China on the other side. The Korean War (1950–1953) ended when both China and the United States decided not to fight a major war against each other, and Korea remained divided.

A similar scenario was enacted in Vietnam but with a different outcome. Vietnam was divided between North and South in 1954, ending a communist-dominated revolt in the north that drove out the French. North Vietnam soon began an effort to take over the South, using the guerrilla warfare tactics that had defeated the French and by inciting revolt in the South. The United States intervened in an effort to defeat a communist takeover in the South, but in this case the North Vietnamese prevailed. The Vietnam War (1961–1973) ended with a negotiated settlement that left the communist regime of North Vietnam in control of a united country.

At one point the Soviet Union and the United States seemed to be on the verge of open war. The United States had placed nuclear missiles in Turkey—an obvious threat to the Soviet Union—and was carrying on a campaign to destabilize the communist regime in Cuba. The Soviet Union retaliated in 1962 by placing nuclear missiles in Cuba—an obvious threat to the United States. The United States countered by imposing a naval blockade on Cuba. After intense negotiations Russia backed down and removed its nuclear weapons from Cuba, and the United States lifted its blockade. Shortly afterwards the United States quietly removed its nuclear weapons from Turkey, and the campaign of subversion against Cuba was eased. The two governments decided that compromise was better than nuclear war. It was a very tense time.

Within the United States the Cold War brought a strong attack on radicals and liberals of all types, their ideas, and their social philosophies. In two famous trials the leaders of the American Communist party were tried for treason and jailed (1949), and Julius and Ethel Rosenberg were sentenced to death and executed for atomic bomb espionage (1950). The Hiss Case (1948–1949) in which Whittaker Chambers, a former Communist party courier, named Alger Hiss, a former State Department official, as a member of a prewar communist group in Washington helped propel Richard Nixon into prominence in Republican party circles. Senator Joseph R. McCarthy of Wisconsin charged that over two hundred State Department employees were communists. As head of the Senate Permanent Investigating Committee he conducted a series of hearings on communism in government and other areas of American life (1953–1954). Another Senate committee investigated communism in education. The House Un-American Activities Committee looked into communism in the entertainment field. State legislatures set up similar investigations of un-American activities. In the hysteria, universities and the movie industry were "purged" of "subversives." In 1953 Robert J. Oppenheimer, wartime head of the Los Alamos atomic laboratory that developed the atomic bomb, was suspended as a consultant by the Atomic Energy Commission as an alleged security risk: he opposed development of the hydrogen bomb. The U.S. Civil Service Commission reported that 2,611 security risks had been fired from government jobs in 1953 and 1954 and that 4,315 more had resigned before investigations were completed. It was a time of ideological witch-hunting.

As the Cold War heated up, American policy toward the Soviet Union began to change. The basic policies of "containment" were put in place under President Truman from 1947 to 1950. Western Europe was to rebuild its economy (Marshall Plan, 1947) and would be protected militarily (NATO, 1949). The United States would assist other nations that were "resisting attempted subjugation by armed minorities or by outside pressures" (Truman Doctrine, 1947), while technical assistance, loans, and private investment in underdeveloped areas would nurture political stability there (Point Four program, 1949). A policy of containment would keep "international communism" in check and protect the "free world."

The theoretical basis for the policy of containment was stated in 1947 by George F. Kennan in an article in the magazine *Foreign Affairs*, written by "X" and titled "The Sources of Soviet Conduct." Kennan was then director of the Policy Planning Staff of the State Department and had held several important diplomatic posts in the Soviet Union and Eastern Europe. Kennan wrote of the hostility of the Soviet leadership toward the United States and the capitalist world, their doctrinaire communist ideology, and the secretiveness, duplicity, and antagonism of Soviet policy. In the face of these ideas and conduct the United States policy should be a "long-term, patient but firm and vigilant containment of Russian expansive tendencies," leading to "either the breakup or mellowing of Soviet power" brought on by serious economic and political weaknesses.

The doctrine of containment was soon confronted by events that seemed to be turning the tide in favor of communist expansion. Soviet-style governments were established in Poland, Czechoslovakia, and Hungary in 1947 and 1948. In 1949 the civil war in China ended in a communist victory, and the invasion of South Korea by the North began in 1950.

The United States government then began a comprehensive review of the policy of containment by the National Security Council (NSC), which was established in 1947 to coordinate and plan national defense policies and programs. The result was a secret memorandum, NSC-68, written by Paul Nitze, one of the Truman administration's foreign policy advisors, and Leon Keyserling, chairman of the President's Council of Economic Advisors.

The memorandum was devoted chiefly to U.S.-Soviet relations and took a hard line against what was felt to be a drive for world dominance by the Soviet Union. This threat was to be countered not simply by containment, but by a three-pronged attack designed to strengthen Europe politically, economically, and ideologically; weaken the Soviet Union economically and loosen its hold on its satellites; and strengthen the United States both militarily and economically.

The economic strategy called for by NSC-68 was a large, threefold increase in U.S. military spending, to be maintained as long as necessary to counter the Soviet threat. The immediate effect would be to greatly strengthen U.S. military capabilities. The Soviet Union would have to follow suit, it was argued, but its increase in military capabilities would be much smaller than that of the United States, because the USSR was already devoting a much larger portion of its national product to military production than the United States. Furthermore, the USSR would soon fall behind the United States in military preparedness, because its output capacity was half that of the United States or less. The United States was sure to win the armaments race, because of its greater ability to produce.

The memorandum went on to argue that the internal effects of an arms race would differ in the two countries. In the USSR, increased military spending in an economy already operating at capacity would force diversion of resources away from either investment or consumption, or both. If investment, economic growth would slow down and the ability of the USSR to continue to match the U.S. military effort would be diminished. If consumption, discontent and unrest would increase. Increased military spending would weaken the Soviet Union. At the very least, the ambitious growth targets of the five-year plans would have to be scaled down.

That would not happen in the United States, the memorandum argued, which by the late 1940s was already suffering from recession and slow growth. Increased military spending would raise consumer incomes, which would stimulate business investment, enabling the private sector to move to full employment. Full employment would stimulate more investment and more rapid economic growth. The entire national economy would be strengthened—while the Soviet economy was weakened—by a stepped-up arms race.

One fundamental assumption of NSC-68 was that the American economy normally operates at some level of output well below capacity. Government spending could be used, therefore, to push the economy to capacity and, while doing so, increase the rate of economic growth. But it had to be military spending, because large increases in other forms of government spending were not politically feasible.

Furthermore, while military spending would stimulate expansion of the private sector in the United States, it would not do so in the USSR, where the private sector was insignificant. NSC-68 argued that the United States could have both swords and plowshares, while the Soviet Union could not.

Most economists would argue today that military spending is economically wasteful. It uses resources that could be used for investment, thereby reducing the rate of economic growth. Alternatively, it uses resources that could be used to increase consumption, thereby reducing living standards. According to this line of argument, using resources to produce guns rather than plowshares or butter makes everyone worse off, especially future generations. Military spending may be necessary in a troubled world, but it is economically wasteful.

The authors of NSC-68 did not accept that reasoning. The experience of World War II showed that the American economy had a far greater capacity to produce after the war than at its start. Conversion to peacetime production was a problem, but it was readily solved. When the first postwar recession came in 1947–1948, many economists, with the experience of the Great Depression in their minds, worried that aggregate demand would be insufficient to maintain high levels of economic activity. That worry was clearly on the mind of Leon Keyserling when he helped Paul Nitze write NSC-68. Both investment and consumption would increase as military spending brought the economy closer to full employment, according to the authors of NSC-68.

That argument was shared by many ordinary people, particularly those working at or living near war plants or military installations. Jobs were created, incomes rose, unemployment fell, business expanded, and property values rose. It was hard to believe the economists who claimed that all this was bad. A climate of public opinion developed that had important repercussions on public policy: military spending was good, not only because it protected against the Soviet Union and the spread of communism, but because it benefited the economy. It could also generate votes for candidates for Congress. Economists could argue that the money could be better spent on other things, such as education, for example, but that did not have either the emotional appeal or the demonstrated economic benefits of military spending.

The Cold War also fostered a climate of opinion that presented the private enterprise market economy as the best possible economic system. This politically conservative doctrine exalted individualism and competition, much like the social philosophy of Herbert Spencer and William Graham Summer in the nineteenth century. Economic freedom was associated with political democracy, in opposition to communism and authoritarian government. Progress came when entrepreneurs and risk takers were given a free hand. Any government interference with market forces would lead to slowed economic growth and inefficiency. It was a return to Adam Smith, bowdlerized to eliminate Smith's qualifications and reservations. These ideas—fundamentalist capitalism—had been current among political conservatives for generations, but, like the British reaction to the French Revolution almost two hundred years earlier, it found new life in the climate of opinion of the Cold War.

High theory in economics reflected this climate of opinion. Applying the principles of mathematical logic to the theory of competitive markets, economists developed a mathematical model of general equilibrium that provided a logical proof of the basic ideas of fundamentalist capitalism. Economic theory became ideology, well suited to the needs of the Cold War and ammunition for economic and political conservatives. Advocates of mathematical general equilibrium theory considered it a great advance in economic science, however. Its pioneers received Nobel Prizes, it became the central theory in mainstream economics, and it continues today to be the economic theory all aspiring economists are taught.

THIRTEEN

CAPITALISM AFTER THE SECOND WORLD WAR

*John Kenneth Galbraith (1908–)
wrote the most incisive critique of
contemporary American
capitalism.*

At the close of World War II capitalism seemed to be in retreat. The postwar settlement left the Soviet Union in control of Eastern Europe and much of Central Europe, including eastern Germany. Communist parties there controlled governments and a variety of programs of economic planning were in effect. In Western Europe, devastated by war, governments moved to economic planning to manage the economic recovery. Social democratic parties, along with communist parties, gained adherents. In England the Labor party won an absolute majority in Parliament in 1946 and began a wholesale transformation of the British economy along socialist lines. Basic industries were nationalized, including steel, coal, and railroads, and a national system of health care was introduced. In France the coal industry was nationalized to assuage labor unrest, and the Renault automobile company was taken over because of its collaboration with the Nazis during the war.

A few years later Nikita Khruschev, then Soviet premier, toasted a group of Americans at a Moscow party with the now famous remark, "We shall bury you." Although the statement was made half jokingly, it symbolized the ideological conflict of the post–World War II era: two economic systems contesting for the loyalties of people. The rivalry existed at all levels: philosophical, economic, diplomatic, and military. It was expressed in the terms used by both sides: "iron curtain," "Cold War," "people's democracies," "neo-imperialism," "evil empire," and the like.

Joseph Schumpeter on the Survival of Capitalism

Joseph Schumpeter (1883–1950) did not think that capitalism would survive. Born in the same year as John Maynard Keynes, Schumpeter was usually bracketed with Keynes as one of the two greatest economists of his time.

Since his death economic theory has developed in directions other than those taken by Schumpeter, but economists will continue to value his three major works. All three sing the praises of the capitalist entrepreneur, described as the innovating profit seeker responsible for the constant change that makes a private-enterprise system dynamic.

In his first important book, *The Theory of Economic Development* (1912), Schumpeter analyzed the function of the entrepreneur in creating economic progress and change. The private-enterprise economy always offers large rewards for new products, new production methods, or new systems of organization. The first person to offer lower costs or new products with customer appeal earns high profits. The entrepreneur is that first person, and his or her continual innovation generates the growth and change that are characteristic of modern capitalist society.

Schumpeter carried the analysis a step further in *Business Cycles* (1939), where he argued that innovations tend to be bunched at certain times—one leading to another—creating large investment booms that promote long periods of prosperity. When investment declines from these high levels, the prosperous years are succeeded by stagnation and bad times. Superimposed on these "long waves" of economic activity are business cycles as we know them: during a long wave of good times the upswings are sustained and strong and the downturns short and shallow, while just the opposite effects occur during the long periods of bad times. In the process, the series of industrial revolutions characteristic of capitalism occur, each one ushering in a long period of good times rooted in a group of related innovations.

The book was one answer to the pessimists who felt that the Great Depression of the 1930s marked the ultimate failure of capitalism. Schumpeter's argument implied that the system was only in one of the troughs of its long waves and that a better future was in store as innovation and technological change turned the wave upward once more. The book also expressed Schumpeter's view of the inner dynamics of capitalism and his answer to Marx. The bad effects of capitalism were not the result of its faults but were caused by its strengths. The innovating, profit-seeking activity of the entrepreneur brought change, growth, and expansion, but the process was erratic rather than smooth and steady, and one result was the business cycle.

The idea of long waves proved to be right. In this chapter we review the fifty years after World War II to show that for twenty years after the end of the war the American economy boomed, and carried the rest of the world with us. Then, about the late 1960s our economy turned to what at best was slow growth that lasted for another two decades. By the early nineties, however, a new wave of business investment in computers and related equipment returned the economy to the start of a new wave of growth.

Schumpeter was a pessimist about capitalism in his finest book, *Capitalism, Socialism, and Democracy* (1942). He believed strongly in the effectiveness of capitalism in producing goods and services for all and estimated that the fifty years from 1928 to 1978 would see a more than doubled output in the United States, making it possible to eliminate poverty for all but the exceptional "pathological" case. In the process, however, several social characteristics of capitalism would become apparent.

One characteristic is the gradual elimination of the entrepreneur. The technology and organization of large-scale production are important innovations of capitalism, leading to big business and monopolistic markets. The bureaucracies created to run large enterprises are not places where individualistic, innovating entrepreneurs can function. These individuals are lone operators, dreamers of large schemes, and risk takers, while bureaucracies tend to be run by committees, by people who conserve the status quo rather than change it. The very organizations created by entrepreneurs dispense with their services.

A second characteristic of developing capitalism predicted by Schumpeter is the alienation of intellectuals from adherence to the system. Thinkers, writers, and teachers are critics of the existing order, even though their position is made possible by the affluence of capitalist society. Their function is to point out faults in an effort to make the world better, and they succeed in creating a climate of opinion antagonistic to the capitalist way of life.

This environment of public opinion engenders a third characteristic, government intervention in economic affairs. The intervention is directed toward the faults of the economy—toward reducing inequality, smoothing out the business cycle, reducing speculation, controlling monopoly, subsidizing agriculture, and so forth. As a by-product, it also reduces the entrepreneur's freedom of action and serves to further reduce the dynamism of the economy.

These trends in economic organization, the climate of opinion, and public policy lead to the gradual elimination of entrepreneurs from economic life, and, with them, the economic advances that give capitalism its appeal. The growth of the economy is hindered, capitalism loses its ability to satisfy new wants, and the predictions of collapse made by the intellectuals are fulfilled. As the performance of the system becomes poorer, government intervention increases, which further reduces the vitality of the system and makes socialism inevitable. Schumpeter believed that socialism would replace capitalism in the long run and that it could be either democratic or authoritarian in political structure—the great choice of the future lay in the political sphere. To the question "Can capitalism survive?" Schumpeter answered, "No, I do not think it can."

Schumpeter was wrong, of course, about the demise of capitalism. It was the Soviet system that collapsed, and private-enterprise capitalism emerged by the end of the century as a vibrant, successful system.

Economic Growth and Economic Change

Schumpeter was correct on one point: innovation, economic growth, and change occur together and reinforce each other. The quarter century after World War II was a period of unmatched world economic growth and sustained prosperity. Contrary to the expectations and fears of many economists during the mid-1940s, the economy did not fall back into the doldrums from which it had been lifted by World War II. Instead of depression or stagnation, the postwar world economy surged ahead. With assistance from the United States, the countries of Western Europe recovered readily from the devastation and dislocation of war. Eastern Europe joined the parade of economic growth after a period of economic and social upheaval, and the Soviet economy continued its forward march. The American economy experienced a steady pattern of growth, with the only major lull coming during the 1950s as the result of old-fashioned monetary and fiscal policies. Japan developed into the world's third major industrial power, and several underdeveloped countries transformed themselves into developing nations.

One of the most important reasons for this advance was an investment boom in electronics, plastics, atomic energy, and motor transportation. The result was a whole new world of automobiles, jet aircraft, computers, automated production, and extended urbanization that created vast areas of economic opportunity.

A second factor promoting growth was the research revolution. Innovation became an integral part of business enterprise and public activity. Basic and applied research expanded many times beyond the level of the 1920s and 1930s and became an accepted function of both business and government. This research and development—the basic ingredient of innovation—provided a new dynamism to the whole economic system, even though much of it was associated with military needs and the race into space.

A third factor in the postwar expansion was the emergence of the consumer to a position of even greater importance. As incomes rose, more consumers had larger amounts of "discretionary income" over and above the amounts needed for satisfying basic wants, which enabled them to invest in homes and home furnishings, automobiles, and other durable goods and in securities and insurance policies. Recreational industries expanded as people gained more leisure time, and service industries grew. The "powerful consumer" was a greater determinant of the level and mix of economic activity than ever before.

A fourth element in postwar economic growth was large government expenditures on armaments and warfare. The Cold War between the United States and the USSR required large increases in military spending, and active war in Korea and Vietnam added to the thrust of government spending. Huge investments were necessary as the technology of warfare changed from guns, tanks, and aircraft to nuclear weapons, missiles, and electronic weaponry.

Business enterprise took advantage of these opportunities for expansion. The postwar years saw a huge increase in investment and plant capacity, which was not restricted to a few nations but became a worldwide phenomenon. World trade expanded, and an international program of reducing barriers to trade brought into being the General Agreement on Tariffs and Trade, as well as the European Common Market and other regional associations of nations.

Economic growth also stimulated rapid technological change. Computers and electronic controls made possible large-scale automation, particularly in manufacturing and business management. As capital was substituted for labor on a growing scale, the nature of work and the work force began to change. At the upper levels of the labor market new types of highly skilled occupations appeared, such as computer programming and operation, and new skills were required of management. New types of scientific education and managerial technique were necessary, and the technical-managerial elite both expanded and became more sophisticated.

At the lower levels of the work force automation eliminated some jobs and transformed others. Tasks on the production line were subdivided into simpler component parts that could be done by machines rather than people. This process had been going on ever since the beginning of the Industrial Revolution, but it was greatly speeded up and applied more widely with the new technology of the years after 1945. Automation, of course, greatly improved the productivity of the work force. However, it also meant that enlarged output could be produced without increasing the number of workers. That is exactly what happened. In the United States after 1950, a greatly expanded manufacturing output was produced with little increase in the work force employed in manufacturing.

Perhaps the most striking example of this relationship between people and jobs occurred in American agriculture. Great increases in farm production made possible by mechanization, hybrid plants, and use of fertilizers were accompanied by a large shift of population from farm to city. Blacks, in particular, were heavily affected. Between 1949 and 1953 workable cotton- and corn-harvesting machines were introduced into southern agriculture; at the same time soybean cultivation, which uses relatively little labor, spread rapidly. The result was a huge decline in the use of unskilled agricultural labor in much of the South and a vast migration of blacks to northern cities. The impact of this migration, together with other social forces, was felt in the urban riots of the 1960s and contributed heavily to the continuing urban and racial crises of the United States.

The international division of labor was also changing. Less-developed countries, particularly those on the western rim of the Pacific, began to industrialize, exporting manufactures produced by large cadres of low-wage workers. Workers in Western Europe and the United States in basic industries such as steel, consumer durables industries such as television sets and automobiles, and soft goods industries such as textiles and shoes began to lose their jobs as imports from the developing countries flooded into world markets.

A persistent shift was taking place in the structure of the labor force. With few new jobs available in manufacturing, which paid high wages, more workers were employed in service industries, which paid lower wages. Other outlets were in government employment, including education and health services, and in the white-collar administrative jobs of expanding corporate enterprise.

Subtle changes took place in the social classes of industrial capitalism. At the upper levels the high-income elite of expensively trained technicians and managers increased in numbers. At the bottom, there was a growing proportion of low-income workers in the expanding service industries. These workers required little training. Their wages remained low because of a surplus population of unemployed and partially employed recipients of welfare, food stamps, and other assistance. In the United States, this part of the work force was heavily black, Hispanic, or immigrant labor, and many were women.

Other changes in the economy were taking place, such as the growth of giant corporate enterprise, the rise and then decline of organized labor, and the expansion of government economic activity. Studies of these trends clearly showed that the traditional pattern of largely self-adjusting markets had changed significantly.

Big Business, Big Labor, Big Government

Capitalism survived the Great Depression, and the economy prospered after World War II as never before. But the price of survival was a change of face. The capitalism we know is hardly that of our grandparents. In the quarter century after World War II big business grew even bigger and, in turn, bred the growth of big labor. Both fostered the growth of government.

These postwar trends had been identified and studied before the war. One of the most important studies of the changing nature of business enterprise was *The Modern Corporation and Private Property* (1932) by Adolf A. Berle, Jr., and Gardner C. Means. It documented the dominant position of the large corporation in the modern economy, the growing dispersion of ownership of corporate stock, and the separation of ownership from control. Emphasis was placed on the new structure of power that had appeared, in which the officers of corporations dominated policies while owning only insignificant portions of the stock. The book also questioned the continued validity of the traditional "logic of profits"; since profits went to stockholders rather than to management, production decisions were no longer necessarily in accord with consumer wishes. The close connections between consumer wants, profits, and business decisions were seriously loosened. Instead, business decisions came increasingly to reflect the needs of management and the ability of firms to control markets.

Gardner Means pursued other aspects of big business in the economy, concentrating on prices and pricing policy. In 1934 he originated the term "administered prices" to describe the type of prices set by firms in monopolized sectors of the economy.* Means showed that such prices were relatively

---

*The term "administered prices" was used in a confidential memorandum to the secretary of agriculture that was leaked to the press and to Congress and later published as "Industrial Prices and Their Relative Flexibility," U.S. Senate Document 13, 74th Congress, First Session.

inflexible and did not respond readily to changes in demand. When demand fell during the depression years, certain firms maintained their prices and cut output and employment. This relative freedom of prices from the effects of market forces, together with the power of large corporations, created a new type of economic system. As Means wrote in a later work, *The Corporate Revolution in America* (1964):

> We now have single corporate enterprises employing hundreds of thousands of workers, having hundreds of thousands of stockholders, using billions of dollars' worth of the instruments of production, serving millions of customers, and controlled by a single management group. These are great collectives of enterprise, and a system composed of them might well be called "collective capitalism."

Means argued that in an economy dominated by giant firms, the interests of management, rather than those of the public, were paramount.

If there was any doubt about the importance of big enterprise and the monopolized nature of many sectors of the American economy, it was dispelled by the reports of the Temporary National Economic Committee (TNEC), published in the early 1940s. This joint congressional committee investigated the concentration of economic power in the United States in the late 1930s. Its hundreds of volumes of testimony and 43 expert monographs documented the overwhelming influence of the large corporation, particularly in finance, transportation, heavy industry, and production of durable consumer goods.

Other governmental studies showed the existence of a closely knit big-business community held together by interlocking directorates, financial ties, large family holdings such as those of the Rockefellers and Mellons, and corporate stockholdings. While a continual struggle for economic advantage, power, and position goes on at even the top levels, the development of a corporate capitalism dominated by a few hundred major firms raised new issues of economic and social power and control. The ends of that power and the goals of the economic system become issues subject to conscious actions. The very organization of productive enterprise made laissez-faire obsolete. Even if government did not seek to control economic activity, big business would.

Organized labor and big business had been in conflict for half a century or more prior to the 1930s, and the battle was often violent. But during the 1930s the National Labor Relations Act (1935) was passed to promote peaceful settlement of labor disputes by mandating collective bargaining between unions and management. The act protected the workers' right to join unions and to strike, sought to prevent employer opposition to union organization, and required employers to bargain "in good faith" with unions. The National Labor Relations Board was established to enforce the act. This legislation was amended in 1947 and 1959 to provide a process for settling strikes that could imperil the national economy, and to protect the rights of individual workers within unions. Class warfare was to be eliminated by peaceful settlement of class disputes.

Labor unions grew rapidly in the new legal environment. By 1950 about 35 percent of all wage and salary employees in the United States were members of unions—before the long decline in union membership began that brought the figure down to less than 15 percent forty years later. The largest growth of union membership was in industries dominated by big business, where administered prices and monopolistic control of markets and prices prevailed.

In those sectors of the economy big firms made more than normal profits from their ability to share markets and influence prices, and from their ability to reduce competition that would drive prices down to just cover production and distribution costs. This meant that labor unions could make substantial gains for their workers by bargaining to share in these monopolistic profits through higher wages, shorter hours, and fringe benefits such as retirement and pension systems. The business firms were willing to bargain because settlement of disputes without strikes enabled them to continue making more than normal profits, particularly if they could pass the added costs on to the public through higher prices. So big labor, protected by national labor laws, grew in the sectors of the economy dominated by big business, and an inflationary bias was introduced into the economy.

The growth of big business and big labor was paralleled by the growth of big government. This was one of the most heavily publicized changes in the American economy, with much of the publicity coming from the business community as part of its opposition to the trend. The opposition sometimes maintained that the growth of government economic activity was an alien development foisted on an unwilling society by political adventurers and demagogues, but economists produced different explanations.

Solomon Fabricant, for example, in his scholarly study *The Trend of Government Activity in the United States Since 1900* (1952), argued that economic growth itself was the chief reason for the expanded role of government. Population growth and its changing structure, the end of the frontier, advancing science and technology, urbanization and industrialization, the growing size of business enterprise, and growing economic interdependence—these developments created new problems that the free market could not easily solve and that demanded new government functions at all levels: federal, state, and local. Added stimuli were provided by recurring depressions, wars, and the increasing possibility of war. Finally, Fabricant pointed out that the climate of opinion changed: there was growing confidence in the ability of government to meet new needs, a confidence inspired in part by improved organization and efficiency within government itself. He noted that by mid-century the government was the nation's biggest banker, operated the largest insurance company, employed one-eighth of the labor force, exerted a major influence on wage and salary levels, and was the largest single buyer of commodities. He expected this share in economic activity to become larger as the economy expanded and income grew.

The growth of big business, big government, and big labor made it clear that the impersonal operation of market forces was at least partially supplanted by the ability of important groups in labor, management, and government to influence significantly the way the economy functioned.

John Kenneth Galbraith: Social Critic

The quarter century after the Second World War were great years for the American economy. It was a period of rapid economic growth, relatively low unemployment rates, rising personal incomes, a falling proportion of families in poverty, and general economic well-being. Nevertheless, this era also saw the publication of the most incisive critique of the American economy and structure of power since Thorstein Veblen wrote over a half-century before.

John Kenneth Galbraith was born in Canada in 1908. He studied agricultural economics at the University of California (PhD, 1934) and spent two years at England's Cambridge University just when John Maynard Keynes was writing his *General Theory of Employment, Interest and Money* and when those ideas were being widely discussed. During World War II Galbraith was in charge of price controls until ousted because of protests from the business community, was involved with economic affairs in the occupied countries, and immediately after the war was director of the Strategic Bombing Survey that evaluated the effectiveness (not very great) of the allied effort to knock out German military production. For five years he was a member of the Board of Editors of *Fortune* magazine before becoming Professor of Economics at Harvard University in 1949.

Galbraith was a strong advocate of activist public policies to promote prosperity. He criticized the economic power of big business and did not believe in the market mechanism as an effective means of allocating resources. He consistently argued in favor of public policies designed to modify the unbalanced distribution of income produced by the market economy.

Galbraith was an active participant in public affairs and acted as an advisor to presidential candidates (all Democrats, of course) and to President John F. Kennedy, who appointed him ambassador to India. Galbraith was elected president of the American Economic Association in 1972, but there would be no Nobel Prize for this strong critic of private enterprise capitalism during the Cold War.

Three major works present Galbraith's argument: *The Affluent Society* (1958), *The New Industrial State* (1967), and *Economics and the Public Purpose* (1973). The first attacked the conventional wisdom that economic growth and greater output are necessarily a good thing, the second sketched the outlines of a society dominated by big enterprise and the "technostructure" that runs it, and the third argued for the dominance of the social good over private gain through democratic socialism and economic planning. Together they comprised a critique of modern society and its values and called for major changes in the ends economic activity ought to seek.

Galbraith argued that modern technology makes possible the abundant society that has always been one of humanity's dreams. But affluence has not brought happiness because people still believe in the doctrine of scarcity and continually seek greater and greater output of material things. The private-enterprise industrial economy creates additional wants, partly by suggestion and emulation, and partly by the deliberate action of producers through advertising and salesmanship. Higher levels of production merely bring higher levels of want creation: wants depend on the process by which they are satisfied. Galbraith calls this the *dependence effect*, and with it disposes of the rational consumer. If he is right, the whole economy becomes irrational: if producers can determine, or even significantly influence, the decisions of consumers, they can determine the forces to which their own decisions respond, and the self-adjusting market becomes merely a device for sustaining and enriching big enterprise.

In such an economy the giant corporation able to manipulate markets is the significant unit. Ostensibly managed by its highest officers, the decisions are really made by a *technostructure* of experts who are able to manipulate the complex technology of modern production and marketing. This hierarchy is interested in the firm's survival and growth and in its own aggrandizement, but maximization of profits is not its chief concern. And without maximization of profits the neat adjustment of production to consumer wants postulated by neoclassical economics would not occur, even in the absence of the dependence effect.

Galbraith's analysis broadens out from there. The giant corporation abhors risk and requires growth and stable markets. This can be achieved only by the use of Keynesian macroeconomic policies. Government becomes one partner of the technostructure. The educational system becomes another partner, because the giant corporation needs trained personnel and the scientific advances it produces, with the costs borne largely by government. Labor unions are a junior partner, gaining security through collective bargaining in exchange for a regular supply of labor for the giant firm. Galbraith pointed out that in the affluent society there was a strong community of interest between big business, big government, and big labor.

The values of the affluent society stress individual wants and starve the public sector. So we drive in our private cars on clogged expressways beside poisoned streams through polluted air to get to public parks that are too crowded for everyone to be admitted—in an affluent society.

The whole system moves toward irrational goals. The consumer continually seeks more and newer products under the influence of an unremitting sales effort; advancing technology creates a growing pool of unemployed and unemployable labor; government policies continually push the economy to higher levels of output; and the only forms of social consumption that get high priority are military needs and special research-and-development programs such as space exploration.

What can be done to bring the economy back toward more humane goals? In the third book of his trilogy Galbraith calls for a "new socialism" that would include, in addition to greater equality of income and wealth, steps to discipline the giant corporation by wage, price, profit, and salary controls, nationalization of the chief military supplying firms, and—surprisingly—nationalization of much of the less-concentrated sectors of the economy, such as health care, in order to achieve the advantages of planning that are already present in the giant corporate sector. Socialization of the "unduly weak industries and unduly strong ones," along with planning of the rest, would enable the public interest to triumph over private interests. All of this could be achieved, however, only if there were a new belief-system that recognized the realities of the modern economy and no longer merely repeated the shibboleths of the past. This would enable a new people's movement to gain political power, bringing with it the new socialism through democratic political change.

The World Economy

While Galbraith and others were describing how a burgeoning American economy could achieve social equality through government supervision, the rest of the world was undergoing rapid economic growth. This era of rapid world economic growth began with economic recovery from the devastation of the war in both Western and Eastern Europe and the Soviet Union, as well as Japan, in the late 1940s. In Western Europe aid from the United States under the Marshall Plan—some $12 billion from 1947 through 1957—spurred the recovery in that region, despite severe inflation and labor strife. In England the Labor party introduced a national health service and nationalized basic industries such as steel, coal, and railroads, and there was agitation on the continent for similar action as the Socialist and Communist parties ran well in national elections. The survival of private enterprise capitalism hardly seemed assured, but a strong economic expansion saved the day.

World trade began a quarter century of strong growth, aided by a stable world financial system established at the Bretton Woods Conference (1944), which also created the International Monetary Fund to aid countries that might run into financial difficulties. Reduction of tariffs and other barriers to trade was begun in 1948 with the General Agreement on Tariffs and Trade (1948), signed by twenty-three important trading nations. By 1993 the agreement had expanded to 122 nations, and the average level of tariffs had fallen from about 40 percent in 1947 to about 5 percent. In Europe several moves were made to promote trade between nations. The European Economic Community was established in 1957, and the European Free Trade Association was formed in 1960. Comecon (1949) was formed to coordinate the economies of the Soviet bloc countries, largely in response to the Marshall Plan in Western Europe.

Meanwhile, Japan began its spectacular rise as a world economic power based on an economic policy designed to promote exports and hinder imports, with control of the domestic market by large manufacturing corporations and financial institutions. The Japanese government, cooperating with major corporations, unions, and financial institutions, imposed restrictions on imports. Elimination of competition from abroad enabled Japanese firms to charge high prices on domestic sales while cutting prices on exports. Jobs were created for workers and profits for business firms. Nevertheless, the chief reasons for Japan's economic growth were high savings and a strong work ethic on the part of ordinary working people. Added to this was a broad-based educational system and development of universities and research centers that would develop new technologies and train the people who could implement them.

The Third World

The postwar world also saw the elimination of colonialism in Asia and Africa. The less-developed nations, including those of Latin America, were caught in a vicious circle of underdevelopment. Low productivity and low incomes meant that savings were inadequate to achieve levels of investment that might accelerate economic growth. Low incomes also meant a consumer demand inadequate to attract capital investment from other countries. Low levels of investment, in turn, completed the circle of low productivity, low incomes, and a tendancy to hold to traditional views. Low incomes also meant poor housing, poor sanitation, and poor health conditions, which reduced both vigor and length of life, resulting in a young population with a large proportion of unproductive dependents. Low incomes, furthermore, prevented innovation in economic affairs. Since innovation requires a surplus on which to rely in case of failure, a peasant family living at subsistence level cannot afford to experiment with new methods or machines; it must be conservative, for one crop failure means death from starvation. Also generating conservatism was the dominance in many less-developed areas of an economic elite with large landholdings and high incomes whose savings were usually not invested for national economic development but used instead for acquiring more land, for moneylending at high rates of interest to the peasants, or for investing in more advanced countries. At the same time, population pressures were created by high birth rates among the peasant families. Birth rates in less-developed nations had always been high, but they were counterbalanced by high death rates until the application of modern methods of sanitation and public health made populations soar.

The less-developed nations began to plan for economic growth, devising various methods to increase savings and mobilize them for economic expansion under the auspices of government. A wide variety of combinations of public enterprise, public subsidies for private enterprise, and economic controls was developed, especially in the years following the Second World War. At one extreme countries such as Mexico and Brazil relied very heavily on private enterprise and foreign capital. At the other extreme the Chinese economy, almost completely socialized, used both central planning of basic industries and local control of much small-scale production.

Many economists were hopeful that the poor nations could set in motion a self-sustaining process of economic growth. For example, the American economist Walt W. Rostow (1916–) argued that any nation goes through stages of economic development as it moves from a traditional society to a modern mass-consumption economy. The process involves establishing certain preconditions: a stable government, improved education, a group of innovators and business people to utilize savings, and expanded trade. Then comes the "takeoff" into sustained growth, when the economy breaks its shackles and economic progress dominates. Crucial to this change, says Rostow, is an increase in savings and investment to 10 percent or more of the national income. Finally, the development of industry and rising living standards lead to economic maturity and mass consumption.

Implicit in Rostow's analysis were policy recommendations that found great favor in the United States. First, social reform was needed to make the less-developed nations more like North America—"Do it the way we did," Rostow said, in effect. Second, the concept of the takeoff implied that economic aid to developing countries could be gradually phased out, even if it had to be initially large to get the takeoff started; this aspect of Rostow's ideas had an obvious appeal to the economy-minded. Third, Rostow's description of the growth process implied that, once begun, it was not dependent on planning or state management; it was self-sustaining. Perhaps for this reason he titled his book *The Stages of Economic Growth: A Non-Communist Manifesto* (1960).

Other economists were less optimistic about the prospects for achieving a natural or self-sustaining process of growth. Gunnar Myrdal (1898–1987), a Swedish economist who helped develop the Swedish version of national income theory concurrently with Keynes and who wrote a sociological classic on the American racial problem, *An American Dilemma*, argued persuasively that the economic gap between advanced and less-developed nations was widening. The already industrialized nations have high incomes that generate large amounts of savings, he pointed out in *An International Economy* (1956), but the savings are not invested in less-developed nations because of higher profit rates at home. The industrial economies reached into some parts of the world with mines and plantations to produce for export, but these economic enclaves drew savings and the most talented people away from the local economy, leaving it more starved for the means of achieving growth than it was in the first place. As a result, Myrdal said, less-developed nations could not model themselves on advanced nations but had to act radically within their own economies to reorganize imports and exports, diversify production, and plan for economic development. In a later study, *Asian Drama* (1968), he argued that economic advancement for the less-developed countries was possible, but only if population growth could be controlled.

Economic planning and foreign capital, however, helped some of the less-developed countries become developing countries during the 1950s and 1960s. Political independence freed some from colonial status and its hindrances to development. Modern health and sanitation facilities and improved nutrition brought greater efficiency in production, although those advances also brought explosive population growth that literally ate up the gains in some areas. Stress on education and literacy also helped. But the biggest economic gains were the result of planning to promote industrialization, with capital coming from government tax receipts, loans from foreign governments and international organizations, investment by foreign firms, and even from domestic savings and business profits. The most successful of the developing countries were those such as Taiwan, Brazil, or Mexico that greatly favored private enterprise in their planning and that were, therefore, able to attract substantial amounts of private capital or assistance from foreign governments.

Although colonialism was brought to an end, a pattern of economic dependency remains in much of the less-developed world. The center of the world economy is in Western Europe, North America, and Japan, particularly in the great financial centers of New York, London, Zurich, and Tokyo. The bulk of the world's manufacturing is there, along with the world's savings and capital accumulation. Research and innovation are dominated by the advanced industrial nations, and most of the world's economic surplus is generated there. Peripheral areas outside the center are dependent on the center for transfers of capital, technology, and managerial expertise—elements essential for economic growth. This means that they must produce a surplus above domestic needs to pay for those transfers, and that in turn keeps living standards low.

The economic surplus generated by the less-developed countries flows to the center in several ways: (1) through the profits made by international corporations that are generated through the sale of or the production of goods in less-developed countries; (2) through payment for import of consumer goods—often luxury items—made by local elites and their business allies; and (3) through the purchase of financial assets in the center by affluent families in the peripheral nations. The flow of this economic surplus from the periphery to the center hinders the development of a self-generating process of economic growth in the less-developed countries and preserves their dependency on the advanced countries of the economic center.

Japan escaped this dependency. Some of her neighbors on the Pacific Rim—South Korea, Taiwan, Hong Kong, Malaysia, Indonesia, and Singapore—followed Japan's example of government cooperation with private business firms (often owned or controlled by political leaders or their families and friends) to promote export-driven economic growth based on low wages. An export surplus brought capital from abroad, which was used for further expansion of export industries. Low wages not only benefited exports, but also kept workers from buying imported foreign goods in large amounts.

This strategy has not been widely adopted outside the Pacific Rim. Most of the less-developed world relied on loans and investments from governments and international corporations to finance economic development. This simply perpetuated dependency by generating a flow of economic surplus from the periphery to the center through payment of interest and principal on the debt.

Despite these difficulties India, Brazil, and Mexico were able to develop strong economic growth. In all three countries there is a modern and highly advanced economic sector encompassing about one-third of the population that is indistinguishable from the economies of the most advanced countries of North America and Western Europe—but much of the population remains poor and backward in the typical condition of a less-developed country. Great wealth exists alongside great poverty.

Problems of Economic Growth

The great era of world economic growth that followed the Second World War began to raise issues of resource use and pollution. A growing economy must have increasing inputs of raw materials as it uses increasing amounts of energy to produce enlarged output and more wastes. Present technology is based very heavily on exhaustible resources and energy supplies and uses the reservoirs of air, land, and water for waste disposal. Both resources and reservoirs are limited. If one resource starts to run out, another can be substituted for it—but it, too, is exhaustible. A continuing buildup of wastes can so burden the environment that health and life can be threatened.

Economists began to examine these issues. Donella H. Meadows and others, in *The Limits to Growth* (1972), reported on a computerized simulation of world economic growth in an environment of limited resources and showed that the economic growth rates of the recent past could not be sustained. While no single limiting factor, such as too little iron ore, could bring growth to an end, the combined effects of a number of interrelated factors would. For example, irrigation of deserts may make available large increases in the food supply, but even if the water can be found, such projects require huge amounts of energy and capital whose production is subject to limits elsewhere. Improvements in technology and inventions still to come may provide further space for growth, but limits are inherent in the finite amounts of resources available on this planet. That point was made in a much-quoted article by Kenneth Boulding, "The Economics of the Coming Spaceship Earth" (1966). Boulding found the solution in the ultimate development of a "closed" economic system, which, like a stable biological system, uses all of its outputs as inputs, including wastes. Herman E. Daly defined the viable economy of the future in somewhat more specific terms. His article "The Steady-State Economy: Toward a Political Economy of Biophysical Equilibrium and Moral Growth" (1971) called for a constant population, constant physical wealth, and socially controlled distribution of goods, with growth taking place in the moral sphere. One further requirement was smaller economic units using technologies that enhance human work skills rather than replacing them with machines, as pointed out by E. L. Schumacher in his book *Small Is Beautiful: Economics As If People Mattered* (1973). There may not be enough time to make the necessary changes, however. Robert L. Heilbroner, in *An Inquiry into the Human Prospect* (1975), contrasted the trajectory of world economic growth with the converging problems of population, food, resources, and pollution and saw a series of potential or actual catastrophes in the future that could bring "convulsive change." The human race could survive this doomsday prospect, he concluded, but only if human society was reorganized on a basis very different from the present.

If these prospects of slowed economic growth are well founded, we should expect some profound changes in our economic institutions. Economic growth has always been necessary to satisfy the acquisitiveness that motivates capitalism. A steady-state economy would require different attitudes toward material things, and that suggests drastic changes in economic institutions. Furthermore, modern capitalism has a highly unequal distribution of income, wealth, and power that is accepted by most people because of the material benefits they obtain. When material gains slow down or stop, the average person, heretofore relatively content, may no longer so easily accept inequality. Without growth, redistribution of income and wealth is far more likely. Capitalism as we know it at present is not likely to survive in a slow-growth or steady-state economy.

Most economists do not fear that resource limits will cause a long-run slowdown in economic growth, however. They feel that the continuing advance of science and technology will enable population growth to continue into the foreseeable future with increasing consumption per person. The earth has a huge reservoir of potentially usable resources, and the price system can satisfactorily manage the rate of consumption of those resources that are conventionally described as exhaustible. As their relative prices rise, people will economize on their use; substitutes will be found and incentives will be provided to discover new supplies and to lower the costs of resource extraction. Science will eventually provide new sources of energy. Pollution can be held in check through technological innovation and use of economic incentives such as taxes on discharge of pollutants. Not to worry: market adjustments, science, and technology will deal with the problems raised by Meadows, Boulding, Daly, Schumacher, and Heilbroner, according to their critics.

A conflict remains, however. The "growth is no problem" school of thought among economists has not been able to silence the "environment is in danger" tenet that calls attention to global warming, loss of tropical rain forests, pollution of air, water, and soil, and other effects of economic growth and technological change.

Population Growth

We pointed out in the discussion of Malthus's theory of population that the advanced industrial nations have avoided the population trap by keeping their rates of population growth below their rates of economic growth. As a result, levels of consumption per person could increase.

Most less-developed countries have not been able to achieve that goal. They seemed caught in a vicious circle of population growth. Birth rates remained high, while sanitation and public health measures brought death rates down. Wage rates fell as a surplus population appeared, attracting foreign investment that attracted more of the surplus population to urban slums, where poverty kept birth rates high and added more downward pressure on wages. Meanwhile, peasant families in rural areas reacted by producing more children. This pattern was seen in much of Latin America, Asia, and Africa. It was worsened by production of agricultural exports such as sugar, cocoa, cotton, tea, or peanuts instead of using the land for production of food for home use. Economic development and modernization seemed to be increasing population pressures and poverty instead of reducing them.

The world's population seems to be soaring upward, from under one billion 200 years ago to six billion in 2000, and if unchecked, seems headed toward more than nine billion in another 50 years. Paul Erlich's *The Population Bomb* (1968) argued that unless measures were taken to slow or halt the population explosion "we will breed ourselves into oblivion."

Then, starting in the 1970s, the more subtle effects of modernization began to take hold. In the less-developed countries, where the problem of population growth was most acute, the average number of births to women of childbearing age fell from six per woman in the period 1965–1970 to three in 1990 to 1995, according to *World Population Prospects: The 1996 Revision,* published by the United Nations. This is still well above the so-called replacement rate of 2.1 children needed to keep a population from declining. For the world as a whole this so-called fertility rate was 2.8 children per woman in 1990–1995. The 2000 census in the United States showed that the population increase came entirely from immigration, while without it the population would not have grown at all. The population bomb is starting to sputter.

No one knows exactly why this is happening, although there are lots of guesses. Urbanization, which reduces housing space per family, may make parents less eager to have large families. Women are marrying later. They are better educated and know more about birth control, and better methods of birth control are available. Greater availability of improved health care means that more children survive, which reduces the incentives for parents to have additional children. Opening of economic opportunities for women in a growing economy may also be part of the answer. No one is now predicting a world population of ten billion or more in fifty years. There are even some demographers who think that the world population may stabilize at about six billion in about fifty years and may even start to fall. The world as a whole, like the advanced industrial nations, may be able to avoid the population trap.

Stagflation, 1970–1990

For a quarter century after World War II the world economy experienced the greatest and most widespread period of economic growth in recorded history. But by the early 1970s the postwar boom began to slow down. The next twenty years was a period of slowed economic growth accompanied by inflation.

The Great Inflation of the 1970s was rooted in large increases in the price of energy and food, supplemented by a huge increase in the world's money supply. The Organization of Petroleum Exporting Countries (OPEC) raised the price of oil tenfold during the period 1973 to 1978, which coincided with increases in the price of food caused by worldwide bad weather and poor crops. Costs of production rose everywhere, and prices responded.

The high price of oil brought a huge shift of income and wealth from oil-importing countries to oil-exporting countries, especially those in the Middle East. This meant economic slowdown in the oil-importing countries as income flowed abroad to pay for needed oil imports. The higher price of energy forced cutbacks in domestic consumption and higher production costs, adding to economic slowdown and rising prices.

A huge expansion of the world money supply accompanied the rising cost of energy and food. Oil-importing countries borrowed heavily to pay for oil needed to keep their economies going. Because the price of oil is denominated in dollars, they borrowed heavily from U.S. banks; even if they borrowed from European banks, the funds had to be converted to dollars. This resulted in a huge expansion of deposits in the so-called Eurobank system (banks that lend to firms engaged in international trade). Eurobank deposits increased from about $50 billion in 1968 to an estimated $1,600 billion in 1982—a huge and rapid increase in the world's money supply. Some $1,200 billion of the total was denominated in dollars.

To a monetarist this confirmed the theory that inflation is caused by an increase in the money supply relative to the amount of goods available for sale. To the Post Keynesian it confirmed the theory that a private-enterprise economy creates the money supply it needs to sustain the processes of production and distribution. There wasn't much that policymakers could do about it, in any case.

The inflationary pressures unleashed by the high price of oil brought high interest rates. Inflation enables borrowers to pay off their debts in money that buys less than when they borrowed. So lenders demand a greater return to make up the difference. At the height of the Great Inflation, interest rates in the United States were in the range of 12 to 15 percent, and for some loans as high as 21 percent. In Western Europe interest rates were even higher, while in some parts of the Third World they reached levels above 50 percent. Central banks were unable to halt the escalation of interest rates, and they adopted tight money policies in an effort to dampen the inflationary pressures that were driving up interest rates. All of this added to the economic slowdown and increasing unemployment. Economists invented the word *stagflation* to describe a stagnant economy accompanied by inflation.

The rise in the prices of oil and food thus reverberated through the world economy. Costs of production rose in what came to be known as "supply side" inflation. Financing purchases of high-priced oil set in motion what was, in effect, a doubling of the world's money supply, leading to an old-style "demand side" inflation, along with high interest rates that brought reduced economic activity and unemployment. Finally, the transfer of income and wealth from oil-importing nations added to the economic stagnation.

An international financial crisis followed. A number of less-developed countries borrowed heavily to pay for oil imports needed to keep their economies going. But the increased debt was used only to maintain output, not to increase it, so nothing was earned to pay principal and interest on the debt. Other imports had to be cut by reducing consumer incomes, which required high interest rates, reduced government spending, and increased unemployment. Banks in the world financial centers, unable to collect on the bad loans, had to reduce their lending both at home and abroad, aggravating the worldwide economic slowdown.

It took years for the world economy to adjust to the rise in the price of oil. Production of other forms of energy increased, but those prices also went up. Oil production outside the OPEC countries rose. Production of oil within the OPEC countries also increased and helped bring down the price. The price of oil finally stabilized in 1985 at about fourteen to eighteen dollars a barrel, which was the approximate cost of exploring for and producing one barrel of new oil.

The world economy began growing once more, but real prosperity did not return to Western Europe. Unemployment rates there were above 10 percent well into the 1990s. The economies of southeast Asia, particularly the "Asian Tigers" of Hong Kong, Singapore, Malaysia, Indonesia, and Thailand, grew rapidly, with economic growth rates of over 10 percent annually, but that couldn't continue. By 1995 there was a pervasive glut of manufactured goods in the world economy, especially in textiles, automobiles, and other durable goods. The international financial system experienced another financial crisis.

The International Financial System

Economic growth after World War II featured a large increase in world trade. Reductions in tariffs and trade barriers helped, and the international financial system established by the Bretton Woods Agreements of 1945 provided a stable financial base for international trade and investment. A new era of world prosperity founded on the benefits of specialization and trade seemed to have arrived.

As world trade grew, a worldwide banking system developed, largely independent of the monetary authorities and controls of any one country, in which large banks deal in loans, deposits, and investments in a wide variety of national currencies. Even though the banks that participate have their home offices in individual countries, such as the United States, Japan, Britain, Switzerland, or Germany, their dealings in other currencies are largely unregulated by monetary authorities. For example, if a Swiss bank lends Italian lire to a Greek firm to buy Italian wine for sale in Germany, the loan does not come under the authority or regulation of the monetary authorities of any of those countries and is not subject to any of their monetary policies. The world monetary system now has a significant component that is substantially free of controls except those provided by the private managers of the international banks themselves. There is a large potential for monetary overexpansion and instability in the world economy.

That potential became reality in the early 1970s when the financing of the oil price increases of that decade helped generate the Great Inflation. Turmoil in international financial markets caused the fixed exchange rate system for trading in national currencies to break down. The Bretton Woods Agreements of 1945 were abandoned. Almost thirty years of stable exchange rates gave way to a new era of flexible exchange rates. The value of any one nation's currency, relative to others, now depended on demand and supply of that currency in world financial markets. That, in turn, depended on economic fundamentals within the country itself: interest rates, the balance of trade, prosperity or depression, political stability, and similar considerations.

The scandal of the Bank of Credit and Commerce International (BCCI) in the early 1990s illustrated how the largely unregulated international banking system could be used for fraud and corruption. BCCI was chiefly a means by which profits from the international drug trade were laundered, along with corrupt gains by political leaders in several less-developed countries. These funds were deposited in BCCI branches, but withdrawals were consistently less than deposits, as the crooks built up their bank balances. This enabled the top executives of BCCI to appropriate the difference between deposits and withdrawals, amounting to more than $20 billion over a few years. In effect, one bunch of crooks stole from another bunch of crooks. BCCI also made some legitimate loans for business purposes, but this was only a sideline to the scam.

The international financial and monetary system introduced a new and as yet uncontrolled source of instability into the world economy. Erratic expansion and contraction of the world money supply is now possible. Economic difficulties in one country can spread quickly to others, through rapid shifting of capital via the Eurobank system and a system of floating exchange rates between national currencies. The central banks of the leading industrial countries, like the Federal Reserve System in the United States, find themselves with considerably reduced influence over economic events.

For example, if the Federal Reserve authorities wished to stimulate investment in the United States by pushing interest rates down, owners of funds in the United States could shift their money abroad to take advantage of higher interest rates in other countries. Less investment in the United States would result, and a policy intended to stimulate economic expansion would lead to a recession instead. This is just one example of how the new international financial system has reduced the effectiveness of domestic economic policy.

The American Economy

The United States emerged from World War II as the dominant economic power in the world. Every other major industrial nation had been devastated by the war. For the first twenty-five years after the war the American economy prospered, sending manufactures, agricultural products, and capital to the rest of the world. The dollar was dominant in world trade and finance, and New York was the financial capital of the world economy.

The period of American economic hegemony began to wither in the 1970s, as the national economy felt the effects of the worldwide slowdown in economic growth. Data from the American economy document the change. Between 1947 and 1969 the nation's gross domestic product, corrected for changes in the price level, grew at an average annual rate of 4.1 percent, well above the long-term growth rate of about 3.3 percent. The growth rate for the next twenty years, 1970 to 1990, was just 2.9 percent. Table 13.1 shows some other relevant figures.

A decline in the rate of savings was an important feature of the era of slow growth. In the rapid growth era of 1947 to 1969, average annual savings as a percent of gross domestic product was 8.5 percent. In the later period of slow growth, the corresponding figure was just 4 percent.

Table 13.1
Economic Indicators, 1947–1969 and 1970–1990

Average Annual Percent Change (Corrected for Changes in the Price Level)

	1947–1969	1970–1990
Gross Domestic Product per Person	2.6%	1.9%
Labor Productivity	2.6	1.2
Weekly Earnings, Except Agriculture	2.0	–0.4
Inflation Rate	3.0	6.0
Unemployment Rate	4.6	6.6

Other factors contributed to the slowdown in growth. Much of the resource base for production advantages was lost, as the best mineral deposits were used up and less rich ores were tapped. For example, the rich iron ores of Minnesota were exhausted shortly after World War II, and expensive processes to enrich poorer ores had to be used. Development of huge ocean-going ore carriers made ocean transport of iron ores from Labrador, South America, and Africa to Europe and Japan competitive with U.S. costs on the Great Lakes.

Large military expenditures diverted capital, labor, and other resources to economically unproductive military uses. The diversion of engineers, scientists, and skilled workers to military production and space exploration during the Cold War pushed up wages and salaries in the private sector and eroded the competitive position of American industry in world markets.

Protected markets had insulated American industries from competitive pressures, due in part to the wartime devastation of Western Europe and Japan, to monopolistic control of prices and output in some major industries, and to private market control under government supervision in other sectors. These conditions enabled labor unions to obtain large wage increases and allowed lax management practices to develop. Those industries were at a disadvantage as world trade grew and competition from foreign producers increased.

Meanwhile, technological advances in computers, communications, and air transport facilitated management control of widely dispersed production and marketing activities. Expansion of international corporations and a shift of production to low-wage economies in the Third World soon followed.

High rates of interest intended to dampen inflationary pressures had the effect of reducing investment and shifting the outlook of business executives to short-run profits rather than long-run development.

Finally, and most important, the Great Inflation of the 1970s raised production costs and reduced consumer buying power.

This is not an exhaustive list, but it will suffice to indicate that the American economy was in trouble. Manufacturing industries in the Midwest and New England were particularly hard hit. By 1992 income per person in the United States, which a quarter century earlier had been the highest in the world, was now tenth highest. The American economy, while remaining strong, was only one of the pack.

These economic problems were not amenable to the traditional analyses and policy prescriptions of mainstream economics. Keynesian budget management and monetary policy were never intended as remedies for the fundamental structural changes occurring in the economy. The theory of self-adjusting markets, with its emphasis on small adjustments at the margin, had little to contribute. In these circumstances one might expect a basic reconstruction of the discipline of economics. That did not happen. The economics profession responded, in the ideological environment of the Cold War, with an even greater emphasis on conventional microeconomics and the theory of competitive markets.

Military Keynesianism

Nevertheless, during the Cold War several periods of substantial economic expansion in the American economy were based on military spending along the lines of the NSC–68 Memorandum. Called *Military Keynesianism,* in its fully developed form the policy embodied a large and sustained increase in military spending combined with tax cuts to stimulate consumer spending and investment incentives to promote business expansion.

The first test of Military Keynesianism came with the Korean War, shortly after the appearance of NSC–68. Military expenditures almost tripled, unemployment fell to below 3 percent, and government revenues increased as the economy grew. Price controls kept prices in check, but they probably had little impact, for prices fell after a short period of increase when controls were removed after the war. The experience of the Korean War period seemed to confirm the theory: military spending and the economy as a whole expanded together, growth of the private sector helped check inflation, and public revenues rose to help balance the increased spending.

The second test came indirectly during the Eisenhower administration of the 1950s. Military spending was stabilized at about $40 billion to $50 billion annually. Three recessions followed, and the administration did little to counter the downturns with either fiscal or monetary policies as unemployment rose and utilization of productive capacity fell.

The next application of Military Keynesianism came during the Kennedy and Johnson administrations, although its policies were not linked directly to NSC–68. Rather, it professed a broader set of goals related to the Cold War and the conflict with the USSR. The best statement of the administration's program was made by Eugene V. Rostow, one of Kennedy's inner group of advisers and later Under-Secretary of State for Political Affairs. His book, *Planning for Freedom,* argued that Keynesian fiscal policy to maintain high levels of economic activity and rapid economic growth, supplemented by a restrictive monetary policy to hold inflation in check, would allow the private sector the freedom needed to meet consumer needs, develop new technologies, and raise living standards for all. The "growth dividend" could then be used to maintain military defenses against the Soviet Union, provide aid to less-developed countries to stimulate their growth and prevent them from falling into the Soviet orbit, and provide additional funds for aid to the disadvantaged within the United States. Keynesian economic policy was to be directed toward both domestic issues and the needs of the Cold War.

Military spending was sharply increased during the Kennedy and Johnson administrations, supplemented by investment tax credits to stimulate investment and income tax cuts to promote consumer spending. Eight years of prosperity and economic growth followed. Escalation of the Vietnam War justified large increases in government spending, and the argument of NSC–68 was once more validated. The private sector expanded, unemployment fell, and economic growth accelerated as the military sector provided a stimulus to the private sector. Expansion of consumer goods production helped check inflation, so a tight money policy was not needed.

Finally, after three administrations—Nixon, Ford, and Carter—that refrained from Keynesian policies, the Reagan administration provided a massive dose of Military Keynesianism. Tight money policies, begun under Carter and continued under Reagan, reduced inflation and brought a serious recession in the early 1980s. But huge increases in military spending, together with tax cuts primarily for the wealthy, stimulated the private sector once more, this time with relatively modest price increases. Military Keynesianism, spurred by Cold War rhetoric and ideology, once again produced eight fat years. The distribution of benefits was lopsided, but the gains were there. We should note, however, that the 1980s differed from the 1960s: private investment did not increase significantly, real wages fell, and the federal budget deficit exploded. Inflation was checked chiefly by restrictive monetary policies and by expansion of production in the private sector of the economy triggered by growth in military spending.

The two episodes of Military Keynesianism under Kennedy-Johnson and Reagan were each successful in triggering seven to eight years of vigorous economic expansion. But the results were different in one important respect. In the 1960s the U.S. economy was still in the era of rapid growth that followed the Second World War. All sectors of the economy benefited from the seven years of Kennedy-Johnson Military Keynesianism, except perhaps the urban poverty areas. But by the 1980s the economy was deep into the era of slow growth that began around 1970. The Reagan administration's Military Keynesianism was not a tide that raised all boats. The unemployment rate never fell to the low levels and close to full employment achieved during the Kennedy-Johnson economic expansion, and the slide in weekly earnings that began in the 1970s continued. The sluggish response of the private sector, together with the tax cuts, meant that government revenues did not rise enough to pay for the large increase in government spending. Huge increases in government debt followed.

The Resurgence of Private Enterprise

In the 1990s the American economy boomed once more, but this time when government spending was falling and inflation had been tamed. The expansion was fueled by private investment in computers, software, and telecommunications, mostly by business firms but also by consumers. Corporate profits rose, aided by downsizing of the workforce, use of temporary workers, shifting of production to nonunionized outside suppliers, and moving of operations to low-wage foreign factories. This made the rising prosperity an uneven one, with many workers worse off as a result of the changing labor market. Nevertheless, the securities markets boomed, and stock prices rose rapidly. It is worth noting that the economic expansion of the 1990s was only the second time in the twentieth-century American economy that an expansion of six to nine years was not accompanied by large increases in military spending. The only other strong private sector expansion was in the 1920s.

Meanwhile, the basic structure of the economy was changing. Technological change shifted the center of gravity of the economy from manufacturing to service industries, from assembly line to computers, software, and telecommunications. Automobiles, trucks, and aircraft were the preferred modes of transportation, replacing the railroads that dominated shipping

THE ECONOMICS OF JOY

So-called supply side economics was popular among conservatives in the 1980s. High taxes, it was argued, held down investment and kept the economy from growing. Cutting taxes would therefore promote economic growth and prosperity. Government revenues would rise despite the lower tax rates, and the government's budget would be balanced. Lower taxes, greater wealth, balanced budgets: Herbert Stein, who was chairman of Richard Nixon's Council of Economic Advisors from 1972 to 1974, called it derisively "the economics of joy."

President Ronald Reagan liked it, and supply side economics became the justification for tax cuts chiefly for upper-income families on the theory that they would save and invest rather than merely spend their larger after-tax incomes. Unfortunately, it didn't work. Individuals with savings "invest" largely in securities and real estate. These are financial investments, not real investments in factories and machinery that put people to work. Normally, some 80 to 90 percent of real investment is made by business firms out of retained earnings—profits that are not paid out to stockholders or are plowed back into the business by individual owners. Some real investment is financed by borrowing or sale of securities, but it is only a small portion of the total. If the Reagan administration had reduced or eliminated the corporate income tax, it might have induced a substantial economic expansion. Instead it relied on a large expansion of military spending—Military Keynesianism—for eight years of rising prosperity.

Supply side theory has merit, however. Economic expansion can be triggered from the business sector, consumers, or government. Government revenues will increase no matter where the stimulus comes from, and lower taxes can help provide the stimulus. But to generate economic growth the tax reductions should focus on real investment in productive plant and equipment, not ones chosen because they chiefly benefit the supporters of one political party.

and travel as late as the Second World War. Seaborne traffic shifted from cargo ships to containers. New technologies permeated older industries, such as textiles, clothing, and shoes. In the 1990s economic expansion business investment in computers and telecommunications amounted to 80 percent of all business investment. The new technologies were heavily capital intensive, and the cost of capital became more important than the cost of labor in most manufacturing industries and many service industries.

Relationships between capital and labor were transformed. Labor unions were strong in the older industries, such as steel, automobiles, and coal; and as those industries declined or changed, the unions were weakened. Union membership fell from 35 percent of the work force to only a little over 10 percent of a much larger work force. New technologies enabled business firms to "downsize" their work force, hire temporary workers, and "outsource" some of their operations by contracting with outside firms. The decline of real wages that began around 1970 forced workers to take second or part-time jobs, and women entered the work force in increasing numbers. Growing feelings of insecurity followed.

Despite its problems, private-enterprise capitalism has no serious rival. The threat of communism disappeared with the collapse of the Soviet Union. Socialism is in retreat. The role of government is diminishing in the industrial nations of Europe and North America, although most of the welfare state programs remain. Capitalism has no rival.

As we look back on the years from the end of World War II to the present we see a typical long wave of growth (1950–1970) followed by a long wave of slow growth (1970–1990). In the booming years of 1950–1970 the U.S. economy pulled the rest of the world along with us, in which little could go wrong. Then came a time of troubles that lasted for twenty years from 1970. Those dates may not be quite accurate. The good times may have begun in the late 1940s and may have ended in the late 1960s. The poor times may have lasted into the early 1990s. But the fifty years as a whole show that Joseph Schumpeter was right about long waves of growth followed by an era of poor economic conditions.

FOURTEEN

A HALF-CENTURY OF HIGH THEORY

Kenneth Arrow (1921–) was one of the originators of modern general equilibrium theory.

High theory in economics during the fifty years after the Second World War passed through several phases from 1945 to the mid-1990s. In the first half of this period, with its rapid economic growth, mainstream economics was heavily Keynesian. The Great Depression of the 1930s was a recent memory, so there was general agreement among policymakers that policies designed to promote economic growth and maintain high levels of employment were necessary. To this was added the need to alleviate poverty and provide for the welfare of working people. In the United States this led to programs such as Medicare and Medicaid, which widened the protections developed during the 1930s under the New Deal. Similar welfare state programs instituted in England and the industrial nations of continental Europe were considerably more extensive than in the United States. Sweden and Norway led the way with their "cradle to grave" welfare systems.

There were several common motivations underlying the Keynesian and welfare programs. One was simple humanitarianism—the desire to counteract the sometimes destructive effects of the capitalist market economy. Others were political—the desire to ease the unrest that led to fascism in the interwar period and might lead to communism in the postwar era. Economic stability, growth, and the welfare state were seen as essential to the triumph of political democracy.

High theory in economics reflected these ideas. A "neoclassical synthesis" of Keynesian economics and the theory of competitive markets appeared, supplemented by a theory of optimal and stable economic growth based on Keynesian concepts.

This majority consensus was not unanimous, however. There was a strong conservative dissent represented by two schools of thought with a strong libertarian base. One originated in the older Austrian neoclassical economics of Karl Menger in the 1870s. The other was the "Chicago School," centered at the University of Chicago. Both championed the merits of the competitive private-enterprise economy.

There were other dissenters. Liberal critics attacked big business and its growing influence on public policy. A group of "neo-Ricardian" economists in England and Italy, and "Post Keynesian" economists in the United States attacked the theoretic and intellectual foundation of the mainstream neo-classical synthesis. And the political and social upheavals of the 1960s generated a new, radical critique of modern capitalism.

As economic growth began to slacken in the late 1960s and the early 1970s, and slowed even more with the Great Inflation of the 1970s, the climate of opinion began to shift. Keynesian economic policies were not effective in dealing with the simultaneous stagnation and inflation of the period after 1970. The Cold War continued, and a conservative reaction gathered strength. The slowdown in economic growth brought a reduced growth dividend, which, together with stagnant real wages, brought political pressure for reduced taxes and a shift in public opinion toward leaner government budgets. There was pressure for deregulation of industry as changing technologies altered economic boundaries in finance, transportation, communication, and energy production. In addition, the growth of world trade enabled business firms to reduce their reliance on domestic markets as they expanded into unregulated markets abroad.

A shift in the structure of power in the United States was slowly taking place. Labor unions were declining. The role of government was reduced. The symbiotic and mutually supportive relationship between big business, big labor, and big government—not without conflict, of course—gave way to a new era dominated by the economic and political power of business enterprise.

High theory in economics reflected these changes in the economic and political environment. A new economic orthodoxy developed, with two major components. One was an extended and more rigorous version of general equilibrium theory. The other was a "new neoclassical macroeconomics" to replace Keynesian interventionism with a laissez-faire explanation of the level of economic activity.

So we turn now to the path of high theory in economics, from the neo-classical synthesis through the rise of competing schools of thought to the triumph of general equilibrium theory and a laissez-faire macroeconomics.

The Neoclassical Synthesis

Following World War II all of the major industrial nations adopted policies to promote high levels of economic activity. In the United States acceptance of the Keynesian point of view was typified by passage of the Employment Act of 1946:

> It was essentially a program in which the economic powers of government would provide a balance to the economy. In simple terms, the private sector

was assumed to be moving to either expansion or contraction, with government moving in the opposite direction. Private investment was assumed to be the volatile factor, either increasing or decreasing, while government spending and/or monetary policy was used to balance the economy. Business cycles would not be eliminated, but they would be largely counterbalanced. Consumer spending would be free to influence output.

A variety of techniques was developed to implement these policies. Monetary policies were used to stimulate the economy in poor times and to dampen economic activity when inflation threatened. Tax laws were changed to increase investment and consumer spending when an economic stimulus was needed. When recessions threatened, government expenditures were increased to fill the gap left by the decline in the private sector, or taxes were reduced to give an added stimulus to private spending and investment. The goal was to balance the economy at full-employment levels rather than to balance government budgets, and the budget was used as a means of achieving that economic balance. The ideal situation was seen as one in which the economy operated at full employment, with stable prices and a balanced government budget that neither stimulated the economy to inflationary levels nor held it back at less than full employment.

Keynesian economics taught that continual prosperity was possible if the government followed proper fiscal and monetary policies. If the private sector showed signs of faltering, it could be stimulated by easy money policies or given a direct boost by increased government spending. The important factor was the level of aggregate demand, which could be kept at full-employment levels by consumer spending and business investment supplemented by whatever levels of government spending were necessary.

If the economy was prosperous, decisions about what should be produced could be left to the private sector. As long as the public sector was adjusted to maintain full employment and to validate the growth pattern inherent in the private decisions to save and invest, the knotty decisions about whether to produce cars or houses, plowshares or butter, refrigerators or snowmobiles—and in what amounts—could be left to the freely made decisions of consumers in the marketplace. Consumers, spending their incomes as they saw fit, would provide signals to producers about what should be produced, and the search for profits would channel resources into those uses. Keynesian macroeconomics seemed to have brought Smith's invisible hand back to life. A grand synthesis of Keynesian macroeconomics and neoclassical microeconomics was forged.

This so-called neoclassical synthesis had to deal with the growth of big business, however. A number of leading economists denied that monopoly was a significant problem. Antitrust laws and public utility regulation were needed, of course, and it was argued that they had helped make for workable competition even in oligopolistic markets. During the 1950s there was an upsurge of such ideas among economists, especially in the United States, the home of the giant corporation. John Maurice Clark argued in *Competition as a Dynamic Process* (1961) that the important criterion was the performance of an industry, not its structure—whether it had a good record of innovation, growth, and labor relations irrespective of whether it met the theoretical criteria of competition. Morris Adelman argued that economic concentration was not increasing (later data showed that it was), but his empirical findings had a wide impact for a time. Gardner Ackley, who was later to be chairman of the President's Council of Economic Advisers, wrote that administered prices were not a significant problem, and much of the profession agreed with his sentiments. Even John Kenneth Galbraith tried to show how an economy of big business and big labor could function effectively. In *American Capitalism* (1952) he argued that "countervailing power" is generated in the private sector. Big business begets big labor, and large manufacturers beget large retailers and large suppliers of raw materials. The power of one will neutralize the power of the other, with government as a balance wheel, ready to step in if any one power center becomes too important. Bargaining between small numbers of equally powerful organizations supplements the system of self-adjusting markets, and a reasonable pattern of production results. All these ideas added strength to the argument that the private sector would function effectively if high levels of total demand were sustained.

The neoclassical synthesis could not ignore the problems of income distribution and poverty, but there was little room in the synthesis for drastic changes. The medicine for poverty was economic growth and full employment. Jobs would be available for all, and economic growth would gradually make the poor better off. Inequalities would still exist, but that seemed to matter little. Economic growth would make everyone rich, and special-assistance programs, particularly in education and vocational training, could bring along even the disadvantaged. Problems associated with change and automation could be resolved by education, growth, and full employment. Economic growth was the key, since growth made more goods available to provide for the good life and ease the problems of an industrial society.

It was not just one or two economists who were primarily responsible for the neoclassical synthesis. It emerged almost as an unspoken consensus among economists and policymakers in the course of applying Keynesian macroeconomics to the policy problems of the period after World War II. The economist most closely associated with the neoclassical synthesis was the American Paul Samuelson (1915–). His textbook *Economics* (first edition, 1947) was the most widely used introduction to economics for college students for more than a quarter century. Its first edition concentrated on presenting the Keynesian analysis, but later editions broadened to give equal emphasis to the neoclassical analysis of markets. The phrase "neoclassical synthesis" first appeared in print in the third edition.

The neoclassical synthesis was as much political economy as it was economic analysis. It supported the comprehensive macroeconomic planning of the Keynesian system and promoted such liberal ideas as antipoverty

PAUL SAMUELSON

Born in 1915 in Gary, Indiana, Paul Samuelson was an academic *wunderkind* from the start. He loved school and was consistently the star pupil from elementary school through college at the University of Chicago. He went to Harvard for graduate work and published eleven papers in scholarly journals while still a student. His doctoral dissertation, *Foundations of Economic Analysis* (completed 1941, published 1947), was a restatement and extension of neoclassical and Keynesian economics, written in the language of mathematical logic and using some of the mathematical concepts of modern physics. Despite the brilliance of the dissertation, a significant minority of the economics faculty at Harvard opposed keeping him on as an instructor. Perhaps that was because Samuelson had been brash enough as a graduate student to point out some of his professors' limitations in open class, a serious academic violation. Persistent rumor has it that one reason for the opposition was the fact that Samuelson was a Jew. So Samuelson accepted a position in the recently formed economics department at nearby Massachusetts Institute of Technology.

Samuelson continued his brilliant career at MIT, writing important and sometimes pathbreaking papers on a wide variety of topics. His *Collected Scientific Papers* (3 volumes, 1966–1968) contains 388 essays written over a period of fifty years, with over 4,000 pages of text. Emphasis on abstract theory did not preclude concern with current issues of economic policy. Samuelson was a forceful advocate of the pragmatic use of monetary and fiscal policy to achieve full employment, stabilize the economy, and promote economic growth. He saw these objectives as the most important goals of public policy, to be achieved by government spending, tax changes, and monetary policy. The particular policy mix at any time would depend on the existing situation, and flexible use of those instruments was highly desirable. Even though any particular situation may be uncertain, Samuelson generally felt that hesitancy is worse than an active policy to push the economy in the proper direction.

His textbook made Samuelson a multimillionaire. He became an important advisor on economic policy to the Kennedy administration and a columnist for *Newsweek* magazine, where his articles tended toward a politically liberal but evenhanded discussion of current economic issues. Together with Milton Friedman and John Kenneth Galbraith, Samuelson was one of the best-known economists of his times. He received the Nobel Prize in Economic Science in 1970.

programs and aid to less-developed countries. At the same time, it accepted the status quo as far as the structure of the economy was concerned: there was no need for significant change in either the distribution of income or the locus of economic power. As long as macroeconomic policies could produce full employment and economic growth, the annual growth dividend of increased output would make additional resources available to meet everyone's needs.

The neoclassical synthesis was well suited to the climate of opinion that prevailed during the Cold War. It showed how the Western democracies, led by the United States, would prosper; full employment and rising living standards would bring contentment; economic growth would solve the internal problems of poverty; aid could be provided to the developing nations; and a growing economy could provide ample resources for a large defense establishment. The new system of political economy validated the position taken by the United States and its allies in the international struggle for world power after World War II, just as it validated the internal structure of power and the existing economic organization within those countries. The neoclassical synthesis defined a policy mix that would allow capitalism not only to survive, but to triumph.

Economic Growth

Economic growth had long been a central concern of economists. It was the subject of Adam Smith's *Wealth of Nations*. David Ricardo argued that limitations on natural resources would gradually retard growth and lead to a stationary economy. Karl Marx sought to show how the relentless growth of the forces of production would lead to the collapse of capitalism. Neoclassical economics, however, was essentially a theory of stationary equilibrium, especially at the hands of Walras and Pareto, and little work was done on economic growth. Joseph Schumpeter was one exception. He sought to show how entrepreneurship and technological change produced economic growth in a pattern of long waves of alternating rapid growth and relative stagnation of some fifty years' duration, accompanied by business cycles of shorter duration.

Meanwhile, a Swedish economist, Gustav Cassel (1866–1944), a neoclassical economist to the core, in his *Theory of Social Economy* (1918, English translation 1923) sought to show how an economy could grow through accumulation of capital while maintaining a general equilibrium. Cassel's analysis, however, assumed simple capital accumulation without new technologies or increases in productivity, so his work had little impact, especially since the great depression shifted the attention of economists to other more pressing problems.

With the development of Keynesian economics, however, the question of whether there could be a moving equilibrium growth path of the economy arose. Roy Harrod (1900–1978), a friend and colleague of Keynes at Cambridge University, provided an answer. In "An Essay on Dynamic Theory" (1939) he showed that there was a unique rate of economic growth at which the savings of the economy would be just absorbed by investment—hence stable growth. There was one catch, however: a slight deviation from this "warranted" rate of growth would send the economy into either explosive growth or continuous decline. A flurry of papers by other economists followed, attempting to show the conditions under which the economy might be stabilized at Harrod's warranted rate of growth, with little success. Harrod was able to show in a "Second Essay on Dynamic Theory" (1960) that there was a rate of interest that would generate the amount of investment necessary for stable growth, which was a step forward, but he could not prove that it would prevail. It appeared that the economy would alternate between unemployment and overexpansion on its growth path.

A different approach to the problem of stable growth was taken by Robert Solow (1924–) who observed in "A Contribution to the Theory of Economic Growth" (1956) that the reason for the instability in Harrod's model was his assumption of a given or fixed technology. If factors of production have to be used in fixed proportions, it is not surprising that some cannot be efficiently employed. The concept that capital and labor can be substituted for each other turned out to be the key to a theory of stable economic growth.

Solow stated the fundamentals of the theory in his 1956 paper, with an expanded version in *Growth Theory: An Exposition* (1970). Stripped to its essentials, he made three assumptions:

> (1) The labor supply grows over time. (2) Consumers save a given share of their income, which determines the rate of capital accumulation. (3) The factors of production, capital and labor, can be substituted for each other in the production process.

There are two possible outcomes. If technology does not change, the new workers will be equipped with the same methods of production as before, and the economy grows without changing its structure. If improved technology (better physical capital) brings about greater productivity, however, or if productivity increases because of better-educated or skilled workers (better human capital), economic growth will increase, and the structure of the economy will change as the factors of production are shifted to the improved technology. In either case the economy will remain in equilibrium. In the first case the rate of economic growth will not change, and income per capita will not increase. With technological change, however, the rate of growth of the economy will increase, and income per capita will rise.

In other words, the rate of economic growth depends on the rate of growth in the supply of labor and the rate of growth of productivity. In terms of the contemporary American economy, where the labor force grows at about 1 percent annually and output per worker at about 1.5 percent annually, the long-term rate of growth of the economy will be about 2.5 percent per year. And so it is. Robert Solow was awarded the Nobel Prize in Economic Science in 1987.

We have to look beyond growth of the labor force and growth of productivity, however. Productivity increases because more capital and less labor is used per unit of output. But capital results from savings. So savings must increase to provide the added capital per unit of output that raises productivity. Now imagine an economy with a stable rate of growth of 2.5 percent a year, of which 1.5 percent results from increased productivity and 1 percent from growth of the labor force. It must have an interest rate at which savings are equal to investment at exactly that amount of investment that generates a 1.5 percent annual increase in productivity. If interest rates are above that level, investment and productivity will be low, the economy will slow down, and output per person will grow slowly. On the other hand, if interest rates are too low, a high rate of capital investment and the high savings rate necessary to achieve it will also result in low output per person: resources will flow into investment rather than consumer goods. Clearly there is an interest rate at which output per person is maximized in the process of economic growth.

This issue was recognized almost immediately after Solow's work on economic growth was published. By the early 1960s some eight papers by different economists, published almost simultaneously, solved the problem: the interest rate that maximized the long-term growth of output per person was equal to the rate of growth of the economy. The earliest paper was written by a graduate student at Yale University, Edmund Phelps, titled "The Golden Rule of Accumulation: A Fable For Growthmen" (1961). The golden rule was "Do unto the next generation what you wish the previous generation had done unto you," referring to the rate of saving necessary to achieve the optimal rate of economic growth. It is a golden rule that applies to many other situations as well.

Unfortunately, we do not apply the golden rule. At the present time the growth rate of the American economy is about 2.5 percent annually. But interest rates are well above that level. The real interest rate (the market rate minus the rate of inflation) for long-term investment is between 3.5 and 5 percent, depending on how one calculates it. High interest rates keep economic growth below the optimum level. Lower interest rates would bring increased investment and wider application of new technologies that would increase productivity, perhaps from 1.5 percent annually to 2 percent. The growth rate of the economy would then rise. As it rises while the real interest rate continues to fall, the two would become equal. The economy would be on the optimal growth path.

Economists will argue about whether changes in current interest rates would affect the long-run rate of savings and investment necessary to sustain an optimal rate of economic growth. Opinions differ. But there seems to be little doubt that the current policies that seek to dampen inflation with high interest rates also dampen economic growth.

The Conservative Dissent

The interventionist fiscal and monetary policies of the neoclassical synthesis and Military Keynesianism were attacked by two groups of conservative economists who reaffirmed the virtues of the competitive private enterprise economy. One group comprised followers of the Austrian neoclassical economics of Karl Menger. One of their themes was that the free market was the only sure antidote to centralized political power and the only way to ensure the survival of individual freedom. We have already examined their attack on socialist economic planning. They condemned equally the rise of modern socialism, Keynesian fiscal and monetary policy, and the welfare state.

The second group of dissenters from the neoclassical synthesis had its home base at the University of Chicago. Like the Austrians they abhorred socialism, Keynesian economics, and the welfare state. They also saw government intervention in the economy as a threat to individual freedom. The best way to describe them is *libertarian*.

In many respects both the Austrians and the Chicago School represent the ideas of *fundamentalist capitalism*. The best economy is the competitive market economy, in which profit-seeking producers maximize their profits by producing what consumers want most. The free play of individual action is unrestricted, and the role of government is minimized. Adam Smith is the high priest of this economy, and business entrepreneurs are his acolytes.

Austrian Economics

Austrian economics began with Karl Menger, whose *Principles of Economics* of 1871 was a central component of the marginalist revolution that ushered in neoclassical economics. Menger was followed at the University of Vienna by Eugen von Böhm-Bawerk (1851–1914), who is best known for vigorous attacks on Marxism and studies of interest rates and capital related to his critique of Marx. In *The Positive Theory of Capital* (1889) Böhm-Bawerk argued that people put a higher value on present consumption than on future consumption. In order to get them to save, they had to be paid a premium that equates the value to them of present versus future goods. This premium is the rate of interest. He went on to argue that a market economy would establish rates of interest based on individual preferences for present and future goods, which would lead to an efficient allocation of resources. But a socialist regime had no mechanism for achieving those goals and would be doomed to inefficiency. This argument against socialism and economic planning was central to the Austrian School's defense of the private enterprise—market economy. Böhm-Bawerk also conducted a famous seminar at the University of Vienna that trained a whole generation of economists in his elaboration of Menger's version of neoclassical economics.

Ludwig von Mises (1881–1973), whose contribution to the debate over socialist planning has already been examined, was a member of that seminar in the years before World War II. After teaching economic theory at Vienna and Geneva (he left Austria in 1934 because of the rising tide of Nazi sentiment there), he came to the United States in 1940. There he worked on his magnum opus, *Human Action: A Treatise on Economics* (1949). This book was a vigorous defense of pure laissez-faire based on individual action coordinated by market forces, leading to an economy that met the needs and desires of individuals at the least cost in human effort. Profit and loss was the motive power of the economy, and profit was the reward for innovative and successful entrepreneurial behavior. Mises taught his libertarian version of economics at New York University between 1948 and 1969, where a younger generation of "neo-Austrian" economists continue in his tradition. A Ludwig von Mises Institute has been established at Auburn University in Alabama.

The foremost representative of the Austrian tradition in the United States was Friedrich von Hayek (1899–1992). His best-known work was *The Road to Serfdom* (1944). Hayek studied at the University of Vienna shortly after the First World War, where the tradition of Menger and Böhm-Bawerk was strong, and where he attended Mises's private seminar. His early work centered on monetary theory and business cycles, in which he elaborated the idea, initiated by Böhm-Bawerk, Mises, and others, that recessions and depressions were caused by easy credit that triggered overexpansion of the capacity to produce and excessive speculation. In 1931 Leonel Robbins invited him to the London School of Economics, where he remained until 1950, when he moved to the University of Chicago. In 1962 he returned to Germany for academic posts at Freiburg and Salzburg.

Where the classical and neoclassical economists centered their attention on the objects being valued, either in terms of labor inputs or costs of production, Hayek, in the tradition of Menger and Mises, focused on the individuals engaged in the process of valuation: the prices of objects and their uses could be understood only in terms of individual human purposes. Hayek argued that the market economy achieves spontaneous, unplanned order that originates in the conscious, unique actions of individuals. Understanding of complex market phenomena must be built on that base. Hayek expressed this *methodological individualism* and the libertarian political philosophy associated with it in his *Individualism and Economic Order* (1949).

Hayek's most important contribution to economics was the concept of the economy as a process of adjustment over time that coordinates the plans and actions of individuals. In this context the price system is a communication network that transmits information from one part of the market system to another. Prices are signals. Competition is an unruly process generated by individual actions taken in response to information obtained from the market process itself. Business plans and entrepreneurial decisions respond to market-generated information, feeding back innovation and changes into the market process. Order emerges from the coordinating function of the market within a continuing process of change and progress.

Hayek accepted the proposition that the coordination of individual action and business plans could falter from time to time. The difficulty lay in capital investment, which can lead to expansion of credit and overproduction that cannot be sustained. This aspect of the market economy was explored in early works on business cycles, *Monetary Theory and the Trade Cycle* (1933), *Prices and Production* (1935), and *The Pure Theory of Capital* (1941).

Hayek's view of how a market economy functions did not have a significant impact on mainstream economic theory. Yet his view of an economy continually changing over time relegates the concept of market equilibrium central to the economics of Walras, Marshall, and their successors to a minor position, if not irrelevance. Hayek's may be a better way to understand the world. When we consider the events of the twentieth century, do we observe a tendency toward equilibrium or a process of sometimes orderly and sometimes disorderly change?

The Chicago School

The conservative dissent of the Chicago School rose to prominence in the 1960s. It was led by Milton Friedman (1912–), a strong advocate of the competitive private enterprise economy who stressed the need for government to establish a framework within which the free market could function most effectively.

Friedman followed in the tradition of Henry C. Simons (1899–1946), who preceded him at the University of Chicago. Simons did not write much—his life's work is a group of essays and papers that comprise only one modest volume—but he was highly influential. A single essay, "A Positive Program for Laissez Faire" (1934), set out a program of reform to bring competitive private enterprise back to life and preserve its vitality:

> Eliminate all forms of monopolistic market power, to include the breakup of large oligopolistic corporations and application of anti-trust laws to labor unions. A Federal incorporation law could be used to limit corporate size, and where technology required giant firms for reasons of low cost production the Federal government should own and operate them. . . .
>
> Promote economic stability by reform of the monetary system and establishment of stable rules for monetary policy. . . .
>
> Reform the tax system and promote equity through the income tax. . . .
>
> Abolish all tariffs.
>
> Limit waste by restricting advertising and other wasteful merchandising practices.

Simons's program was directed against artificially maintained privilege and market restrictions as much as it was in favor of competition and individualism. It did not ignore instability, inequity, and wasteful spending but sought measures that would reduce if not eliminate them.

A contemporary of Simons at the University of Chicago, Frank H. Knight (1885–1972), was also important in helping formulate conservative neoclassical economics in the United States. He was the theorist who balanced Simons's policy emphasis. Neoclassical economics had come under attack in the 1920s from those who advocated a more egalitarian income distribution and greater government intervention in the economy. Knight's career was devoted primarily to answering those attacks by more careful definition of terms and greater precision in analysis. The result was an enriched statement of the theory of the free market based on the economic individual as the key actor. Knight recognized that the theory was not all-inclusive and that it was sometimes at variance with reality, but he argued that it was *useful*. This methodological position was a cornerstone of the Chicago School and the approach developed later by Friedman, who received the Nobel Prize in 1978.

Milton Friedman was an important representative of the classical liberal philosophy that went back to Adam Smith's economics. He argued that the benefits derived from a laissez-faire policy are far more desirable than those obtained from interventionist policies that modify the operation of free markets in the interest of solving some immediate problem. Take minimum-wage laws, for example. Designed to benefit low-wage workers by raising their incomes, Friedman argued that they have the opposite effect. By making it too expensive for employers to hire such workers, the laws increase unemployment and worsen the economic position of all those at the bottom of the economic pyramid. A series of similar examples is given in Friedman's widely read *Capitalism and Freedom* (1962), in which the root of the argument is that those measures that restrict the free market bring losses rather than gains, while economic freedom pays off in greater benefits in the long run.

The most significant example of government intervention in the economy was Keynesian macroeconomic planning. Friedman's strongest criticisms were directed against the use of fiscal policy to stabilize the economy, and his strongest advocacy was in support of monetary policy—but of a special type that goes back to Simons's policy proposals for its base.

Friedman argued that it is extremely difficult to counterbalance the swings of the private sector by using government spending or tax changes. Not only is it difficult to forecast the movement of the business cycle, but, in Friedman's words:

> There is likely to be a lag between the need for action and government recognition of the need; a further lag between recognition of the need for action and the taking of action; and a still further lag between the action and its effects.

The result is that "corrective action may itself turn into a further error," with a stimulus coming when spending should be dampened, or vice versa.

Friedman believed that the monetary system has a far more pervasive effect on economic activity than fiscal policy. To support his position he revived and gave new life to the quantity theory of money—the idea that the quantity of money determines the general level of prices—by showing that the monetary system affects the level of aggregate demand and the national output in a wide variety of subtle ways. The Keynesians had never denied the importance of monetary policies and sought to use them as one of the twin arms of macroeconomic policy in coordination with fiscal policies. But even on that point Friedman parted company with the Keynesians. He did not like the active use of monetary policy. He wanted neither easy money to promote full employment nor tight money to prevent inflation. The long-run effects of each, he argued, might be just the opposite of their intended short-run effects. He wanted a neutral monetary policy oriented toward long-run growth needs. Friedman prescribed a gradual and steady increase in the money supply at a fixed percent annually as an aid to economic expansion and growth.

But what about business cycles and depressions? Would not Friedman's policies leave the economy wide open to another severe depression? He argued that they would not, and in support of this point he and Anna Schwartz (1915–), a colleague at the National Bureau for Economic Research, analyzed the monetary history of the United States in an attempt to show that instability in the monetary system had always been the chief cause of instability in employment and output. These findings were published in *A Monetary History of the United States* (1963). A large section of that book was devoted to arguing that the monetary policies of the Federal Reserve System first helped to bring on the Great Depression of the 1930s and then made it much worse after it came. The implication was clear: stabilize the monetary system, and economic stability will follow.

Friedman and his supporters, who are called "monetarists" because of their emphasis on monetary factors, also contend that government spending designed to prevent recessions is a significant cause of inflation. Government securities sold to finance a deficit during a recession represent additions to the private and public debt that the economy normally generates. Thus, when the economy moves back to a full-employment level of activity, they argue, the money supply must be increased in order to support the extra debt. With a larger money supply the price level will be forced up as full employment is approached. Thus a recession-created deficit is "monetized" by action of the monetary authorities as the economy moves toward full employment, and prices rise. Recessions can be avoided but only at the cost of inflation, in this view.

The attack on Keynesian policies by Friedman and the Chicago School broke the almost complete dominance of Keynesian macroeconomics in the formulation of government economic policy. It showed that money is important, and much of the work of the monetarists was integrated into the larger body of economic theory. But there remains a strong area of disagreement. It centers on the fundamental differences between the activist liberal who advocates strong government action to solve society's problems and the laissez-faire liberal who sees that path as wrong. The latter wants government to follow only the path of establishing and maintaining a framework within which the free market can function effectively.

Neo-Ricardian and Post Keynesian Economics

Another dissent from the neoclassical synthesis appeared in the 1960s and 1970s. It is called "neo-Ricardian" in England and "Post Keynesian" in the United States. It takes from Keynes a heavy emphasis on the instability of a modern private-enterprise economy and the uncertainty that surrounds much economic behavior. In particular, it stresses the volatility of the level of investment that results from changes in anticipations and expectations about the future.

The investment decision must be made in the present, but, because capital equipment is long-lasting, the payoff can never be accurately known at the time the investment is made. As expectations about the future change—and they can change widely in a short time—investment decisions can also fluctuate widely and cause large swings in the level of economic activity.

These ideas derived from Keynes's writings were further developed by Joan Robinson (1903–1983), whose contributions to the theory of imperfect competition were noted in an earlier chapter. She taught at Cambridge, England, and was a younger compatriot of Keynes. A brilliant theorist, she should have received a Nobel Prize in economics but never did.

In a paper published in 1953 with the esoteric title "The Production Function and the Theory of Capital," Robinson mounted an attack on a highly vulnerable part of neoclassical economics, its treatment of capital and the time-consuming process of production. The issue was the role of capital goods in the production process. In the neoclassical theory of production, producers are presumed to minimize their costs of production. But costs of production are only the prices of inputs, such as capital. Capital goods, however, derive their value from the value of the final products they produce. This makes the argument circular: the cost of inputs depends on the value of the goods they produce, but the goods they produce cannot be priced until the costs of inputs are determined. The circularity would make no difference if all this were happening simultaneously, but that is not the case. Production takes place over time, and the business firm must value its inputs before it has information about what it can get for its outputs. Furthermore, since capital cannot be adequately valued in independently measurable units, how can we show that it earns a return equal to its contribution to production? The only ways out of this difficulty are to define capital as Marx did—as an intermediate product only, standing midway between labor and final output—or to find some way to define and measure capital independently of the value of final output—and this cannot be done. These issues raised by Joan Robinson started a long and acrimonious debate on the nature of capital and its relationship to economic growth, prices, and the distribution of income.

Robinson's emphasis on capital and the production process fitted in well with the writings of several other economists. One was Piero Sraffa, an Italian economist who went to Cambridge at Keynes's invitation after fleeing Mussolini's fascism in the 1920s. In 1960 he published a ninety-page book with the unlikely title of *Production of Commodities by Means of Commodities*. It was a highly abstract mathematical description of a simplified competitive economy in which technological relationships rather than supply and demand determined the production of commodities. Prices, however, resulted from the tradeoff between wages and profits imposed on the production system by collective bargaining, conflict between labor and management, or the edicts of a central planning agency. Note the conceptual breakthrough here. The entire emphasis was shifted from market adjustment to production technology, which was also the emphasis in Robinson's seminal paper.

A major "capital controversy" followed the publication of Robinson's and Sraffa's works, as advocates of mainstream economics sought to answer the heretics. But the neo-Ricardians and the Post Keynesians, that is, the supporters of Robinson and Sraffa—won the day. Prevailing ideas about the determination of prices and the distribution of income were shown to be logically inconsistent and of little or no relevance, particularly in a modern world of long-lasting capital goods and a complex technology. As long as the theoretical questions asked by economists were limited to exchange of goods within a market, the older ideas retained their robust conclusions: the interaction of demand and supply determined market price. But when production involved the use of capital goods in a time-consuming process determined by the technologies available, the neoclassical synthesis no longer provided adequate answers.

The critics claimed victory in the theoretical wars, but they lost on the field of ideology. Even Paul Samuelson, leader of the American economists who attacked the Robinson-Sraffa supporters, admitted that they were right on key theoretic matters, but he continued to present the mainstream neoclassical synthesis in his textbook and other writings. One could not expect, in the midst of the Cold War, that the foundations of Western ideology would be significantly modified simply because of flaws in the theory.

Post Keynesian economics in the United States developed further. A new view of the financial system emerged. Where monetarists saw the supply of money as a major determinant of prices, and traditional Keynesians argued that management of the money supply can help stabilize the economy, Post Keynesians argued that the level of economic activity determines the money supply and that little can be accomplished by attempting to manage or control the monetary system. Inflation is seen as the result of big unions, big business, and big government all attempting to enlarge or maintain their incomes in the face of changing levels of output and changing rates of economic growth. The economy is analyzed as a dual system, the more important sector being dominated by big business and monopoloid pricing, with the competitive, small-business sector being less important and diminishing in significance, even though the traditional theory of competitive markets is still relevant there. The labor market is also analytically

PIERO SRAFFA

Piero Sraffa (1898–1983) published relatively little in his professional career. A paper in 1924 analyzed the concept of perfect competition and started the modern theory of imperfect competition. A few years later, when John Maynard Keynes wanted an economist to write an article on the Italian economy for a special issue of the *Manchester Guardian* newspaper, he called on Sraffa, who wrote a stinging critique of fascist economic policies under Mussolini. Mussolini ordered Sraffa's arrest, but Sraffa's father, a professor of law at the university in Turin, was an old friend of Mussolini's. As soon as the arrest order was given, Mussolini telephoned Sraffa's father and urged him to have Piero leave Italy immediately. Piero Sraffa fled to England, where Keynes got him a position in the economics department at Cambridge. Sraffa spent the next ten years editing the works and papers of David Ricardo, now the standard edition, including an introductory essay that is the best single essay on Ricardo as an economist. He also began work on his *Production of Commodities by Means of Commodities,* which played such an important role in the capital controversy of the 1960s.

But this quiet, soft-spoken, unassuming scholar also played a key role in the publication of one of the important contributions to Marxist political theory in the twentieth century, Antonio Gramsci's *Letters from Prison.* Gramsci and Sraffa had been boyhood friends in Turin. While Sraffa landed in Cambridge, Gramsci became the leader of the Italian Communist party and was imprisoned by the Mussolini regime. Sraffa made arrangements with a bookseller in Milan to provide Gramsci with any books or newspapers he wanted, billing Sraffa for the cost. In prison Gramsci began writing long letters to his wife in Rome, a Russian whom he had married while in the Soviet Union in the early 1920s. The letters contained Gramsci's analysis of the proper political tactics for a revolutionary party under a dictatorship.

Gramsci's wife worked as a secretary in the Soviet Embassy in Rome. When she received a letter from her husband, she took it to the embassy, where it was sent by diplomatic pouch to the Soviet embassy in London. There the letter was mailed to Sraffa in Cambridge, who sent it by mail to the headquarters of the Italian Communist party in exile in Paris. This was the scheme that evaded the comic opera security system of Mussolini's Italy to bring the famous *Letters from Prison* to light.

divided into two chief parts, a primary sector in the industries with advanced technology, labor unions, and big business, and a secondary sector with more labor-intensive technology, few unions, and relatively small, competitive business enterprise. There is no presumption of a general equilibrium; the level of economic activity is volatile; the process of growth is unbalanced; and income distribution is the result of conflicts between the chief claimants, labor and capital, and the strength of their organized power.

This view of the economy implies that any tendency toward a harmonious and orderly outcome of the economic process is swamped by countertendencies toward fluctuation, conflict, and disorder. If orderly and desirable outcomes are to be achieved, government must intervene.

Radical Economics

The problems of a changing economy also triggered a revival of Marxism and an increased interest in socialism. Gathering force through the 1960s, the resurgence of radicalism was less an attack on the dominant economic theory and policy as it was a critique of the economic system and its effect. A new interest in Marxism appeared, along with a wide range of non-Marxist radical analyses of the modern world.

One book led the way in the United States for the resurgence of Marxism as a tool for analyzing the contemporary economy. It was *Monopoly Capital* (1966) by Paul Baran (1910–1964) and Paul Sweezy (1910–). Baran, who died two years before the book was published, was professor of economics at Stanford University. An earlier book, *The Political Economy of Growth* (1957), had already marked him as a major contributor to Marxist economic theory. In it, he focused attention on monopoly as the distinguishing feature of highly developed capitalism, on the production of an economic surplus that had to be disposed of, and on a drive toward economic imperialism leading to inevitable conflict between the advanced and the underdeveloped economies. All of these themes were developed in the later book. Baran's co-author, Paul Sweezy, had begun an academic career, teaching at Harvard University from 1934 to 1942 and writing two important pieces, one on interest groups among American corporations and the other on the theory of oligopoly. After government service in World War II, he helped found in 1949 the leading American Marxist journal, *Monthly Review*, and was one of its editors until a few years ago. He also wrote an important Marxist work, *The Theory of Capitalist Development* (1942), which is still one of the best restatements of basic Marxist economic theory for the contemporary reader.

Monopoly Capital made a major contribution to Marxist theory by shifting attention away from the assumption of a competitive economy, which was basic to the original analysis developed by Marx, and by focusing on the monopolistic aspects of giant enterprise in the contemporary economy. In doing so it also deemphasized the role of the working class and the class struggle, as it worked out the logic of an economy dominated by privately owned big corporations.

The argument runs as follows: monopolistic large corporations are able to maintain selling prices at relatively high levels while competing with each other to cut costs, advertise and sell, and develop new or modified products, all in a gigantic race for profits. An economic surplus is the result, which can't be absorbed by consumer spending, however wasteful, or business investment, which only increases the surplus. Part of the surplus is absorbed in mammoth sales and marketing efforts and part through government employment. But the major thrust of monopoly capital is toward imperialism and militarism as the easiest and surest ways of utilizing otherwise surplus productive capacity. In the process, exploitation centers on low-wage workers at home, especially blacks and other minority groups, and on underdeveloped areas overseas that provide opportunities for profit even larger than in the home economy. For the average person the profit nexus and exchange relationship destroy meaningful human relationships, leading to widespread alienation, hostility, and purposelessness. The entire system is essentially irrational, for although individual economic units may be operated with the utmost emphasis on rational decisions, the system as a whole is directed toward irrational goals. Nevertheless, the system continues to function effectively because of military spending and Keynesian full-employment policies. It will continue to do so until the less-developed countries throw off the yoke of neocolonialism and the worldwide system of industrial capitalism collapses.

This brief summary can only suggest the richness and breadth of the analysis and the angry condemnation of modern life the book contains. If it had been written by anyone other than the two leading American Marxists, it might have become a major best-seller, just as some non-Marxist critiques have been. Baran and Sweezy were clearly describing the same economy as Galbraith, and much of their analyses were parallel. As it is, *Monopoly Capital* has had a steadily widening influence both in the United States and abroad.

Perhaps equally influential in stimulating radical analyses of modern society was an earlier book, *The Power Elite* (1956), written by the Columbia University sociologist C. Wright Mills (1916–1962). Mills argued that the United States is ruled by an elite group of business, political, and military leaders who manage the large bureaucratic organizations that dominate modern life. Recruited from a relatively narrow stratum of society, this group of several thousand elite managers selects itself by an informal process in which the older leadership passes on a value system that stresses acquisition of wealth and private enterprise. Oligarchy, rather than democracy, dominates modern America, along with the corrupt values of individualistic materialism, according to Mills.

These themes—dominance of the economy by giant corporations led by a self-selecting elite, and the problems of the capitalist economy—are the distinguishing features of radical analyses of the modern economy. In the United States, the Union for Radical Political Economics publishes a journal, sponsors national and regional conferences, and participates in the annual meetings of the American Economic Association. There are similar groups in England and other countries of Western Europe.

The Marxist revival and related radical economic thought were not particularly associated with support for the Soviet Union and its brand of socialism. Many radicals, including strong Marxists, looked with dismay upon the centralized bureaucratic methods of planning of the Soviet Union. They are more favorably inclined toward decentralized administration, market socialism, and workers' management. A search is under way among radicals for alternatives to both private-enterprise capitalism as practiced in the United States and Western Europe and the centralized state planning of the Soviet Union.

A Brief Overview

Adam Smith had developed two chief lines of analysis. One centered on economic growth and its relationship to the distribution of income. This theme was taken up by David Ricardo and Thomas Malthus, and later by Karl Marx. Smith's second theme was the competitive marketplace, in which the interaction of demand and supply determined the "natural" price of commodities.

This second theme was developed further by the neoclassical economists. One group, led by Léon Walras, expanded Smith's analysis of individual markets into a theory of general equilibrium in all markets. These theorists concentrated on the conditions necessary for the existence of a general market equilibrium but paid little attention to how it could be achieved. They gave even less attention to problems of economic growth.

A second group of neoclassical economists headed by Alfred Marshall, sought to extend the analysis of demand and supply in individual markets in greater detail by developing a partial equilibrium theory that could be applied to specific economic problems, rather than the more general equilibrium of the followers of Walras. This was the situation, greatly simplified, that prevailed in conventional or mainstream economics at the time Keynes loosed his macroeconomic bombshell on the profession.

Economic theory is never isolated from politics and ideology, however. We have already seen how proponents of the neoclassical synthesis of the 1960s argued that competitive markets driven by consumer demand could continue to allocate resources and produce what the public wanted as long as Keynesian budget and monetary policies provided a stable economy at or near full employment. This, it was argued, would enable the U.S. economy to prosper while the inefficient authoritarian planning of the Soviet Union would slowly lead to economic stagnation there. Keynesian macroeconomic management plus free markets would lead to victory in the Cold War.

The limits of this approach became apparent with the ending of the long postwar boom in the late 1960s and the Great Inflation of the 1970s. Keynesian management of aggregate demand seemed to have little impact on the relative stagnation and the worsened recessions in the new era of slow economic growth. Unemployment increased and tended to last longer despite the best efforts of Keynesian-oriented policies. Worse yet, severe inflation, fueled by increased energy costs, monetary expansion, and military spending, seemed completely out of control. Once again, events brought a change in economic thought. High theory in economics provided a new rationale for the desirability of private-enterprise capitalism in the form of general equilibrium theory, a new neoclassical macroeconomics, and a theory of real business cycles.

General Equilibrium Theory

The general equilibrium theory that came to dominate the analysis of competitive markets in the last fifty years was a further development of the neoclassical economics of Walras and his follower, Vilfredo Pareto, which had been largely dormant in the interwar period. It came back to life in the era of the Cold War, when capitalism and communism were in combat. Here we examine the essentials of the theory, some of its limitations, and its larger significance.

Picture a closed economy (no foreign trade) with a given number of consumers who seek to maximize their satisfaction, a given number of producers who seek to maximize their profits, and a given amount of resources, which are divided among the consumers and producers. The question to be explored is whether there is a system of prices at which consumers succeed in optimally satisfying their preferences, within the limits set by their resources, and producers succeed in maximizing their profits, solely through the operations of competitive markets and without any government intervention. The theory then proves that such a price system exists. We do not go into the proof here, since it uses such mathematical exotica as vectors, convex spaces, and fixed point theorems. Two books present the analysis, using the mathematical logic developed in Whitehead and Russell's *Principia Mathematica*: Gerard Debreu, *Theory of Value: An Axiomatic Analysis of Economic Equilibrium* (1959) and *General Equilibrium Analysis* (1971) by Kenneth Arrow and Frank Hahn. They argued that there could exist in a perfectly competitive system of markets a general equilibrium of prices brought about solely by the voluntary action of consumers and producers.

The analysis was an improvement over the earlier theory of market price. Recall in our discussion of the beginnings of mathematical economics that Augustin Cournot pointed out that the demand for a commodity was a function of its price: $D = F(p)$ in his terminology. That would be true if everything else in the economy remains the same. But everything else does not remain the same. As Irving Fisher showed in 1892, a change in one price reverberates throughout the price system. Thus, the demand for lox will be affected not only by the price of lox, but by the prices of bagels and cream cheese as well. Cournot's equation expands to $D_a = F(p_a\ p_b\ p_c \cdots p_n)$ in algebraic notation. That is, the demand for commodity a is a function of its price, as well as the prices of commodities b, c, and all other commodities. Cournot's equation defined a partial equilibrium in a single market, while the expanded equation defines a general equilibrium of all markets. The fundamental idea is that the system of markets is a unified whole.

The concept of a market system of interrelated parts led economists to examine some complex market relationships. Markets for complementary products such as lox, bagels, and cream cheese, for example, or products that can substitute for each other, such as tin or aluminum cans, were explored. The concepts of competition and monopoly were broadened from examining a single industry, such as steel or chemicals, to studying competition for the consumer's dollar by more than one product. The economics of general equilibrium theory enabled economists to broaden their field of analysis to include many areas of economic activity that previously had not been thought of as economics. Viewing households and families as utility maximizing units, their production and distribution decisions became items to be analyzed. Marital status, the number of children, education, and health care were all subject to the desire to optimize. Criminal activity, drug addiction, and inheritance were also topics to be analyzed. In other areas, game theory was applied to all kinds of personal relationships. Growth theory was broadened to include the complex relationship between past and present investments in human capital and research and development expenditures. The core assumption of general equilibrium theory, that individual preferences determined individual choices, was developed. These choices were subject to the constraints imposed by social norms and by existing technology, and they were qualified by human expectations.

Despite these advances, general equilibrium theory has serious limitations. Perhaps the most serious flaw is a failure to show how the equilibrium could be achieved. The theory defined the system of prices at which all consumers and all producers were able to optimize, but it failed to show how the economy could move from an initial disequilibrium to an equilibrium. Nirvana may be there, but how does one get to it? Debreu and Arrow/Hahn had no answer.

A second and perhaps more serious flaw involved the distribution of income and wealth. The theory postulated an initial distribution of income and wealth among consumers and producers. If the initial distribution gave half of all resources to 5 percent of the participants and half to the remaining 95 percent, the resulting equilibrium would provide many luxuries to the few and little subsistence to the many. Was this optimal? Indeed, for every possible initial distribution of resources there would be a unique equilibrium set of prices and a unique distribution of income. So even if a general equilibrium were achieved, the desirability of the result was still at issue.

Finally, the theory included assumptions that were clearly unrealistic. For example, it required that all producers and consumers have "perfect knowledge" of all prices, including all future prices, in order to make optimizing decisions about the use of their resources. This ruled out all uncertainty. Theorists took up the challenge. Some used the concept of "expected utility" to convert uncertainty into risk whose probability could be determined, but this resulted in temporary equilibria only. Others built true uncertainty into general equilibrium models only to end up with a variety of disequilibria. These and other explorations on the frontiers of general equilibrium theory tended to undermine the very concept of a general equilibrium.

The presence of unrealistic assumptions in general equilibrium theory was strongly attacked by critics. They pointed out assumptions about the rational behavior of consumers and producers that could be neither proven nor disproven, reflecting Gödel's undecidability theorem in systems of mathematical logic. Other assumptions about the absence of uncertainty and the presence of full employment were clearly unrealistic. It was a static theory. Some critics argued that these aspects of general equilibrium theory placed it in the realm of metaphysics rather than reality. The problem may be that the mathematics used is not able to fully account for the great complexity of the real world market economy. Perhaps the underlying issue is whether a concept of the economy as a stable system in equilibrium, or tending toward equilibrium, is meaningful in a world that seems to be continually changing and sometimes in turmoil. Perhaps we should be thinking in terms of continuous disequilibrium and conflict instead of equilibrium and harmony.

Despite its flaws, general equilibrium theory swept through the economics profession in the 1970s in the same way that neoclassical economics displaced classical economics a century ago, and as Keynesian economics had swept the field a generation before. General equilibrium theory was studied by graduate students in every economics department in the English-speaking world. The books by Debreu or Arrow and Hahn, or textbooks derived from them, were required reading, and they still are. The leading journals in the field are filled with papers based on general equilibrium models of the economy, bolstered by econometric studies that support the hypotheses developed in the model.

The time was ripe for the general equilibrium revolution. The ideology and climate of opinion of the Cold War extolled the market economy and economic freedom in opposition to the economic planning and authoritarian government of the Soviet Union. As if by an invisible hand, high theory in economics responded by describing the competitive market economy as one in which every need or want of consumers, insofar as their resources would allow, would be met by the voluntary actions of producers. It also fitted the needs of political conservatives who believed in eliminating government from economic affairs. Political events and the ideological needs of the Cold War created a fertile environment for general equilibrium theory.

This is not to say that those who originated or developed general equilibrium theory were political conservatives or Cold Warriors. The political leanings of the individuals involved are not particularly relevant to the social and political processes by which ideas move to prominence. Walras was a socialist, Pareto a right-wing conservative. Debreu is reputed to be a political conservative, Arrow a political liberal; the two are close friends. The important point is that the political and ideological climate of opinion is always an important factor in the development of ideas.

New Neoclassical Macroeconomics

For fifty years and more after the end of the Second World War, the American economy, and the world economy as well, was afflicted by a continuing inflation of prices. At times the inflation slackened while at other times it accelerated. Economists argued about the causes, the cure, and appropriate policies. Furthermore, the rise of general equilibrium theory raised the question of whether inflation, a phenomenon of disequilibrium, could prevail in an economy supposedly in equilibrium.

The debate began in the 1950s. Paul Samuelson's neoclassical synthesis, in order to simplify the analysis, contained the assumption that prices would not start to increase until full employment of labor and capital was achieved. This "fixed price model" was adopted in order to show exactly how much the gross national product (now renamed the gross domestic product) would change if there were an increase or decrease in any of the variables that affected it. The assumption of fixed prices was made to isolate the impact of changes in the Keynesian variables solely on output and employment.

John Robinson, the English economist and a younger colleague of Keynes at Cambridge University, called this "bastard Keynesianism." It ignored the later chapters of Keynes's *General Theory* in which Keynes explained that prices would tend to rise as an expanding economy approached full employment and markets tended to tighten. Price increases while unemployment persisted were quite consistent with this "flexible price" Keynesian theory. The real danger, according to Keynes, would come if expansion of purchasing power continued after full employment was achieved. This could occur in wartime, he pointed out in his pamphlet, *How to Pay for the War* (1940). This is where macroeconomic theory stood—the fixed price and flexible price Keynesian analyses—when three recessions hit in rapid succession in the 1950s. Prices continued to rise when the economy faltered. Reduced aggregate demand did not bring the general price level down.

At this point the Phillips Curve appeared. An English economist, A. W. Phillips, published a study in 1956 on the relationship between unemployment and wage rates in England between 1861 and 1940. The study showed that wages tended to rise when unemployment rates fell, and that wages fell when unemployment rose. American economists, led by Paul Samuelson, immediately incorporated the Phillips Curve into the fixed price Keynesian model. Because wages were an important element in the cost of production, it was argued that wage increases would result in price increases. So the Phillips relationship was changed to the idea that reduced rates of unemployment would cause prices to rise.

KENNETH ARROW

Kenneth Arrow was born in 1921, the son of immigrants. His business-man father prospered, but lost everything in the Depression of the 1930s. After high school Arrow went to the City College of New York, chiefly because it was free. At commencement he was awarded a medal as the graduate with the highest grades. He started graduate work at Columbia University and obtained a master's degree in mathematics in 1941. World War II interrupted his graduate work. As a weather officer in the U. S. Air Force, Arrow published his first paper on the optimal trajectory for aircraft. Returning to Columbia after the war, he completed his graduate work with a dissertation on *Social Choice and Individual Values* (1951).

Few scholars in any field manage to write even a single major work. Arrow produced two. One was his doctoral dissertation, which bridged the fields of economics and political theory. In it Arrow argued that a majority consensus may not be possible in a democratic society if there are three or more political groups of relatively equal size. Shifting coalitions among these competing groups could prevent a majority from emerging. For example, group A could agree with group B to form a majority that defeats group C. But group C could break that coalition by offering B a better deal, leaving A in the cold. A, in turn, could form another coalition with C that excludes B, only to discover that allying with B against C, as in the original coalition, would be better. An endless cycle of legislative deadlock could easily follow. Arrow then went on to analyze how a democratic process might solve the problem. He found that although deadlocks could be broken, satisfying all of the differing groups simultaneously was not possible. This became known as Arrow's impossibility theorem. It became the starting point for a rapidly expanding literature on social choice.

Arrow's second pathbreaking work was *General Competitive Analysis* (1971), which he wrote in collaboration with Frank Hahn. Both books were cited when Arrow was awarded the Nobel Prize in Economic Science in 1972. Like Samuelson, Arrow wrote extensively on a wide variety of topics. His *Collected Papers* (six volumes 1983–1985) are overwhelming in number, diversity, and scientific significance. Unlike Samuelson, Friedman, or Galbraith, Arrow did not engage in public debates over public policy. He taught at Stanford University from 1949 to 1969, before moving to Harvard. When in the 1970s the Harvard economics department purged itself of the brilliant young radicals on its faculty, Arrow quietly left Harvard and returned to Stanford, where he ended his academic career.

Two policy prescriptions were developed from the Phillips Curve analysis. One came from business interests and political conservatives: zap labor unions. The other came from liberals: supplement Keynesian policies designed to reduce unemployment with actions to keep wages from rising, like the wage-price guidelines of the Kennedy administration in the 1960s. Somehow or other, economists lost sight of the Keynesian flexible price analysis that rising aggregate demand would cause the general price level, including wages, interest rates, and prices, to rise together as the economy approached full employment. The growing economy would generate an increased flow of output as well as an increased flow of income. Inflation would result if the flow of income increased faster than the flow of output. According to the flexible price Keynesian theory, prices (and wages) rise when the flow of spending grows more rapidly than the flow of output.

The Phillips Curve analysis was discredited when, during the Great Inflation of the 1970s, prices rose and continued rising no matter what happened to the unemployment rate. For example, in both 1972 and 1974 the unemployment rate was 5.6 percent. According to the Phillips Curve theory, the rate of inflation should have been the same in both years. It wasn't. In 1972 prices rose by 3.3 percent, in 1974 by 11 percent. The unemployment rate also fell between 1971 and 1972, from 5.9 to 5.6 percent. The theory said that price increases should accelerate. They didn't. Instead, the rate of inflation fell from 4.3 to 3.3 percent. So much for the Phillips Curve theory!

Of course, something else was fueling the Great Inflation of the 1970s: the Organization of Petroleum Exporting Countries (OPEC) raised the price of oil tenfold, from about $2.50 per barrel to about $25.00 per barrel. The price of food also escalated in the 1970s, and the financing of oil purchases at the new higher prices brought a huge increase in the world's money supply.

Economists began to reexamine the causes of inflation. Emphasis shifted from "demand side inflation" caused by increased purchasing power relative to the goods available for sale, as in wartime, to "supply side inflation" caused by increased costs of production. A new concept also emerged, called "core inflation." In measuring inflation, if we leave out the cost of energy and the cost of food, which can be influenced by noneconomic factors such as OPEC and weather, the residual is core inflation that results solely from the way the economy functions—a continuing and steady increase in prices. There has been much speculation about the causes of core inflation, including military spending, government deficits, increasing use of credit, increasing demand for skilled workers, and so on, almost indefinitely. The new neoclassical macroeconomics attributes core inflation to expectations that prices will continue to rise at the same rate as in the recent past, but no one really knows. So when you hear economists discussing core inflation, remember that it is an economic phenomenon that is known to exist, but no one knows why.

Despite the facts, the Phillips Curve refused to die. It fitted neatly into the arsenal of political conservatives who used it to attack not only labor unions, but also government policies designed to reduce unemployment and dampen recessions. One result was the concept of a "natural rate of unemployment," say 6 percent, at which the core inflation rate would be stable. If government tried to reduce unemployment below that level, using Keynesian fiscal and monetary policies, the reduced unemployment would be only temporary. Lower unemployment would generate higher prices, according to Phillips Curve theory. The higher prices would then bring about an increase in unemployment back to the "natural rate" of 6 percent. The attempt to reduce unemployment by stimulating the economy would only result in higher prices. If the Keynesian policies designed to reduce unemployment continued, a process of accelerating inflation would ensue.

The next step was to bring "rational expectations" into the analysis. If consumers, business executives, and financiers expect stimulation of the economy to bring higher prices, they will anticipate that result and act accordingly. Consumers, expecting higher prices in the future, will buy now, pushing prices up. Business managers, observing the increase in consumer buying and expecting prices to rise, will raise prices now. Bankers, observing the increase in demand for loans as consumers spend now and producers borrow to increase output, will raise interest rates. All this will happen very quickly as everyone acts on their expectations. The result, according to rational expectations theory, is that price increases quickly absorb all or almost all of the effect of stimulative fiscal and monetary policy. Little or no change is felt in reduced unemployment or increased output.

The "new neoclassical macroeconomics" had arrived. The economy would be in equilibrium at the natural rate of unemployment. All of the Keynesian variables are in equilibrium at that point: aggregate demand and supply are equal, desired saving and desired investment are equal, and cash balances held by the public are equal to the money supply. It is not a full employment equilibrium, however, unless one defines full employment as the natural rate of unemployment. Prices are not stable either, for the price level rises at the rate of core inflation. Meanwhile, the economy expands at the growth rate defined by the growth of the labor force, the rate of savings and accumulation of capital, and increased productivity due to technological change.

The policy prescriptions of the new neoclassical macroeconomics are in the laissez-faire tradition. Any effort by government to reduce unemployment could set an accelerating inflation into motion. Balanced budgets should be the rule for government, in order not to disturb the equilibrium. If the growth rate of the economy should grow rapidly, causing unemployment to fall and prices to rise, the central bank should raise interest rates to slow down the rate of growth and raise unemployment to the natural rate. These are exactly the policy initiatives that were adopted during the economic boom of the 1990s.

Unfortunately for the new neoclassical macroeconomics, however, the theory faces the same problem that discredited the Phillips Curve in the 1970s. It doesn't fit the facts. As the upward swing of the economic boom of the 1990s gathered steam, the unemployment rate began to drop. As it fell toward 6 percent, then regarded as the natural rate of unemployment, predictions abounded that prices would soon start rising. The Fed raised its short-term interest rate. Nothing happened. The boom continued apace, the unemployment rate fell below 6 percent, and the rate of inflation did not rise. The unemployment rate continued to decline, approaching 5.5 percent, and the same scenario was reenacted. As this is written (mid-2001) the unemployment rate has risen from below 4 percent to above 4.5 percent, the Fed is reducing interest rates and the rate of inflation has not changed. The economy is not in an equilibrium. The theory of a natural rate of inflation is in serious trouble, and with it the entire edifice of the new neoclassical macroeconomics.

Equilibrium Business Cycles

One problem remained in the theory of an economy characterized by general equilibrium microeconomics and the new neoclassical macroeconomics. How do business cycles fit into the picture of an economy in equilibrium? Do they fit at all? A series of papers by Robert Lucas (1937–), culminating in "An Equilibrium Model of the Business Cycle" (1975) sought to fill that gap. The essence of his argument was that business cycles were caused by random disturbances not anticipated by consumers and producers. For example, consumers and producers base their decisions to buy and produce on past experience. They have "rational expectations" about the future based on previous events. But the expectations of consumers may not fit well with the expectations of producers. The two groups may arrive at incompatible conclusions about how much to spend and how much to produce. The equilibrium is disturbed. A recession can result if planned consumption falls short of planned production, for example, or a temporary boom can occur if planned consumption is excessive. The economy will return to equilibrium, however, as expectations take the events of the recession or boom into account.

As for policy prescriptions, the Lucas model predicted that monetary policy would not affect the level of output and that fiscal policy would set a Phillips Curve inflation in motion. The best policy seemed to be an expansion of the money supply to meet the needs of a growing economy while enduring the business cycles created by random events.

Lucas's work led to the concept of "real business cycles" (in contrast to business cycles related to events in the financial and money markets). The rational expectations of individuals can lead to random disturbances in the level of output, due to such factors as imperfect information, lags in obtaining information, short-term changes in wages and incomes, introduction of new products, technological change, or other unanticipated events. For example, introduction of a new children's toy just before the Christmas season could disrupt the entire toy market at the busiest time of year, with unanticipated shortages and surpluses. The equilibrium can be disturbed by these random shocks, but it would be reestablished when the shocks subsided. In this view the coordinating function of the market economy stressed by Hayek may not work perfectly.

The argument can be carried one step further. General equilibrium theory tells us that the normal condition of markets is that supply is equal to demand at the market price. That is, if the supply of a commodity rises relative to demand, the price will fall until supply is once more equal to demand. This rule applies to all markets, including labor markets. So if a shock disturbs the economy, and output falls, with a corresponding decline in employment, wages will fall until the supply of labor is once more equal to the demand. There will be no involuntary unemployment—those who do not work are unwilling to accept the lower wage. In this version of the theory of real business cycles, the economy is always at full employment because a perfectly competitive economy is always in equilibrium.

High theory in economics presents a utopian vision of the market economy of modern capitalism. General equilibrium theory pictures an economy in which the goods most wanted by consumers are willingly produced at the least cost by profit-maximizing producers. All markets, including labor markets, are in an equilibrium at which supply equals demand at the market price. New neoclassical macroeconomics defines the level of economic activity at which unemployment is consistent with a stable rate of inflation. The theory of real business cycles shows that the level of economic activity can rise or fall in response to shocks of various kinds without disturbing the general economic equilibrium, as long as market prices are flexible.

Equilibrium growth theory can be added to this picture, defining the rate of growth in terms of population growth and increases in productivity generated by savings and investment. Schumpeter's entrepreneur creates new products, new technologies, and new forms of organization. The economy grows and changes.

Two lines of policy derive from this view of the economy: government should get out of the way, and a stable monetary policy should be used to avoid disruptions originating in the financial sector.

Economics, Politics, and Ideology

The rise of the new neoclassical economics coincided with a political shift away from the liberal-reformist ideas that had come to dominance during the Depression of the 1930s. As long as the economy enjoyed stable prosperity, Keynesian economics and its interventionist emphasis prevailed, and growth of public spending on both arms and social programs was not a significant burden. But those ideas and policies were discredited when, in the 1970s, growth slowed and inflation escalated. As the new conservatism moved to power in 1980 with the election of Ronald Reagan as president, the new neoclassical economics spread widely within the economics profession. It also dominated the economic policies of the new administration. This was a pattern often seen in the past: economic doctrines move with the tides of politics and provide the intellectual letters of credit that justify specific political strategies.

The economic theory of the Reagan administration provided a rationale for fundamentalist capitalism and its political program. Forged in the heat of the Cold War and hardened in the era of slow growth and inflation, it extolled the virtues of capitalism over socialism, communism, or, indeed, any movement that seeks to manage, reform, or humanize the workings of the economy.

Serious economic issues were not dealt with: the distribution of income and wealth, the dislocations of the lives of people and communities caused by economic change, the effect of economic growth on the natural environment, the anomie and alienation created by an impersonal and uncaring market economy—and more. Could such problems be solved by the panaceas used in the past, or did the times require a new approach?

FIFTEEN

THE NEW
ECONOMY

*Alan Greenspan is the Chairman
of the Board of Governors of the
Federal Reserve System.*

In the last few years the world economy developed a new way of operating, using new technologies that are based on mathematics and computers. The computer age began with Mark I (1939), the first modern computer, and ENIAC (1943), the first electronic computer without moving parts. During World War II the United States government funded research into tools for calculating trajectories for artillery shells. The result was the development of the first digital computers with remarkable capabilities for calculation. Computers are not "number crunchers." They are symbol processors. The same basic technologies can be used to store, retrieve, organize, transmit, and transform any information that can be digitized. This is fortunate because most problems are not numerical problems. The everyday activities of most managers, professionals, and information workers involve other types of thinking.

The economic role of computers becomes clear if you think about organizations and markets as information processors. Our economic institutions developed in eras of high communication costs and limited computing capability. Computers have the capability to reduce the costs of such coordination, communication, and information processing. It is not surprising, therefore, that the massive reduction in computing and communication cost has triggered a substantial restructuring of the economy.

Because of its role in restructuring the economy, information technology is not considered a traditional capital investment, but rather a general purpose technology. Such technologies are beneficial chiefly because they facilitate other innovations. For example, electricity made possible radio and television, the telegraph facilitated the development of geographically displaced enterprises, and the steam engine triggered many technological and organizational changes. Computers play a similar innovative role today, and investments in information technology are linked to higher productivity and organizational transformation. Computers enable processes and work practices to be organized more closely, reducing production costs. These processes allow firms to produce new products or to enhance convenience, timeliness, quality, and variety.

Traditional economic measurements do not account for all of these improvements. As a result, the economic contributions of computers are likely to be understated: returns to computers may be substantially higher than a first appears. New business processes, new skills, and new industry structures are all important outcomes of information technology, and compared to their share of capital stock or investment, the computers' contribution to economic growth is disproportionately large.

In the second half of the nineties the investment in computers and other information processing equipment enabled companies to reduce costs, generate revenue in new ways, empower employees, and provide the agility needed for the rapid expansion of the Internet. Productivity rose in the information technology industry, increased output that kept inflation from rising. A new era seemed to be developing, and the stock market began to rise. Technology stocks boomed, with Internet stocks leading the way. Unemployment fell to 4 percent, with no sign of rising prices. The Fed, under the leadership of Alan Greenspan, kept raising interest rates to head off inflation. The stock market responded with increased prices for most computer, information technology, consumer industries, and industrial stocks in a classic boom. It seemed as if a new era of prosperity had arrived.

It was not to be. The boom created the conditions that turned the stock market around. Technology stocks lost 60 percent of their value from mid-2000 to early 2001. The Internet was devastated and billions of dollars were lost. Other stock indexes fell 10 to 20 percent. Banks that had led the way in stock market investments cut back in an effort to recoup large losses. Consumers changed their ways from spending and borrowing to at least stopping the borrowing. By the first quarter of 2001 unemployment was rising, gross domestic product was down to zero growth, and the Fed was reducing interest rates. Was the economy turning down?

The boom in the American economy was not matched by the rest of the world economy. Western Europe was in a downturn for the last half of the nineties. The Japanese economy was in a depression, and it had stopped its flow of capital to southeast Asia. The countries there had been growing under the influence of low wage labor producing manufactures that by the late nineties were overproduced, and the economies of the whole region fell into crisis. The American economy imported more than it exported, financing the debt by imports of capital from the rest of the world economy that added to the rising stock market and kept the dollar high in value.

We turn now to the role of free trade during this period, to see how it fits into the scene.

ALAN GREENSPAN

Alan Greenspan has been chairman of the Federal Reserve Board longer than anyone else. Appointed by President Ronald Reagan in 1987, he has served under five other presidents and as this is written (2001) he remains in office. The Fed is the central bank of the United States. Its principal function is monetary policy, which it controls using three tools: reserve requirements for member banks (seldom used), the discount rate (rate of interest paid by member banks to the Fed), and open market operations (buying and selling of government bonds). It operates chiefly through open market operations.

The Fed seeks to establish a Federal Funds Rate, which is the rate of interest at which banks borrow overnight from other banks. The Fed tries to influence that rate through open market operations. If it wants to lower the Federal Funds Rate, it will sell government securities at the New York Federal Reserve Bank. That will make more loanable funds available, and if all goes well and the calculations are correct, the Federal Funds Rate will go down. Look it up in the newspaper: a year ago, the bank's prime rate was 9.5 percent, the discount rate was 6 percent, and the Federal Funds rate was 6.56 percent; yesterday (May 17, 2001) they were 7 percent, 3.5 percent, and 4.04 percent, respectively. The Fed had announced that the target for the Federal Funds Rate was 4 percent. Good enough, they almost made it.

Alan Greenspan is the man who manages all this. At the present time he is lowering interest rates because of the dearth of lending that seems to be a cause of poor times and falling stock prices. The financial markets are waiting, and hoping, that Alan Greenspan is right. Until about six months ago he raised interest rates because of fear of inflation and was criticized for not changing the policy.

The Move Toward Freer Trade

The breakdown of the Soviet economy in 1989–1991 brought an end to the Cold War; the battle between socialism and capitalism was over. For a quarter century after the Second World War there had been a contest between the economy of control and the economy of free markets, and at the end of this period the market economy of the West emerged as the clear winner.

The idea of free trade was based on neoclassical economics, supplemented by the classical doctrine of the law of comparative advantage: if every nation adopted free international trade, each would move ahead in tandem. Underdeveloped countries would become developed and disparities would diminish. Capital would move freely, bringing advantages of modernization. As capital moved into countries of the old Soviet system, the world would move toward peace. The economies of Asia, already starting to develop, would become prosperous, with the opportunity to become more like the West or Japan. It was a grand theory of international economic development leading to a peaceful world.

From the close of World War II, freer trade was the goal of the nations of Europe and North America. The Bretton Woods Agreement of 1944 established stable financial arrangements among nations. The International Monetary Fund was established to assist nations that ran into financial difficulties, and the General Agreement on Tariffs and Trade reduced tariffs and other barriers to trade. The European Community (1957) and the European Free Trade Association (1960) led to the establishment of the Euro (launched in 1999) as a single currency for western Europe. Not only did trade expand, but international banking grew. From the 1980s some $1 trillion was invested in Southern Asia, Korea, Brazil, Mexico, and China. The international economy experienced a new era of growth.

The new economy of free trade experienced periodic crises, but it was able to maintain its stability. In 1997 a large-scale financial crisis hit the world economy. It came at a time when world markets were suffering from an oversupply of many manufactures, particularly textiles, automobiles, and other durable goods. The crisis began in southeast Asia, in Thailand, Malaysia, Singapore, Hong Kong, and Indonesia, and spread quickly to South Korea and Japan. The fundamental problem was that banks and business firms in those areas, except Japan, had borrowed huge amounts abroad to finance their rapid economic growth.

Beginning in the late 1980s and through the 1990s, investors in the United States, Japan, Europe, and elsewhere poured about $1 trillion into poor countries. China, Brazil, Thailand, Indonesia, Malaysia, Singapore, Hong Kong, and Korea were big recipients. Some money came as direct investment in factories, some as bank loans or purchases of bonds, and some as investment in local stock markets. The investors were multinational companies, banks, business tycoons, and mutual fund managers. These investments were the fuel that generated the "Asian miracle" of growth rates of over 10 percent annually, with even better profits on the regional stock markets. The basis of the growth, the bait that attracted the capital, was low wages, which meant that the Asian economies relied on exports rather than on domestic consumer demand. Thus when a worldwide glut of manufactured goods developed by the mid-1990s, the rapidly growing Asian economies were in trouble.

Speculators were the first to leave the sinking ship. They realized that debtors in the southeast Asian economies would have to buy dollars to pay their foreign debts (because of lagging exports), which would cause their currencies to fall in value relative to the dollar. Speculators began selling those currencies and buying dollars, setting off a financial panic. Everyone started selling the falling currencies, demanding payment of debts in dollars, and selling securities on the local stock markets. Currency exchange rates collapsed, stock prices fell, banks stopped lending, business firms laid off workers, and the gloom of economic depression spread. The economy of the whole region unraveled.

The International Monetary Fund, which had been organized as a result of the Bretton Wood Agreements in the mid-1940s, became the lender of last resort in an effort to stem the crisis. Its original purpose had been to help individual nations stabilize their currencies in the era of fixed exchange rates. That purpose changed when the flexible exchange rate system followed in the 1970s. The IMF played a prominent role in alleviating the problems of oil-importing countries in the 1970s, insisting that its loans be supplemented by balanced government budgets and high interest rates to control inflation. These IMF loans were based on funds obtained chiefly from the advanced industrial countries in North America and Europe, which had a natural self-interest in preventing serious problems for their banks, which were the largest lenders to the countries in difficulty.

When the 1997 crisis broke, the IMF stepped in to provide financial assistance to the southeast Asia countries, pledging up to $100 billion to that area alone and additional amounts to South Korea. Fortunately, the crisis was restricted to Asia, with relatively little impact on the economies of Europe and North America. Japan continues in a recession, and South Korea and Taiwan are once again moving ahead. But southeast Asia is still feeling the effects of the financial crisis. Hong Kong has recovered, largely the result of the trade with the Chinese mainland, and Singapore is doing well. But the Philippines is not, Thailand, Cambodia, and Malaysia are marking time, and Indonesia is still in crisis.

There are two lessons to be learned from this. One is that the world economy and the international financial system is a seamless web; what happens in one sector affects the whole. The second is that a private-enterprise economy is subject to very large speculative booms and equally large speculative busts unless there is a regulatory agency that enforces good banking practices and a lender of last resort able to curtail a speculative crash if one develops. In the United States the Office of the Comptroller of the Currency in the Treasury Department and the Federal Deposit Insurance Corporation (FDIC) supervise banks, and the Federal Reserve System is the lender of last resort. Thus when the U.S. stock market crashed in October 1987, the Fed announced that U.S. banks could borrow as much as they needed to avert any spread of the crisis. The danger then quickly subsided.

The international financial system, however, has no regulatory agency to enforce good banking practices. Banks and other financial institutions in southeast Asia engaged in reckless and speculative lending with little constraint. The corrupt Bank of Credit and Commerce International was able to operate freely. Nor was there a true lender of last resort when crisis developed. The International Monetary Fund did not have enough resources to fill that role. The world economy badly needs greater stability in its financial system.

Rich Nations and Others

In the 1980s and 1990s, free markets, even in the West, certainly did not provide the only economic system. All the countries of western Europe had varying systems of free markets with controls that were designed to keep the market economy within bounds and to provide individuals with jobs, health insurance, unemployment insurance, and pensions. The United States provided Social Security, Medicare, unemployment insurance, and other protections against the risks of market behavior. Japan, by comparison, had a system of job protection in exchange for work, and a system that protected industrial production at home and freedom overseas. Whatever critics said about free trade abroad, all major nations protected their economies with systems of control at home. The move toward free trade was bound to come into conflict with efforts to protect people and resources.

Unfortunately the theory extolling the merits of free trade did not pass the test of empirical verification. It held up for trade between rich, advanced countries such as the United States and western Europe, where most world trade centered. When barriers to trade were reduced, the rich countries shared the gains more or less equally. But it did not work out that way for the poor nations. If a rich country mutually reduced trade barriers with a poor country, the rich country would benefit and the poor country would lose. Capital going to a poor country to take advantage of low wages, as in the case of the United States and Guatemala. The recipient had to repay the capital, the machinery, and the cost of managerial skills. Guatemala must restructure itself from an agricultural economy producing food for its workers to a manufacturing economy producing for export. Meanwhile the profits were accruing to foreign enterprise that supply the capital. According to a 1999 report of a United Nations Development Program, the difference between the richest and poorest countries increased from 35 to 1 in 1950 to 72 to 1 in 1992. The rich nations benefited from trade liberalization while the poor nations fell behind.

With trade between developing nations and rich nations, however, developing nations tended to gain. In the case of NAFTA (North America Free Trade Association), the rich nation exported capital to the developing nation to take advantage of low wages for manufacturing. Low-wage jobs were lost in the United States but were gained in Mexico. It was only the multinational firms that benefitted by controlling the jobs in those low-wage countries.

This raises another aspect of the problem: who gets the benefits when capital moves within two states? In the case of the advanced nations, it may be that large corporations benefit while workers lose. In the developing country business groups gain while low-wage workers lose. Furthermore, the business gainers are well organized and politically adept and workers are poorly organized, the business interests can get the advanced nation to adopt a strategy that may not be in its national interest. The fallout from such a relationship cuts several ways, and the outcomes are not clear.

However, freer trade has always been favorable to the dominant, business-oriented nation.

Globalization

The changes in the world economy in the 1990s have been so great that terms such as "new economy" and "globalism" have come into use. It is a very particular kind of capitalism that has emerged victorious; one that is much harder, more mobile, more ruthless, and more certain about what it needs. Its overriding objective is to serve the interests of property owners and stockholders, and its assertion is that all obstacles to those ends—regulation, controls, unions, taxation, public ownership—are unjustified and should be removed. Individuals should be free to invest and disinvest capital in industries and in countries at will. This ideology has become a very effective transmission agent for new technologies and for creating the new global industries and markets. It is a tool both of job generation and of job degeneration: it is a classic example of what Joseph Schumpeter called capitalism's creative self-destruction.

The infrastructure for this new economy is based on innovation that began during World War II and continued through the Cold War. Microelectronics telecommunications and network-oriented computer software, which seem so new and original, had their roots in mathematical activity analysis, input-output studies, and game theories of the 1940s and 1950s. Network-oriented information and communication, which allow for unprecedented speed and complexity in the management of the economy, is another application of the mathematical principles that appeared in that earlier development. Knowledge generation and information processing have made economics global: firms are organized into networks of production, management, and distribution within regions of planetary scope. In addition, capital has been organized into a global market, operating twenty-four hours a day and seven days a week, with hundreds of billions of dollars trading instantly among the financial capitals of the world. Capital markets accommodate risk, experiment over investment for the future, and daily coordinate millions of buying and selling decisions.

Economic globalization has several characteristics. First, it is part of a worldwide expansion and liberalization of trade. Eight rounds of tariff reductions led in 1995 with the formation of the World Trade Organization with power to resolve disputes and punish violation of the rules. This has been supplemented by smaller scale agreements—such as the North American Free Trade Agreement (NAFTA)—that have continued to push toward liberalized trade.

Increased mobility of capital is a second characteristic of the new economy. Borrowing and lending, trading of currencies and other financial claims, provision of commercial banking and other financial services has increased rapidly. This includes capital flows associated with foreign domestic investment. One recent study put the daily turnover of currency markets at over one trillion dollars, more than 50 times the volume of daily trade and greater than the foreign exchange reserves of the world's central banks.

A third characteristic of the new economy is the emergence of multinational corporations. These corporations are key contributors to the new finances—as well as principal beneficiaries of the process of financial globalization. They have no country to which they owe more loyalty than any other, nor any country where they feel completely at home. Recent debates have focused on how multinationals are uniquely well equipped to exploit the revolution in communication and information technology and the greater ease of market penetration characterized by the new economy. Multinationals form part of the global web of interconnected economic transactions that is becoming increasingly separated from the territorial nation state.

Finally, we note the contribution of information technology to the recent increase in productivity and output. Information technology is disproportionately associated with intangible assets such as the costs of developing new software, populating a database, implementing a new process, acquiring a more highly skilled staff, or undergoing a major organizational change. One estimate is that for every dollar of information technology, the typical firm has accumulated $9 in intangible assets.

There is tension, however, between the market for capital and the markets for other resources and labor. Capital may be free to move in response to the needs of manufacturing and distribution, but resources are fixed in place, and labor can move but is usually socially constrained. Low-wage labor, in particular, is limited largely to its place of residence, although the large amount of migration that does occur shows that it cannot be totally fixed. Like labor, production is also constrained. Financial assets such as stocks and bonds, which can move instantly, can participate in capital movements and increase or decrease in value, but production, labor, and resources do not have that ability.

Where Are We Heading?

It is beyond doubt that the American economy has been changed by new technology. Faster and faster computers connected through high-speed networks and embedded in almost everything people use are making their imprint on the nation, just as the automobile, the electric motor, and the railroad once did. The earlier innovations are still with us, and so are banking and finance, but on a larger scale. Each of these enriched America, but none could arrest the endless cycles occurring in a market economy. New technology has never been a match for the forces that periodically overwhelm the economy: forces such as falling profits, high interest rates, shrinking consumer demand, plunging stock prices, too much debt, or bankruptcies. The new technologies will make our lives richer, and opportunities for greater wealth will appear at the same time that the economic activities that are displaced will wither away.

As we move into the twenty-first century, however, the whole world is in the midst of a period of rapid technological change, a developing system of global markets and financial systems, shifting relationships between capital and labor, and the effects of economic growth. A changing world is forcing all of us to rethink where the world is heading, how to understand it, and what to do about it. Economics, too, will change, and the next fifty years will undoubtedly show as much intellectual ferment as the last half-century has shown. The historical record suggests that the economics of fifty years hence will be as different from the economics of today as today's economics differs from that of fifty years ago.

SUGGESTED READING

General Works

The literature of economics is vast and complex. It is no longer possible for even professional economists to be familiar with all of it, although a century ago Karl Marx could devote a lifetime to the subject and read just about everything that had been written in the field. Following are some suggestions to get you started:

There are good textbook surveys of the history of economics. The more readable of these comprehensive works are Eric Roll, *A History of Economic Thought* (fourth edition, 1973); John F. Bell, *A History of Economic Thought* (second edition, 1967); Charles Gide and Charles Rist, *A History of Economic Doctrines* (second edition, 1948); Irene H. Rima, *Development of Economic Analysis* (fourth edition, 1986); and Robert B. Ekelund, Jr., and Robert F. Herbert, *A History of Economic Theory and Method* (second edition, 1983). Note the emphasis on theory, analysis, and method in the titles. William J. Barber, *A History of Economic Thought* (1967), focuses on the classical, Marxist, neoclassical, and Keynesian schools of thought, while Mark Blaug, *Great Economists Before Keynes* (1986), provides short sketches of one hundred economists from the history of the profession. Two surveys interesting for their points of view are Leo Rogin, *The Meaning and Validity of Economic Theory* (1956), which emphasizes the political and ideological uses to which economic theories are put, and Joseph Schumpeter, *A History of Economic Analysis* (1954), an encyclopedic volume that stresses the development of economics as a theoretical science. Mark Blaug, *Economic Theory in Retrospect* (fifth edition, 1996), although written for the advanced student, contains chapter-by-chapter summaries of the key writings of Smith, Ricardo, John Stuart Mill, Marx, Marshall, Walras, Keynes, and others. Robert Heilbroner, *The Worldly Philosophers* (sixth edition, 1992) covers much the same material as this book but stops about 1945.

Several books resurvey the history of economics from the viewpoint of critics of orthodoxy, indicating how changing ideas bring about reexamination of the past: Maurice Dobb, *Theories of Value and Distribution Since Adam Smith* (1973); Phyllis Deane, *The Evolution of Economic Ideas* (1978); and Guy Routh, *The Origin of Economic Ideas* (1975). For those who would like more detailed discussions of almost every topic discussed in this volume, *The New Palgrave: A Dictionary of Economics* (London: Macmillan, 4 vols., 1987) can be extensively mined. A recent supplement to the surveys noted above is *New Ideas from Dead Economists* by Todd G. Buchholz (1999). The author presents a view of the personal lives of past economists and their economic beliefs that hold true in our world today.

Chapter 1 Economics and the Market Economy

The early history of capitalism is covered in the standard treatises on the economic history of Europe, but few analyze the rise of the market economy. Two books that do are Karl Polanyi, *The Great Transformation* (1944; published in paperback 1957), and Richard H. Tawney's great work, *Religion and the Rise of Capitalism* (1947). Two multivolume accounts of the rise of capitalism are: Immanuel Wallerstein's *The Modern World System* (2 vols., 1976–1980) and Fernand Braudel's *Civilization and Capitalism* (3 vols., 1981–1984). Both are important historical studies, full of new ideas and interpretations.

Chapter 2 The Early Days

A good compendium that provides the flavor of mercantilism, physiocracy, and early economic liberalism is Arthur E. Monroe, *Early Economic Thought* (1945). A paperback edition of Bernard Mandeville's *The Fable of the Bees* (1962) has made this work available to modern readers. Two books that deal with economics before Adam Smith are Edgar A. Johnson, *Predecessors of Adam Smith* (1937), and William Letwin, *The Origins of Scientific Economics* (1963).

Chapter 3 Adam Smith

John Rae, *The Life of Adam Smith* (1965; first published in 1895) is rich in information but not written in a very interesting style. There are no good biographies of either Malthus or Ricardo, but useful brief accounts of their lives are Keynes's essay on Malthus in his *Essays and Sketches in Biography* (1956), which also contains interesting accounts of Alfred Marshall and William Stanley Jevons, and "A Memoir of Ricardo," written by one of his brothers and published with addenda in Piero Sraffa, ed., *The Works and Correspondence of David Ricardo,* Vol. 10 (1955). A fine account of Jeremy Bentham and his influence is Elie Halevy, *The Growth of Philosophic Radicalism* (1952), and classic accounts of Bentham, James Mill, and John Stuart Mill are in Leslie Stephen, *The English Utilitarians* (1900; reprinted in 1950). Recent reinterpretations of classical economics include Samuel Hollander, *The Economics of Adam Smith* (1973); Thomas Sowell, *Classical Economics Reconsidered* (1974); Robert V. Eagly, *The Structure of Classical Economic Theory* (1974); and D. P. O'Brien, *The Classical Economists* (1975).

Chapter 4 Classical Economics

There is a large literature on classical economics. The very best discussion is Wesley Mitchell, *Lecture Notes on Types of Economic Theory* (1966), which originally appeared in mimeographed form during the 1930s; it consists of notes taken by students from Mitchell's lectures at Columbia University and has the unique characteristic of being equally absorbing for both specialists and the general reader. A more demanding book, but one well worth studying, is Werner Stark, *The Ideal Foundations of Economic Thought* (1944). The best readily available editions of the major works of classical economics are the Modern Library Giant edition of Adam Smith's *Wealth of Nations;* the Ann Arbor Paperbacks edition of Thomas Malthus's *Population: The First Essay;* and the Cambridge University Press paperback edition of David Ricardo's *Principles of Political Economy and Taxation.* Smith is not easy to read, Malthus is a delight, and Ricardo is quite difficult. Samuel Hollander, *The Economics of Thomas Robert Malthus* (1997) tells you more about Malthus than you might want to know. Perhaps the best overall statement of classical economics for the general reader is John Stuart Mill, *Principles of Political Economy,* which is available in most good libraries. Mill's *Autobiography* is a fascinating account of his education and early life, and *The Life of John Stuart Mill* by Michael St. John Packe (1954) is well worth reading. There are three quite different books on the relationship between Harriet Taylor and John Stuart Mill. Friedrich von Hayek, *John Stuart Mill and Harriet Taylor* (1951) is a collection of letters between the two and Hayek's perceptive comments; H. O. Pappe, *John Stuart Mill and the Harriet Taylor Myth* (1960); and Josephine Kamm, *John Stuart Mill in Love* (1977).

Chapter 5 Socialism and Karl Marx

There are several good introductions to socialist thought. Probably the most interesting is Edmund Wilson, *To the Finland Station* (1953). Two more comprehensive surveys are Harry W. Laidler, *Social-Economic Movements* (1948), and Philip Taft, *Movements for Economic Reform* (1950). Donald Sassoon, *One Hundred Years of Socialism* (1996) carries the history of socialism to the late twentieth century.

The most readily available edition of Marx is the Modern Library Giant edition of the first volume of *Capital,* and fine translations of all three volumes are available in paperback from International Publishers and Vintage Books. The novice should not tackle *Capital* directly, however. A good place to start is Ernst Mandel, *An Introduction to Marxist Economic Theory* (1969), Chapters 1–2. Two pamphlets by Marx provide an excellent introduction to his economic analysis of capitalism: *Wage-Labour and Capital* (1849) and *Value, Price, and Profit* (1865), Chapters 6–14. Two early writings by Marx, which were not published until recently, provide the flavor of his humanist concern for people and his dialectical-historical way of thinking: "Estranged Labor," in *Economic and Philosophical Manuscripts of 1844;* and *Pre-Capitalist Economic Formations,* which consists of extracts from early unpublished notebooks. A good supplement is Anthony Brewer, *A Guide to Marx's Capital* (1984), which provides brief chapter-by-chapter summaries of the three volumes.

Most of the writings on Marx's dialectical and historical method are biased toward the author's preconceptions or political prejudices. Marx published almost nothing on these matters in his lifetime other than a few brief paragraphs in the "Author's Preface" to *A Contribution to the Critique of Political Economy* (1859). His early training was in philosophy, and the philosophical background to his economic thought is analyzed in Sidney Hook, *From Hegel to*

Marx (1950). Reading Marx's early unpublished writings on his conceptual framework, followed by Engels, Lenin, and the Stalinists, provides an education in how rich philosophical ideas can be reduced to political dogma. There are, however, two useful survey-critiques of Marx and his economic interpretation of social change: M. M. Bober, *Karl Marx's Interpretation of History* (1927), which is a bit outdated, and Melvin Rader, *Marx's Interpretation of History* (1979).

Basic Marxist theory was further developed by V. I. Lenin in *Imperialism: The Highest Stage of Capitalism* (1933), and his *State and Revolution* (1932) is the bible of orthodox communist political action. "Revisionist" Marxism received its classic statement in Eduard Bernstein, *Evolutionary Socialism* (English translation 1961), and was refined in Karl Kautsky, *Social Democracy Versus Communism* (English translation 1946). David McClellan, *Marxism After Marx* (1979) takes the story up to 1975.

Chapter 6 The Philosophy of Individualism

There are a variety of interesting books on the philosophy of individualism and the environment out of which it emerged. My favorite is Sidney Fine, *Laissez Faire and the General-Welfare State* (1964), closely followed by Richard Hofstadter, *Social Darwinism in American Thought* (1955). A more specialized but equally interesting study is Edward C. Kirkland, *Dream and Thought in the Business Community* (1956). Brief collections of the writing of the individualists and their antagonists include two works by E. David Cronon, *Government and the Economy: Some Nineteenth-Century Views* (1960) and *Democracy and the Gospel of Wealth* (1949). The flavor of individualism can best be obtained from the protagonists themselves: Herbert Spencer, *Social Statics* (1851); William G. Sumner, *Essays* (1934); and Andrew Carnegie, *Triumphant Democracy* (1886), *The Gospel of Wealth* (1900), *The Empire of Business* (1902), and *Autobiography* (1920). There are some fascinating histories of the era of great wealth: Charles Francis Adams, Jr., and Henry Adams, *Chapters of Erie* (1956); Gustavus Myers, *History of the Great American Fortunes* (1936); and Matthew Josephson, *The Robber Barons* (1934).

Chapter 7 Neoclassical Economics

There is no good general survey of neoclassical economics as a whole, and very little interpretive literature below the scholarly level. Alfred Marshall's *Principles of Economics* (eighth edition, 1920) is ponderous but not difficult; it remains an authoritative statement of the neoclassical system. The last three chapters are a moving statement of Marshall's concern for human welfare and his preoccupation with socialism and England's economic decline. Three small volumes in the Cambridge Economic Handbook series are a better introduction: Hubert Henderson, *Supply and Demand* (1958); E. A. G. Robinson, *The Structure of Competitive Industry* (1959); and Dennis H. Robertson, *Money* (1959). All three were written by eminent economists, students and followers of Marshall, and all were intended for the person who has no prior knowledge of economics.

Lionel Robbins, *An Essay on the Nature and Significance of Economic Science* (1932) is easy to read and is very important for the idea that deductive theorizing from correct premises is the only way to achieve a scientific economics. Mathematical logic at the hands of Alfred North Whitehead and Bertrand Russell, *Principia Mathematica* (3 vols., 1910–1913) is not for mere mortals like you and me. Try Bertrand Russell, *Introduction to Mathematical Philosophy* (1919) instead. Kurt Gödel's undecidability theorem is best approached through Earnest Nagel and James R. Newman, *Gödel's Proof* (1958).

Chapter 8 The Human Family

The papal encyclicals on social problems, *Rerum Novarum, Quadragesimo Anno,* and *Mater et Magistra,* are readily available in pamphlets published by The American Press or the Paulist Press. The best introduction to the Fabian socialists is still George Bernard Shaw, ed., *Fabian Essays* (1948). Nearly all of John A. Hobson's books have been reprinted in hardbound editions; the only one available in paperback is *Imperialism* (1965). Three major works by Richard H. Tawney are available in inexpensive editions: *Religion and the Rise of Capitalism* (1947), *The Acquisitive Society* (1960), and *Equality* (1961).

The best of Thorstein Veblen's thought is in *The Theory of the Leisure Class* (1899; published in paperback 1954) and *The Theory of Business Enterprise* (1904); his essays in *The Place of Science in Modern Civilization* (1919) are also interesting. Allan G. Gruchy, *Modern Economic Thought* (1947) is a laudatory survey of Veblen and other institutionalists. Gruchy's *Contemporary Economic Thought: The Contribution of Neo-Institutional Economists* (1972) expands on the earlier volume. Rexford G. Tugwell, ed., *The Trend of Economics* (1924) presents essays by the leading American institutional economists that emphasize both their criticisms of orthodox economics and their advocacy of economic reforms. Two books by J. M. Clark, *Preface to Social Economics* (1936) and *The Social Control of Business* (1939), develop those themes further, as do the essays of Wesley Mitchell in *The Backward Art of Spending Money* (1937). John R. Commons was a prolific, obtuse, and turgid writer; his books are almost impossible to read—with one exception, his fascinating autobiography, *Myself* (1934; published in paperback 1963). For contemporary institutional economics in the United States look at recent issues of the *Journal of Economic Issues.* Geoffrey M. Hodgson, et al., eds., *The Elgar Companion to Institutional and Evolutionary Economics* is insightful and thorough.

Chapter 9 Women and the Economy

M. A. Dimand, R. W. Dimand, and E. L. Forget, eds., *Women of Value: Feminist Essays on the History of Women in Economics* (1995) has essays on Jane Marcet and Harriet Martineau, Mary Paley Marshall, Harriet Taylor, Barbara Bodichon, Charlotte Perkins Gilman, and American women economists before 1940. Dorothy L. Thomson, *Adam Smith's Daughters* (1973) covers most of the women economists discussed in this book. Millicent Fawcett, "The Position of Women in Economic Life" appeared in W. H. Dawson, ed., *After-war Problems* (1917), pp. 191–215, and her "Equal Pay for Equal Work" in the *Economic Journal*, Vol. 28 (1918), pp. 1–6. Francis Y. Edgeworth's paper on the crowding hypothesis, "Equal Pay to Men and Women for Equal Work," *Economic Journal*, Vol. 32 (1922), pp. 431–57, appeared soon after. G. Martin, *Madame Secretary Frances Perkins* (1976) is particularly good on the years before Perkins became secretary of labor. Four books by Jane Addams illustrate her chief interests: *Democracy and Social Ethics* (1902), *Twenty Years at Hull House* (1910), *A New Conscience and an Ancient Evil* (1912), and *Peace and Bread in Time of War* (1922). The best of Ayn Rand's work are *The Fountainhead* (1940), her best-seller novel, *For the New Intellectual* (1961), and *Capitalism: The Unknown Ideal* (1967), which also contains essays by Alan Greenspan.

Two books discuss the changing role of women in the economy: Barbara R. Bergmann, *The Economic Role of Women* (1986) and Daphne Spain and Suzanne M. Bianchi, *Balancing Act: Motherhood, Marriage and Employment Among American Women* (1996). Both show how the contemporary economy is changing the family and the role of women.

Chapter 10 The Keynesian Revolution

Keynes's *General Theory of Employment, Interest, and Money* (1936) is far too difficult for the ordinary reader. One might start with *The Economic Consequences of the Peace* (1920), *The Means to Prosperity* (1933), or *Essays and Sketches in Biography* (1956). Two good summary-introductions to the *General Theory* are Dudley Dillard, *The Economics of John Maynard Keynes* (1948), and Alvin Hansen, *A Guide to Keynes* (1953). R. F. Harrod, *The Life of John Maynard Keynes* (1951) is a full-scale biography, while Seymour Harris, *John Maynard Keynes* (1955) is shorter and contains a more extensive evaluation of Keynes's ideas. Robert Lekachman, *The Age of Keynes* (1966) is an excellent book for the general reader. Robert Skidelsky has completed two of three volumes of a great biography of *John Maynard Keynes* (1986, 1992), and a third is on the way. Donald E. Moggridge, *Maynard Keynes* (1992) is another good one.

Discussions of economic policy in the United States from the Keynesian viewpoint include James Tobin, *National Economic Policy* (1966); Walter W. Heller, *New Dimensions of Political Economy* (1967); and Arthur M. Okun, *The Political Economy of Prosperity* (1970). The monetarist-Keynesian argument is illustrated by Milton Friedman and Walter W. Heller, *Monetary vs. Fiscal Policy: A Dialogue* (1969), which reproduces a debate between the two authors. Friedman's monetary theories are presented in *The Optimum Quantity of Money and Other Essays* (1969), in the long and difficult *Monetary History of the United States, 1867–1960* (1963), which he coauthored with Anna Schwartz, and in essays published in *Dollars and Deficits* (1968). His methodological position is stated in the first chapter of his *Essays in Positive Economics* (1953).

Probably the best presentation of the social philosophy of the Keynesian synthesis and its relation to American Cold War strategy is Eugene V. Rostow, *Planning for Freedom* (1959), in which "planning" is Keynesian economic policy and "freedom" is the private-enterprise economy.

Chapter 11 Economic Planning

There is a huge literature on the Soviet economy. Maurice Dobb, *Soviet Economic Development Since 1917* (1948) is old, but unexcelled in its treatment of the policy debates of the 1920s that preceded adoption of the strategy of planning for rapid economic growth. Much of the debate itself has been translated and published in Nicolas Spulber, *Foundations of Soviet Strategy for Economic Growth* (1964). Three older surveys of the Soviet economy are Robert W. Campbell, *Soviet-Type Economies* (third edition, 1974); Alec Nove, *The Soviet Economy* (revised, 1969); and Nicolas Spulber, *The Soviet Economy* (revised, 1969). Robert W. Campbell has also provided us with a good summary of the changes taking place in the former Soviet bloc in *The Socialist Economies in Transition: A Primer on Semi-Reformed Systems* (1991). David Kotz and Fred Wier, *Revolution from Above: The Demise of the Soviet System* (1997) describes the breakdown of the Soviet economy and the breakup of the Soviet Union. For the latest view on current happenings in Russia, *The Tragedy of Russia's Reforms: Market Bolshevism against Democracy* by Peter Reddaway and Dmitri Glinski (2001) is recommended.

The debate over the theory of planning is best represented by Oskar Lange and Fred M. Taylor, *On the Economic Theory of Socialism* (1938); Friedrich A. Hayek, *The Road to Serfdom* (1944); and John M. Clark, *Alternative to Serfdom* (1948). There are several interesting books on the practical applications of the theory of market socialism, including Branko Horvat, *Towards a Theory of Planned Economy* (1964), and Ota Sik, *Plan and Market Under Socialism* (1967) and *The Third Way* (1976). The Chinese economy changes so rapidly that almost anything written about it is out of date before it can be published. Nevertheless, John G. Gurley, *China's Economy and the Maoist Strategy* (1977) is an excellent analysis of developments under Mao Zedong. There are two excellent books on the Chinese economy since Mao: Barry Naughton, *Growing Out of the Plan* (1995) and Susumi Yabuki, *China's New Political Economy* (1995).

Chapter 12 World War II and the Cold War

Economic planning in the United States during World War II is described in Bureau of the Budget, War Records Section, *The United States at War: Development and Administration of the War Program by the Federal Government* (n.d.). The events of the Cold War are chronicled by Thomas G. Paterson, *Meeting the Communist Threat: Truman to Reagan* (1988) and Dian B. Kunz, *Butter and Guns: America's Cold War Economic Diplomacy* (1997). What is sometimes called "the warfare state" or "the national defense state" of the Cold War is analyzed from various points of view by Tibor Scitovsky, Edward S. Shaw, and Lorie Tarshis, *Mobilizing Resources for War* (1951), Fred J. Cook, *The Warfare State* (1962), Norman A. Graebner, ed., *The National Security: Its Theory and Practice, 1945–1960* (1960), and Seymour Melman, *The Permanent War Economy: American Capitalism in Decline* (1974). George F. Kennan's famous "X" article, "The Sources of Soviet Conduct" was published in *Foreign Affairs*, Vol. 25 (July 1947), pp. 566–82. NSC-68, "United States Objectives and Programs for National Security," April 14, 1950, is reprinted in Earnest R. May, *American Cold War Strategy: Interpreting NSC68* (1993), pp. 23–82.

The classic work on game theory is John von Neumann and Oscar Morgenstern, *The Theory of Games and Economic Behavior* (second edition, 1947). E. Roy Weintraub, *Conflict and Cooperation in Economics* (1975) and Morton D. Davis, *Game Theory: A Nontechnical Introduction* (1983) are relatively simple explanations of game theory. There are two excellent books on *The Prisoner's Dilemma* by Anatol Rapaport and Albert Chammah (1965) and William Roundstone (1992).

Look into Wassily W. Leontief, *The Structure of the American Economy, 1919–1929* (1941) for the pioneering work on input-output analysis. Leonid V. Kantorovich's 1939 paper on linear programming was translated as "Mathematical Methods in the Organization and Planning of Production," *Management Science*, Vol. 6 (1960), pp. 366–422. Tjalling Koopmans, *Three Essays on the State of Economic Science* (1957) provides a systematic overview of the relationship between activity analysis and economic theory as a whole.

Chapter 13 Capitalism After the Second World War

Joseph Schumpeter's pessimistic forecast of the decline of capitalism and the victory of socialism is to be found in *Capitalism, Socialism and Democracy* (1942). But the dynamic aspects of capitalism that led to its resurgence after World War II are brought out in his *The Theory of Capitalist Development* (1912). Schumpeter also emphasized the uneven and often costly process of economic growth in the private-enterprise economy in his two-volume *Business Cycles* (1939), in which he laid out the theory of long waves. John Kenneth Galbraith provides an equally perceptive analysis of post–World War II capitalism in his major works: *American Capitalism* (1952), *The Affluent Society* (1958), *The New Industrial State* (1967), and *Economics and the Public Purpose* (1973). Galbraith argued that financial markets and the monetary system created instability in *The Great Crash, 1929* (1955) and *Money: Whence It Came and Where it Went* (1975, revised 1995). Andrew Shonfeld, *Modern Capitalism: The Changing Balance of Public and Private Power* (1965) looked at the international aspects of big business. Issues raised by big business in the United States are explored in Walter Adams and Horace M. Gray, *Monopoly in America: The Government as Promoter* (1955); Gardner C. Means, *Pricing Power and the Public Interest* (1962); John Blair, *Economic Concentration* (1972); John Munkirs, *The Transformation of Industrial Organization* (1990); and two books by Walter Adams and James W. Brock, *The Bigness Complex* (1986) and *Antitrust Economics on Trial: A Dialogue on the New Laissez-Faire* (1991).

Two excellent books chronicle American economic policy since World War II: Herbert Stein, *Presidential Economics: The Making of Economic Policy from Roosevelt to Reagan and Beyond* (1984) and Lynn Turgeon, *Bastard Keynesianism: The Evolution of Economic Thinking and Policymaking Since World War II* (1996). Both books, written from opposite sides of the political spectrum, are highly critical. Benjamin M. Friedman, *Day of Reckoning: The Consequences of American Economic Policy* (1989) criticizes the Reagan era policies while Martin Feldstein, ed., *American Economic Policy in the 1980s* (1994) defends them.

The conservative economics of the post–World War II years is presented in highly simplified form in Henry Hazlitt, *Economics in One Lesson* (fourth edition,

1979). Milton Friedman and Rose Friedman, *Free to Choose: A Personal Statement* (1980) is a similar paean of praise for the laissez-faire philosophy. The rationale for the policies of the Reagan administration, which are laid out in the administration's own statement, *America's New Beginning: A Program for Economic Recovery* (1981) and in the *Economic Report of the President* for the years 1981 through 1988.

The underdeveloped countries were an important field of study for economists during the Cold War, when the United States and the Soviet Union were contesting for their loyalty. Three widely different approaches are presented by Barbara Ward, *The Rich Nations and the Poor Nations* (1962); Pierre Moussa, *The Underprivileged Nations* (1963); and L. J. Zimmerman, *Poor Lands, Rich Lands: The Widening Gap* (1965). Gunnar Myrdal's *An International Economy* (1956) deals with problems of underdevelopment and is one of the most important economics books of the post–World War II years; an abridged version was published in 1957 under the title *Rich Lands and Poor*. Myrdal's concept of circular causation with cumulative effects was an important contribution to understanding economic backwardness as a self-reinforcing condition that was not subject to simple solutions. Several other important analyses of economic backwardness appeared in the 1950s and 1960s. Alexander Gerschenkron, *Economic Backwardness in Historical Perspective* (1962) is a minor classic. Raoul Prebisch argued that the terms of trade and financial ties between the center and periphery nations reinforced and perpetuated backwardness, in "The Economic Development of Latin America and Its Principal Problems" (1949), published by the United Nations Economic Commission for Latin America. W. Arthur Lewis took up the issue in a highly influential paper, "Economic Development with Unlimited Supplies of Labor" (1954) in the *Manchester School of Economics and Social Studies*, Vol. 22, pp. 139–91, and in *The Theory of Economic Growth* (1955). These and other ideas were brought together in Bert F. Hoselitz, ed., *Theories of Economic Growth* (1965) and Albert D. Hirschman, *The Strategy of Economic Development* (1958).

Edward F. Denison, *The Sources of Economic Growth in the United States and the Alternatives Before Us* (1982) is a seminal empirical study of U.S. economic growth. Jacob Schmookler, *Inventions and Economic Growth* (1966), Nathan Rosenberg, *Perspectives on Technology* (1976), and Gerald Silverberg and Luke Soete, eds., *The Economics of Growth and Technical Change* (1994) provide a broad account of the role of technology in economic growth. Three books by Alfred D. Chandler make the case for changes in business organization and management in raising productivity: *Strategy and Structure: Chapters in the History of the Industrial Enterprise* (1962), *The Visible Hand: The Managerial Revolution in American Business* (1977), and *Scale and Scope: The Dynamics of American Capitalism* (1990). Two broader studies of institutional change should also be examined by anyone interested in the process of economic growth: Richard R. Nelson and Sidney G. Winter, *An Evolutionary Theory of Economic Change* (1982) and Douglass North, *Institutions, Institutional Change and Economic Performance* (1990).

A number of important writings on the relationship between growth, population, food, resources, and pollution are reprinted in *Growth and Its Implications for the Future*, Part I, Hearings, Subcommittee on Fisheries and Wildlife, U.S. House of Representatives (1973). An older book with new relevance is K. William

Kapp, *The Social Costs of Private Enterprise* (1950). Lester R. Brown, *In the Human Interest: A Strategy to Stabilize World Population* (1974) has an excellent treatment of population problems. Readings on the steady-state economy are included in Herman E. Daly, ed., *Toward a Steady-State Economy* (1973) and Mancur Olson and Hans H. Landsberg, eds., *The No-Growth Society* (1973). Two very provocative little books, Robert L. Heilbroner, *An Inquiry into the Human Prospect* (1975) and E. L. Schumacher, *Small Is Beautiful* (1973) deal with those larger issues at the level of the general reader, while Nicholas Georgescu-Roegen, *The Entropy Law and the Economic Process* (1971) is slowly coming to be recognized as a key treatise on the physical limitations to economic growth. Herman E. Daly, *Beyond Growth, The Economics of Sustainable Development* (1996) argues for a compromise between economic growth and protection of the environment. Susan Baker et al., eds., *The Politics of Sustainable Development* (1997) and Nick Mabey, et al., eds., *Argument in the Greenhouse: The International Economics of Controlling Global Warming* (1997) discuss the pros and cons of these hot topics.

Chapter 14 A Half-Century of High Theory

The neoclassical synthesis was so frequently discussed throughout the writings of a wide variety of economists that it is impossible to give just a few references. The interested reader might look at Paul Samuelson's textbook *Economics* (third edition, 1980) for his initial statement of the concept. The classic statement of Keynesian fiscal policy, together with a restatement of neoclassical welfare economics, is Abba P. Lerner, *The Economics of Control* (1944). Beyond that, three books were influential in providing the theoretic and intellectual foundations for the drive to deregulate the American economy that began in the late 1970s. They were William Fellner, *Competition Among the Few* (1949), which used ideas from the theory of games; Alfred Kahn, *The Economics of Regulation* (2 vols., 1970–1971), which pointed out that regulation had evolved into a system that protected the regulated industries rather than the public; and William J. Baumol, *Contested Markets and the Theory of Industry Structure* (1982), which argued that the threat of competition was often enough to control the market power of large firms.

The persistence of poverty in America was forcefully presented in Michael Harrington, *The Other America* (revised edition, 1970). The other extreme of the distribution of income and wealth is shown in G. William Domhof, *Who Rules America?* (1967) and Ferdinand Lundberg, *The Rich and the Super Rich* (1968). The problem of achieving equitable income distribution is discussed in Arthur M. Okun, *Equality and Efficiency: The Big Tradeoff* (1975). David Griffith, *Low-Wage Labor in the United States* (1993) and John E. Schwarz and Thomas J. Volgi, *The Forgotten Americans* (1992) document the working poor.

Key works in the development of modern growth theory include Roy Harrod, "An Essay in Dynamic Theory," *Economic Journal*, Vol. 49, no. 193 (March 1939) pp. 14–33, and "Second Essay in Dynamic Theory," *Economic Journal*, Vol. 70, no. 278 (June 1960); Evsey Domar, "Expansion and Employment," *American Economic Review*, Vol. 37, no. 1 (March 1947), pp. 34–55; Robert M. Solow, "A Contribution to the Theory of Economic Growth," *Quarterly Journal of Economics*, Vol.

70, No. 1 (February 1956), pp. 65–94, and *Growth Theory: An Exposition* (1978); Edmund Phelps, "The Golden Rule of Accumulation: A Fable for Growthmen," *American Economic Review*, Vol. 51, no. 4 (September 1961), pp. 638–43; and Frank H. Hahn and R. C. O. Matthews, "The Theory of Economic Growth: A Survey," *Economic Journal*, Vol. 74, No. 296 (December 1964), pp. 779–902, with an inclusive bibliography.

Friedrich von Hayek's concept of the market economy as a coordinating mechanism is presented in his *Individualism and Economic Order* (1949). His broader economic and political philosophy is set out in *The Constitution of Liberty* (1960), and his attack on socialism in *The Road to Serfdom* (1944). G. R. Steele, *The Economics of Friedrich Hayek* (1993) emphasizes his studies in monetary theory and business cycles. John C. Wood and Ronald Woods, eds., *Friedrich A. Hayek: Critical Assessments* (4 vols., 1991) is a very valuable collection of essays on Hayek by renowned international scholars. There are two recent collections of papers on the contemporary Austrian school: Stephen Littlechild, ed., *Austrian Economics* (3 vols., 1990) and Peter J. Boettke, ed., *The Elgar Companion to Austrian Economics* (2 vols., 1994).

There is no good general survey of contemporary high theory in economics outside of textbooks and scholarly accounts. Frank Hahn presents an excellent summary and critique of "General Equilibrium Theory" in Chapter 3 of his *Equilibrium and Macroeconomics* (1984). E. Roy Weintraub, *General Equilibrium Theory* (1974) is a useful account and critique for those with limited mathematics, while Bent Hansen, *A Survey of General Equilibrium Systems* (1970) is for those with more mathematics. The reader without a strong grounding in mathematics could get the flavor of axiomatic mathematical general equilibrium theory by reading the short introductory sections of each chapter in Gerard Debreu's *Theory of Value* (1959). Readers with a more sophisticated knowledge of mathematics can go beyond that, but it will be slow going. The same is true of Kenneth Arrow and Frank H. Hahn, *General Competitive Analysis* (1971).

Piero Sraffa's *Production of Commodities by Means of Commodities* (1960) offers an alternative theoretical system based on "objective" technological relationships instead of "subjective" individual preferences. Closely related to Wassily Leontief's input-output analysis, it was rejected by the defenders of the neoclassical faith in a vitriolic "capital controversy" of the 1960s, chronicled in Jeffrey Harcourt, *Some Cambridge Controversies in the Theory of Capital* (1972) and Mark Blaug, *The Cambridge Revolution: Success or Failure?* (1974). American developments of Post Keynesian ideas are Sidney Weintraub, *Capitalism's Inflation and Unemployment Crisis* (1978); Paul Davidson, *Money and the Real World* (second edition, 1978); and Alfred S. Eichner, *The Megacorp and Oligopoly* (1976). *The Journal of Post Keynesian Economics* provides current ideas from this branch of economic thinking. Other important works in this tradition include Michael Kalecki, *Essays in the Theory of Economic Fluctuations* (1939) and Joan Robinson's paper "The Production Function and the Theory of Capital" (1953).

The new neoclassical macroeconomics is best pursued through individual papers rather than a single source. A good statement of the natural rate of unemployment hypothesis is Milton Friedman, "Nobel Lecture: Inflation and Unemployment," *Journal of Political Economy*, Vol. 85 (June 1977), pp. 451–72, especially pp. 456–59. The seminal paper on the tradeoff between unemployment and wage rates, which the new conservatives modified to a tradeoff between unemployment and prices, is A. W. Phillips, "The Relationship Between Unemployment and the Rate of Change of Money Wage Rates in the U.K., 1861–1937," *Economica*, Vol. 25 (November 1958), pp. 283–99. The theory of rational expectations is presented in Thomas J. Sargent and Neil Wallace, "Rational Expectations and the Theory of Economic Policy," *Journal of Monetary Economics*, Vol. 2 (April 1976), pp. 169–83. John F. Muth, "Rational Expectations and the Theory of Price Movements," *Econometrica*, Vol. 29, No. 3 (July 1961), pp. 315–35, originated the theory. The general reader may find these articles in professional journals rather tough going. Portions of G. K. Shaw, *Rational Expectations: An Elementary Exposition* (1984) are not all that elementary.

The theory of real business cycles, or equilibrium business cycles, can be explored in three scholarly papers: Robert Lucas, "An Equilibrium Model of the Trade Cycle," *Journal of Political Economy*, Vol. 83, No. 6 (1975), pp. 1113–44; John B. Long, Jr., and Charles I. Plosser, "Real Business Cycles," *Journal of Political Economy*, Vol. 91, No. 1 (February 1983), pp. 39–69; and N. Gregory Mankiw, "Real Business Cycles: A New Keynesian Perspective," *Journal of Economic Perspectives*, Vol. 3 (Summer 1989), pp. 79–90. For a critique, look at Lawrence H. Summers, "Some Skeptical Observations on Real Business Cycle Theory," *Federal Reserve Bank of Minnesota Review*, Vol. 10, No. 4 (Fall 1986), pp. 23–27.

Chapter 15 The New Economy

Although surveys of modern economics tend, of necessity, to be highly selective, there are two general works: T. W. Hutchison, *A Review of Economic Doctrines: 1870-1929* (1953), which is essentially a historical summary of major trends, and Ben B. Seligman, *Main Currents in Modern Economics* (1962), a broad and inclusive volume full of useful insights into the social theories and political assumptions underlying the doctrines of academic economics. G. L. S. Shackle, *The Years of High Theory: Intervention and Tradition in Economic Thought* (1967) deals with economic theory between 1920 and 1940. William Breit and Roger L. Ransom, *The Academic Scribblers* (1971) is an excellent survey of economics in the 1950 to 1970 period. Sidney Weintraub, ed., *Modern Economic Thought* (1977), with essays by outstanding economists, covers the period since World War II.

Most of the works on globalization in recent years have been wholly optimistic: globalization will provide dramatic progress for all peoples worldwide. Typical is John Micklethwait and Adrian Wooldridge, *A Future Perfect* (2000), which defends globalization as leading to the advance of individual freedom—while recognizing its faults. One book, *Globalization and History* (1999), by Kevin O'Rourke and Jeffrey Williamson explains how a form of globalization occurred in the Atlantic world in the late nineteenth century and stresses the fact that globalization can sow the seeds of its own destruction. On somewhat larger issues, Paul Krugman, *The Age of Diminishing Expectations* (1990) and Robert Kuttner, *Everything for Sale: The Virtues and Limits of Markets* (1997) agree that the market economy has virtues but with important qualifications.

Finally, here are five books that deal incisively with some of the long-range topics that we often lose sight of in the hurly-burly of current affairs. Paul

Kennedy, *The Rise and Fall of the Great Powers: Economic Change and Military Conflict from 1500 to 2000* (1987) argues that nations project their military power on the basis of their economic resources and in defense of their economic interests, and that the shifting economic base of the world's economies causes shifts in world power. On the other hand, Mancur Olson, *The Rise and Decline of Nations* (1982) found the driving forces of rise and decline within nations themselves. Charles P. Kindleberger, *World Economic Primacy, 1500–1990* (1996) provides an analysis by one of the world's experts on economic development and world trade. Kindleberger's *Manias, Panics and Crashes: A History of Financial Crises* (revised edition, 1989) should be read by anyone who thinks the stock market will rise forever. David H. Fischer, *The Great Wave: Price Revolutions and the Rhythm of History* (1996) also looks at the future by examining the past, arguing that long inflations like that of the twentieth century always end with a lengthy period of troubles and social upheaval.

Name Index

Subject Index